PassKey EA Review Workbook

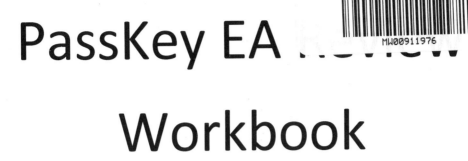

Six Complete

Enrolled Agent Practice Exams

2013-2014 Edition

Authors:
Collette Szymborski, CPA
Richard Gramkow, EA
Christy Pinheiro, EA ABA®

PassKey Publications
Elk Grove, CA

Recent Praise for the PassKey EA Review Series

Kari Hutchens (Canon City, Colorado)

I passed all three exams with the cheapest study materials out there! Easy to understand and comprehensive. Even from Part 1 of the book (Individuals), I learned so much that I am going to amend two prior year tax returns and get over $1,000 back. Passing all three parts of the EA exam on the first try and getting some extra cash in my pocket gets this book an A+!

Ken Smith (Chicago, Illinois)

I studied like crazy, night and day, and passed all three parts of the EA exam in just eight days. And I passed on the first try!

Michael Mirth (North Las Vegas, Nevada)

I am happy to say I am now an enrolled agent. This was the only source I used to study besides some extra practice tests. The way the book presented the materials made it easy to comprehend. If you are looking for a detailed study guide, this one is for you.

Oliver Douglass

I found this book to be the least expensive and the best guide around. The tests are on the money and the explanations are so easy to comprehend. Thanks for a great book.

Baiye Zebulone

Great books. Straight to the point, and very good examples for SEE preparations. I used all three parts to prepare for the SEE and passed Parts 1 and 3 on the first sitting and Part 2 on the second sitting. I will recommend it to anybody who wants to pass the rigorous EA examination.

Carl Ganster (Wyomissing, Pennsylvania)

I passed all my tests on the first try in five months using the PassKey books. Every topic is covered. It is easy reading, with plenty of examples. I have recommended the books to others who have to take the test. Thanks, PassKey, for writing great test guides. So many of the ones out there are hard to understand.

Tammy the Tax Lady ®

I think you need to find new tax software.

Editor: Cynthia Willett Sherwood, EA, MSJ

PassKey EA Review Workbook, Six Complete Enrolled Agent Practice Exams 2013-2014 Edition

ISBN 978-1-935664-25-3

First Printing. PassKey EA Review
PassKey EA Review® is a U.S. Registered Trademark

PassKey Publications Licensing Inc., PO Box 580465, Elk Grove, CA 95758

www.PassKeyPublications.com

Table of Contents

Introduction

Welcome to the PassKey EA Exam Review Workbook. This workbook is designed to be an additional study tool to your existing study guide. It is not designed as a stand-alone workbook, although you will not be required to refer back to the Pass-Key study guides in order to use this book. The test questions are all unique and not found in the PassKey study guides. This is intentional—so candidates can have a more true-to-life test-taking experience when they go through the workbook questions.

Any EA exam candidate will benefit from the exam questions and detailed answers in this workbook. We suggest that you use this workbook to prepare for the exam in a realistic setting. Set aside an uninterrupted time block and test yourself just the way you would if you were actually taking the EA exam at a testing center.

Score yourself at the end, and go through the answers carefully. Unlike the Prometric exam, you will have a complete, clear answer for each question. If you miss a question, you will know why. Use this workbook to uncover your weak points and concentrate on those. You should answer at least 70% correctly. Any score below 70% means you probably need to study more.

This workbook is designed for the 2013-2014 testing season that lasts through February 28, 2014. All of the questions are based on 2012 tax law until the current exam is retired. If you have any questions about the actual exam, or if you want to sign up for it, contact Prometric directly at 1-800-306-3926 or www.prometric.com/IRS.

If you wish to find out more about the Complete Enrolled Agent study guides and other books by PassKey Publications, visit our website at *www.PassKeyPublications.com.*

Successfully passing the EA exam can launch you into a fulfilling and lucrative new career. The exam requires intense preparation and diligence, but with the help of PassKey's EA Review, you will have the tools you need to learn how to become an enrolled agent. As the authors of the PassKey EA Review, we wish you much success.

Good luck on your exam!

Ten Steps for the IRS EA Exam

STEP 1-Learn

Learn more about the enrolled agent designation and explore the career opportunities that await you after passing your three-part EA exam. In addition to preparing taxes for individuals and businesses, EAs can represent people before the IRS, just like attorneys and CPAs. Many people who use the PassKey study guides have had no previous experience in preparing taxes, but go on to rewarding new professional careers.

STEP 2-Gather information

Gather more information before you launch into your studies. The IRS publishes basic information about becoming an EA on its website at www.irs.gov/Tax-Professionals/Enrolled-Agents. You'll also find valuable information about the exam itself on the Prometric testing website at www.prometric.com/see. Be sure to download the Candidate Information Bulletin, which takes you step-by-step through the registration and testing process.

STEP 3-Obtain a PTIN

A PTIN stands for *Preparer Tax Identification Number.* Before you can register for your EA exam, you must obtain a PTIN, which is issued by the IRS. The sign-up system can be found at www.irs.gov/ptin. You'll need to create an account, complete an on-line application, and pay a required fee.

STEP 4-Sign up with Prometric

Once you have your PTIN, you may register for your exam on the Prometric website. After creating an account and paying the required testing fee, you can complete the registration process by clicking on "Scheduling."

STEP 5-Schedule a time, date, and location

You'll be able to choose a test site and time and date that are convenient for you. Prometric has test centers in most major metropolitan areas of the United States, as well as certain other parts of the world. You may schedule as little as two days in advance—space permitting—through the website or by calling 800-306-3926 Monday through Friday. Be aware that the website and the phone line have different inventory of available times and dates, so you may want to check the other source if your preferred date is already full.

STEP 6-Adopt a study plan

Focus on one exam part at a time, and adopt a study plan that covers all the tax topics on the EA exam. You'll need to develop an individualized study pro-gram based on your current level of tax knowledge. For those without prior tax experience, a good rule of thumb is to study at least 60 hours for each of the three exam sections, committing at least 15 hours per week. Start well in advance of the exam date.

STEP 7-Get plenty of rest, exercise, and good nutrition

Get plenty of rest, exercise, and good nutrition prior to the EA exam. You'll want to be at your best on exam day.

STEP 8-Test day has arrived!

On test day, make sure you remember your government-issued ID and arrive early at the test site. Prometric advises to arrive at least 30 minutes before your scheduled examination time. If you miss your appointment and are not al-lowed to test, you'll forfeit your exam fee and have to pay for a new appointment.

STEP 9-During the exam

This is when your hard work finally pays off. Focus, don't worry if you don't know every question, but make sure you allocate your time appropriately. Give your best answer to every question. All questions left blank will be marked as wrong.

Step 10-Congratulations. You passed!

After celebrating your success, you need to apply for your EA designation. The quickest way is by filling out Form 23, *Application for Enrollment to Practice Before the Internal Revenue Service*, directly on the IRS website. Once your application is approved, you'll be issued a Treasury card, and you'll be official—a brand new enrolled agent!

Essential Tax Figures for Tax Year 2012

Part One: Individuals

Here is a quick summary of all the tax figures for the current exam cycle:

Income Tax Return Filing Deadline: April 15, 2013

The Personal Exemption: $3,800 (up $100 from 2011) ***Note:** In the 2012 tax year, the personal exemption and itemized deductions do not phase out at higher income levels.

Social Security Taxable Wage Base: $110,100

Medicare Taxable Wage Base: No limit

Standard Deduction Amounts:

- Married filing jointly (or qualifying widow/widower) $11,900
- Head of household $8,700
- Single $5,950
- Married filing separately $5,950
- Dependents $950
- Blind taxpayers and senior citizens (over 65) qualify for an increased standard deduction. Additional amounts for 2012 per taxpayer are:
  - $1,450 for single or head of household
  - $1,150 for married filing jointly, married filing separately, or qualifying widow

Retirement Plan Contribution Limits: Traditional or Roth IRA: $5,000 ($6,000 for taxpayers age 50 or over by the end of 2012.)

Roth IRA Phase-out AGI limits:

- Married filing jointly: $173,000 to $183,000
- Single or head of household: $110,000 to $125,000
- Married filing separately: $0 to $10,000

Alternative Minimum Tax Exemption (AMT):

- $78,750 (MFJ or QW)
- $50,600 (Single or HOH)
- $39,375 (MFS)

Earned Income Credit (EIC) Income Thresholds:
Earned income and adjusted gross income must each be less than:

- $45,060 ($50,270 MFJ) with three or more qualifying children
- $41,952 ($47,162 MFJ) with two qualifying children
- $36,920 ($42,130 MFJ) with one qualifying child
- $13,980 ($19,190 MFJ) with no qualifying children

Maximum EIC credit (for all filing statuses except MFS):

- $5,891 with three or more qualifying children
- $5,236 with two qualifying children
- $3,169 with one qualifying child
- $475 with no qualifying children

Investment income must be $3,200 or less in 2012 in order to qualify for the EIC.

Estate and Gift Tax Exclusion Amount: $5,120,000 (up from $5 million in 2011)

Gift Tax Annual Exclusion: $13,000

Non-Citizen Marital Threshold for Gift Tax: $139,000

Kiddie Tax Unearned Income Threshold: $1,900

"Nanny Tax" Threshold: $1,800

Foreign Earned Income Exclusion: $95,100

Child Tax Credit: $1,000 per child

Adoption Credit: $12,650 nonrefundable (credit was refundable in 2011)

Education Credits and Deductions:
- American Opportunity Credit (AOC): maximum of $2,500 per student
- Lifetime Learning Credit: maximum of $2,000 per return
- Tuition and fees deduction: maximum of $4,000
- Student loan interest deduction: maximum of $2,500

Mileage Rates:
- Business miles: 55.5¢ per mile
- Medical or moving miles: 23¢ per mile
- Charitable purposes: 14¢ per mile

Section 179 Expense: $500,000 of qualified expenditures/phase-out at $2 million

New Tax Law Affecting Individuals

The *American Taxpayer Relief Act of 2012* extended a majority of tax cuts already in place. The legislation also made permanent certain other tax provisions that had been temporary. The major changes are as follows:

Alternative minimum tax: The exemption amount on the AMT on individuals is permanently indexed for inflation starting in 2013. The AMT exemption amounts were increased for 2012.

Marriage penalty relief: The increased size of the 15% bracket and the in-creased standard deduction for married taxpayers filing jointly has been made permanent.

Personal exemption phase-out: This repeals the personal exemption phase-out and the limitation on itemized deductions for taxpayers with adjusted gross income at or below a certain threshold.

Reduced rates on capital gains and dividends: The current maximum tax rate of 15% (or 0% for those below the 25% bracket) has been extended permanently, ex-cept that the rate will be 20% for taxpayers above a certain threshold starting in 2013.

Child and Dependent Care Credit: The rules allowing the credit to be calculated based on up to $3,000 for one dependent or up to $6,000 for one has been made permanent.

Child Tax Credit: The $1,000 credit per child was made permanent.

American Opportunity Credit: This credit was extended through 2017.

Adoption Tax Credit: This credit was made permanent. It is nonrefundable for tax year 2012.

Education tax relief: An increase in the annual contribution to Coverdell Education Savings Accounts; an extension of the exclusion for employer-provided educational assistance; and an increase in the phaseout ranges for the student loan interest de-duction have all been made permanent.

Estate and gift tax: The estate tax portability election has been made permanent. This is when the surviving spouse's exemption amount is increased by the deceased spouse's unused exemption amount.

Individual provisions extended retroactively to 2012 include the following:

Deduction for certain teacher expenses; exclusion from gross income of discharge of qualified principal residence indebtedness; deduction for mortgage insurance; parity for exclusion from income for employer-provided mass transit and parking benefits; deduction of state and local general sales taxes; above-the-line deduction for qualified tuition and related expenses; the credit for energy-efficient existing homes; the credit for two-or-three-wheeled plug-in electric vehicles; and the credit for installing alternative vehicle refueling property in a main home; and in some cases, the American Taxpayer Relief Act of 2012 Act modified certain provisions of these items.

Also for 2012:

- Schedule 8812 is now also used for the Additional Child Tax Credit, replacing Form 8812.
- Taxpayers who converted amounts to a Roth IRA or designated Roth account in 2010 must report half of the resulting taxable income on their 2012 returns, unless they reported the full amount on their 2011 returns.
- An employee's W-2 must now report both the employer and employee portion of health care insurance costs for 2012.

Part Two: Businesses

2012 Social Security Taxable Wage Base: $110,100.

In 2012, the Social Security portion of the FICA tax for employees only is reduced from 6.2% to 4.2%. The employer's portion remains 6.2%. The Social Security tax rate for self-employed persons is similarly reduced, from 12.4% to 10.4%. Therefore, the tax rate for self-employment income earned in calendar year 2012 is 13.3% (10.4% for Social Security and 2.9% for Medicare).

2012 Medicare Taxable Wage Base: No limit.

Section 179 Expense: $500,000 of qualified expenditures/phase-out at $2 million; up to $250,000 in expense for qualified leasehold improvement, restaurant, and retail improvement property.

Bonus Depreciation: Up to 50% for new assets placed in service in 2012.

Mileage Rates:

- Business miles: 55.5¢ per mile
- Medical or moving miles: 23¢ per mile
- Charitable purposes: 14¢ per mile

Exclusion for Employer-Provided Mass Transit:

- $240 per month for parking benefits
- $240 per month in combined highway vehicle transportation and transit passes (increased retroactively for 2012)

Employer Contribution Limits to 401(k) Participant's Plan: $17,000 maximum.

Estate and Gift Tax Exclusion Amount: $5,120,000 (up from $5 million in 2011).

Gift Tax Annual Exclusion: $13,000.

New Tax Law Affecting Businesses 2012 Tax Year

S Corporation Built-In Gains Tax (BIG tax): The American Taxpayer Relief Act of 2012 extends the reduced five-year recognition period to sales occurring in 2012 and 2013. The Act also provides that gain on installment sales during these years are subject to the five-year recognition period when it is recognized in future years.

Business Credits: The American Taxpayer Relief Act of 2012 extends and in some cases modifies many credits, including the following:

- Research and Experimentation Credit
- Work Opportunity Tax Credit (expanded target groups that qualify for 2012)
- Employer Credit for Differential Military Pay
- Indian Employment Tax Credit
- New Markets Tax Credit
- Empowerment Zone Employment Credit
- Low Income Housing Credit
- Credit for Alternative Fuel Vehicle Refueling Property
- Credit for Construction of New Energy Efficient Homes
- Credit for Manufacture of Energy Efficient Appliances
- Various credits for producing cellulosic biofuel, alternative fuel mixtures, and wind electricity

Other Extensions Under the Taxpayer Relief Act:

- Enhanced charitable deduction for contributions of food inventory
- Special rules allowing U.S. film and television producers to expense up to $15 million of production costs incurred in the United States ($20 million in economically depressed areas in the U.S.)

Estate and Gift Tax: The estate tax portability election has been made permanent. This is when the surviving spouse's exemption amount is increased by the deceased spouse's unused exemption amount. The single lifetime exemption extending unification of the estate and gift tax has been made permanent.

Other Business-Related Tax Changes:

- **W-2s:** An employee's W-2 must now report both the employer and employee portion of health care insurance costs for 2012.

- **Farmers' Tax Deadline:** Because of delays created by the late tax changes of the fiscal cliff legislation, the IRS will waive penalties for farmers and fishermen who miss the March 1, 2012 tax filing deadline, so long as they file their returns and pay the tax due by April 15.

- **Cell Phones:** The value of employer-provided cell phones has been ruled as excludable as a de minimis fringe benefit, if provided primarily for noncompensatory business reasons.

- **Nonprofit Relief:** Small organizations that lost their tax-exempt status by failing to file e-postcards were eligible for transitional relief in 2012, including possible retroactive reinstatement and a reduced user fee.

- **Reporting of Nontaxable Exchanges of Property:** Both the corporation and certain stockholders involved in a nontaxable exchange of property for stock must attach to their income tax returns a complete statement of all facts pertinent to the exchange. The reporting requirement now applies to stockholders that own 5% or more of a public company or 1% or more of a privately held company.

Part Three: Representation

RTRP Program Suspended: On January 18, 2013, the U.S. District Court for the District of Columbia directed the IRS to stop enforcing the requirements for registered tax return preparers. In accordance with this order, RTRPs are not required to complete competency testing or secure continuing education. This ruling does not affect the practice requirements for other enrolled practitioners (CPAs, attorneys, enrolled agents, enrolled retirement plan agents, or enrolled actuaries). The IRS has stated that they plan to appeal this decision.

Mandatory PTIN Requirement: Beginning in 2011 all paid preparers were required to have a Preparer Tax Identification Number (PTIN) before preparing returns. The mandatory PTIN requirement was suspended for a short time due to pending litigation, and was reinstated February 1, 2013.

PTIN Helpline: PTIN applicants can obtain (and renew) their PTIN online using the IRS website (www.irs.gov/ptin). The fee is $64.25. The PTIN helpline is 1-877-613-7846.

OPR Mailbox Suspended: Effective in 2012, the former OPR e-mail address is no longer in operation. This is because many preparers were receiving fraudulent e-mails that purported to be from the Office of Professional Responsibility.

Reporting Preparer Violations: Starting in 2012, taxpayers are able to report tax preparers in violation of Circular 230 guidelines using the new Form 14157, Com-plaint: Tax Return Preparer. This form is appropriate for reporting violations of both enrolled and unenrolled preparers.

TAC Refusing Bulk Returns: Starting in 2012, IRS offices will no longer accept bulk returns for processing. The IRS wants to eliminate the practice of tax preparers dropping off completed returns for processing, especially during peak operating periods. However, TACs will still accept returns with imminent statute implications, with remittances or other time-sensitive situations.

ITIN/SSN Mismatch: For tax year 2012, it is now possible to e-file returns with an ITIN/SSN mismatch. The IRS made this change on June 22, 2012.

ITIN Application Requirements Changed: Starting in 2012, Forms W-7, Application for IRS Individual Taxpayer Identification Number, must include original documentation such as passports and birth certificates. Notarized copies or photocopies of documentation are no longer sufficient.

Stockpiling: The IRS announced on January 4, 2013 that the stockpiling of 2012 re-turns is allowed. The Internal Revenue Service temporarily lifted its prohibition against stockpiling tax returns before e-filing due to the late tax law changes.

Practice Exams

Test tip: Time yourself. Set up a watch or other digital timer while you read and answer the questions. You will have 3.5 hours to take the EA exam, with approximately two minutes to answer each question. Do not spend an inordinate amount of time on any one question. Don't run out of time! It's the number one reason why first-time test takers fail.

Part 1: Individuals Practice Exams

#1 Individuals Sample Exam

1. Pam works in New York. She travels to New Orleans to attend a one-week conference at the suggestion of her employer. The conference is educational and is designed to supplement her current job requirements. While in New Orleans, she does some sightseeing and visits friends. On the last day of the conference, Pam flies home. Pam had the following expenses during her trip:

Roundtrip airfare to the conference	$360
Parking at the airport	$24
Meals while at the conference	$220
Meals while sightseeing	$72
Hotel costs during the conference	$450

How much of these costs are deductible, before the consideration of any AGI limitations?

A. $1,054.
B. $980.
C. $944.
D. $360.

2. Rusty, age 66, is married and will file jointly in 2012 with his wife, Paula, age 54. Rusty has gross income of $19,500, all from investments. Paula received an $8,000 inheritance during the year. Are they required to file a return?

A. Yes, they are required to file.
B. No, they are not required to file.
C. Filing requirements are not based on income level.
D. Insufficient information to answer.

3. Which of the following taxpayers would not be considered self-employed?

A. An independent contractor.
B. A general partner of a partnership.
C. The estate of a deceased taxpayer that carries on a trade or business.
D. A person who works full-time and also has a part-time business.

4. Darryl wants to contribute to his traditional IRA for 2012. He files an extension to file his 2012 tax return. What is the latest that Darryl can contribute to his traditional IRA and still take a deduction on his **2012** tax return?

A. October 15, 2013.
B. October 15, 2012.
C. April 15, 2013.
D. December 31, 2012.

5. Mateo received two **Forms W-2:** one showing wages of $5,000, and the other showing wages of $18,500. He also had $4,000 in long-term capital losses from a stock sale, and a $130 early-withdrawal penalty from a certificate of deposit. He had no other items of gain or loss during the year. What is his adjusted gross income (AGI) on Form 1040?

A. $20,370.
B. $20,500.
C. $21,500.
D. $19,500.

6. Which of the following is not an AMT preference item for individual taxpayers?

A. Investment interest expense on Schedule A.
B. Taxes on Schedule A.
C. Personal exemption.
D. Casualty losses on Schedule C.

7. All of the following are deductible medical expenses except:

A. Treatment for drug addiction.
B. Transportation to a medical conference related to the chronic disease of a dependent.
C. Smoking-cessation programs.
D. Cost of child care while a parent is in the hospital.

8. Which of the following filing statuses would prevent a taxpayer from qualifying for the Earned Income Credit?

A. Head of household.
B. Single.
C. Married filing separately.
D. Qualifying widow(er).

9. Which of the following taxpayers would not be able to file jointly in 2012?

A. A married couple with one spouse who is a nonresident alien and not eligible for a Social Security Number.
B. A couple living together in a common law marriage recognized in the state where they live.
C. A married couple who are legally separated under an interlocutory decree of divorce.
D. A couple whose marriage was annulled and finalized on January 12, 2013.

10. Angela and Donald are married and file jointly. However, on December 22, 2012, Donald dies. For filing status purposes, the IRS considers Angela to be _____ all year.

A. Married.
B. Unmarried.
C. Single.
D. Legally separated.

11. Wayne is unmarried and owns a residential rental property. In 2012, his wage income was $82,000, and his losses from the rental property were $27,000. He materially participated in the rental activity. Wayne is not a real estate professional. How much of the rental loss is he allowed to take on his individual return?

A. $0.
B. $25,000, with a $2,000 passive loss carryover.
C. $27,000.
D. $25,000 with no carryover.

12. Ellie and Timothy are married and file jointly. In 2012, they have the following items of income and loss:

W-2 wages for Ellie	60,000
W-2 wages for Timo	105,000
Income from a pass	_____
Rental losses from r	165,000

They materially participat   , what is
their adjusted gross incor

Passive income 4000
Passive losses (4500)
500 Loss carry forward

A. $164,500.
B. $160,500.
C. $165,000.
D. $169,000.

13. Frank purchased 200 shares of Global Marine Corporation stock three years ago. On January 10, 2012, Frank gives his son, Ryan, 200 shares of Global Marine stock. Frank's adjusted basis in the stock immediately before the gift is $950. On the date of the transfer, the fair market value of the stock was $1,100. Ryan sells all 200 shares for $1,320 on November 16, 2012. What is the amount and nature of Ryan's gain?

A. $370 short-term capital gain.
B. $150 long-term capital gain.
C. $370 long-term capital gain.
D. $220 short-term capital gain.

14. Which of the following items is taxable income to the recipient?

A. Life insurance proceeds.
B. Traditional IRA distributions to a beneficiary after the death of the IRA owner.
C. Accelerated death benefits for a terminally ill individual under a life insurance contract.
D. Canceled debt from qualified principal residence indebtedness.

15. Stan owns a residential rental and materially participates in the rental activity. The cost basis of the building is $210,000. According to the property tax rolls, the value of the property is allocated as follows:

- $150,000 to the building
- $60,000 to the land

The building was placed into service two years ago. Stan chose to depreciate the building using MACRS straight-line depreciation. Residential rental property is always depreciated over 27.5 years. Based on this information, how much depreciation expense may Stan claim per year?

A. $5,455.
B. $5,000.
C. $12,500.
D. $17,500.

16. Gary has three kids in college. They are all his dependents:

1. Brianna, age 22, a college sophomore working on her first bachelor's degree
2. Devon, age 19, a college freshman working on his first bachelor's degree
3. Keisha, age 23, a graduate student, working on her first master's degree

Based on the above scenario, what is the **maximum** in American Opportunity Credits (AOC) Gary can claim on his 2012 return?

2500 per student

A. $2,500.
B. $6,000.
C. $5,000.
D. $7,500.

17. The Lifetime Learning Credit is limited to $2,000 per _Tax Return_.

A. Qualifying student.
B. Tax return.
C. College.
D. Dependent.

18. During 2012, Matthew paid $1,700 for medical expenses. His AGI for the year was $20,000. What is Matthew's allowable medical expense deduction on **Schedule A** *after the AGI limit is applied?*

A. $1,500.
B. $1,700.
C. $500.
D. $200.

19. Amelia died in 2012. Which of the following assets would be included in the calculation of her gross estate?

A. Life insurance proceeds payable to Amelia's beneficiaries.
B. Property owned solely by Amelia's spouse.
C. Lifetime gifts that are complete.
D. All of the above would be includable in Amelia's gross estate.

20. Irene owns a residential rental condo. In 2012, she trades her existing rental property with an adjusted basis of $17,000 (FMV $50,000) for a new condo costing $68,000. As part of the exchange, she pays $20,000 to the owner of the other property. This is a qualified section 1031 exchange. What is Irene's basis in her new rental property?

A. $37,000.
B. $68,000.
C. $70,000.
D. $51,000.

21. During 2011, Brandy had gross medical expenses of $1,400, but could only deduct $300 on **Schedule A** due to the 7.5% of AGI limit. In 2012, Brandy received a $900 reimbursement from her insurance for a portion of the medical expenses. How much of this recovery must be included on her 2012 return?

A. $0.
B. $900.
C. $300.
D. $600.

22. Aiden bought his primary residence on September 1, 2009. He lived in the home until March 30, 2012 when he moved in with his girlfriend. On September 15, 2012, Aiden decided to sell the home. He had a $23,000 gain on the sale of the home. Is Aiden required to report any of the gain on the home, and, if so, what is the nature of the gain?

A. Aiden must report $23,000 in long-term capital gain.
B. Aiden must report $23,000 in short-term capital gain.
C. Aiden must report $23,000 in ordinary gain.
D. All the gain is excludable from income.

23. Which of the following types of nontaxable income is required to be reported on a taxpayer's return, even though it is exempt from tax?

A. Gifts and inheritances.
B. Municipal bond interest.
C. Life insurance proceeds received by a beneficiary.
D. Employee reimbursements made under an accountable plan.

24. Donna received the following income for the year. Determine which sources of Donna's income are taxable and which are nontaxable, and then figure the gross income shown on her return.

SOURCE	TAXABLE?
Wages	$26,200
Interest	$5,400
Child support	$6,200
Alimony	$7,400
Inheritance	$12,600
Workers' compensation	$2,300
Unemployment compensation	$5,300

Based on the figures above, what is Donna's gross income before adjustments and deductions are applied?

A. $52,800.
B. $63,100.
C. $41,300.
D. $44,300.

25. Which of the following types of income is considered qualifying compensation for purposes of a traditional IRA contribution?

A. Rental income.
B. Dividend income.
C. Alimony income.
D. Annuity income.

26. Individuals who receive _____ or more per month in cash tips from one job must report their tip income to their employer.

A. All tip income must be reported to the employer, no matter how small.
B. $10.
C. $20.
D. $100.

27. Allie converted her home to a residential rental several years ago. On the date she converted the property, her cost basis in the home was $375,000 and the fair market value was $230,000. She had claimed $18,000 in total depreciation on the rental. In 2012, Allie sells the rental property for $205,000. What is the amount of Allie's deductible loss?

A. $152,000 loss.
B. $43,000 loss.
C. $25,000 loss.
D. $7,000 loss.

28. What is the main difference between **Form 1099** and **Form 1098**?

A. **Form 1098** reports expenses taxpayers have paid, while **Form 1099** reports income that a taxpayer has received.
B. There is no real difference between **Form 1099** and **Form 1098**.
C. **Form 1099** is used to report wages, while **Form 1098** is not.
D. **Form 1099** is used for taxpayers, while **Form 1098** is used for entities.

29. Herb has the following dispositions in 2012:

- $1,000 loss on ABC Co. stock he purchased on January 15, 2012 and sold on November 15, 2012
- $5,000 gain on the sale of an empty lot that he inherited on February 2, 2012
- $2,000 gain on the sale of XYZ Co. stock he purchased on March 15, 2011 and sold on June 15, 2012

What is the amount and nature of Herb's net gains and net losses?

A. Herb has a $1,000 short-term capital loss and a $7,000 long-term capital gain.
B. Herb has a $1,000 short-term capital loss, a $2,000 long-term capital gain, and a $5,000 short-term capital gain.
C. Herb has a net $1,000 short-term capital loss and a $5,000 long-term capital gain.
D. Herb has a net $2,000 short-term capital loss and a $5,000 long-term capital gain.

30. Natalie is a U.S. citizen who lives and works in England, which is where her tax home is. She does not maintain a residence in the U.S. In 2012, she received the following income:

- $12,500 in annuity income
- $2,000 in taxable interest
- $90,000 in wages

Natalie wants to take the foreign earned income exclusion on her individual tax return. What is the total amount of qualifying foreign earned income that Natalie must report on her **Form 2555** (Form 1040)?

A. $102,500.
B. $92,000.
C. $90,000.
D. $95,100.

31. Martina works as a secretary during the week and works as a hairdresser on the weekends, where she is paid an hourly wage plus tips. She also receives some other items of income. Based on the figures below, what will Martina show as her **wage income** on her individual **Form 1040?**

Secretary, Form W-2 wages	$25,600
Hairdresser, Form W-2 wages	$4,950
Hairdresser, unreported tips	$300
Unemployment compensation	$3,700
Taxable state tax refund	$2,000

A. $36,550.
B. $30,850.
C. $30,550.
D. $34,250.

32. Larry owns a $500 U.S. Series EE savings bond. He paid $250 for the bond earlier in the year. When the bond matures, Larry will receive $500. At the end of the first year, the bond is worth $257. How should Larry report this interest on his tax return?

A. Larry must report the bond interest as it is earned. Therefore, on his current year return, he would report $7 in interest income.
B. U.S. Series EE savings bonds are exempt from federal income tax.
C. Larry may report $250 of interest income once when the bond matures, or he may choose to report $7 of interest income at the end of the year.
D. Larry is required to report the interest when the bond reaches maturity, regardless of the redemption date.

33. A taxpayer dies on March 31, 2012. For estate tax purposes, what is the alternate valuation date for the taxpayer's estate?

A. September 30, 2012.
B. December 31, 2012.
C. April 15, 2013.
D. March 31, 2013.

34. Karen owns a residential rental duplex. Both units were vacant at the beginning of the year. On April 1, 2012, Karen begins renting the first unit for $1,300 per month. She also collects a $1,000 refundable cleaning deposit from the first tenant. On October 1, 2012, Karen is finally able to rent the second unit for $600 per month. Karen obtains a $300 refundable cleaning deposit from the second tenant. On December 12, 2012, Karen's second tenant leaves on vacation and pays his January 2013 rent in advance. Karen accepts the check for $600, but does not cash it until January. Based on this information, how much rental income should Karen report on her **Schedule E** in 2012?

A. $13,500.
B. $15,400.
C. $14,800.
D. $14,100.

35. Which of the following items is not an adjustment to income?

A. Alimony paid.
B. Bad debt deduction.
C. Moving expenses.
D. Employee business expenses. Sch A

36. Sandy's unmarried son, Greg, lived with her all year. Greg was 27 years old at the end of the year, and his gross income from wages was $5,200. Greg is not disabled. Sandy paid all the costs of keeping up the home. Can Sandy claim Greg as a dependent and also file as head of household?

A. Sandy can claim Greg as a dependent and also claim head of household filing status.
B. Sandy can claim Greg as a dependent, but she cannot claim head of household filing status.
C. Sandy cannot claim Greg as a dependent, but she can file as head of household.
D. Sandy cannot claim Greg as a dependent, and she does not qualify for head of household filing status.

37. John and Bree are going through a divorce. The divorce decree states that John must transfer a portion of his traditional IRA to Bree as part of their settlement. Bree is 48 and John is 62. For tax purposes, how is this transfer treated?

A. The transfer is tax free.
B. The transfer is subject to tax, but exempt from the 10% early withdrawal penalty.
C. The transfer is exempt from income tax as long as the amounts are rolled over, but Bree must pay an early withdrawal penalty because she is younger than 59½ years old.
D. The transfer is subject to tax and also subject to the 10% early withdrawal penalty.

38. Which of the following is a **prohibited transaction** relating to a traditional IRA?

A. Early withdrawal of IRA funds.
B. Using the IRA as security for a loan.
C. Making excess contributions.
D. Failing to take required minimum distributions.

39. Tina is 32, unmarried, and files head of household. Her AGI was $115,000 in 2012. Is she allowed to contribute to a Roth IRA?

A. No, she may not contribute to a Roth.
B. Yes, she may contribute to a Roth, but her contribution is limited by AGI.
C. Yes, she may contribute to a Roth, and her contribution is not limited by AGI.
D. Insufficient information to answer.

40. In 2012, taxpayers are allowed to convert their traditional IRA to a Roth IRA. The conversion is treated as a _____.

A. Prohibited transaction.
B. Early withdrawal.
C. Rollover.
D. Special distribution.

41. Theo works as an independent bookkeeper for several clients. His biggest client, Danville Construction Company, sends Theo a **Form 1099-MISC** that shows he received $12,400 for bookkeeping work in 2012. Theo also received other cash payments of $2,500 from several different individuals for the work he completed. He did not receive **Forms 1099-MISC** for the $2,500. Based on this information, how much of his income is subject to regular income tax, and how much is subject to self-employment tax?

A. $12,400 is subject to income tax and self-employment tax. The remaining $2,500 is only subject to income tax.
B. $12,400 is subject only to income tax. The other $2,500 is subject to income tax and self-employment tax.
C. $14,900 is subject to income tax. None of the amounts is subject to self-employment tax, because Theo qualifies as a statutory employee.
D. The full amount, $14,900, is subject to self-employment tax and income tax.

42. Which of the following would be a qualified adoption expense for purposes of the Adoption Credit?

A. Expenses paid in an unsuccessful adoption attempt to adopt an eligible child.
B. Expenses for adopting a spouse's child.
C. A surrogate parenting arrangement.
D. Adoption expenses reimbursed by an employer.

43. Which of the following corporate distributions must be reported on Form 1040 as taxable income?

A. Capital gain distributions.
B. A return of capital.
C. Stock dividends.
D. Dividends paid to cash-value life insurance policyholders.

44. Which of the following credits is partially refundable?

A. The American Opportunity Credit.
B. The Lifetime Learning Credit.
C. The Adoption Credit.
D. The Child Care and Dependent Care Credit.

45. Lupe received ordinary dividends in the amount of $175. She also had a $700 capital gain from the sale of stock. How should this income be reported?

A. Both amounts should be reported on **Form 1040, Schedule B.**
B. Lupe's ordinary dividends should be reported on **Form 1040**, and the capital gain from the stock sale should be reported on **Schedule D.**
C. Lupe's ordinary dividends should be reported on **Schedule B**, and the capital gain from the stock sale should be reported on **Schedule D.**
D. Both amounts should be reported on **Form 1040, Schedule D.**

46. Danni is 26 and unmarried. She and her 4-year-old daughter, Jennifer, lived with Danni's father, Fred, all year. Fred paid all the costs of keeping up the home. Danni provides her own support, but Fred helps support Jennifer, his granddaughter. Danni's AGI is $19,000. Fred's AGI is $45,000. Based on these facts, may Danni file her own return and claim her daughter as her dependent?

A. Yes, Danni may file as head of household, claim her daughter as a dependent, and claim the Earned Income Credit.
B. Yes, Danni may file as single, claim her daughter as a dependent, and claim the Earned Income Credit.
C. No, Danni may not claim her daughter as a dependent because she did pay the costs of keeping up the home.
D. None of the answers are correct.

47. Leslie files single and has no refundable credits. Based on the figures below, is Leslie required to pay estimated tax in 2013?

AGI for 2012	$73,700
Total tax on 2012 return	$9,224
Anticipated AGI for 2013	$82,800
Total 2013 estimated tax (using the 2013 estimated tax worksheet)	$11,270
Tax expected to be withheld in 2013	$10,250

A. Yes, she is required to make estimated tax payments.
B. No, she is not required to make estimated tax payments.
C. She is not required to make estimated tax payments, but she should increase her withholding at her job.
D. None of the above is correct.

48. In general, royalties from copyrights, patents, and oil, gas, and mineral properties are taxable as:

A. Capital gains.
B. Ordinary income.
C. Self-employment income.
D. Exempt income.

49. Dave has a loss from worthless securities. How many years does Dave have to amend his tax returns in order to take this loss?

A. Two years.
B. Three years.
C. Six years.
D. Seven years.

50. Pearl bought tickets for a fundraising dinner at her local church. She paid $280 for six tickets. The value of the dinner (printed on the ticket) was $20 per person. All the proceeds from the dinner will go to the church. How much can Pearl deduct as a charitable gift on **Schedule A**?

A. $0.
B. $280.
C. $120.
D. $160.

amt that exceeds value

$20 x 6 = $120 value

$280 - 120 = $160

51. Paul is an Army veteran. He was injured while serving in a combat zone and was later awarded Veterans Affairs (VA) disability benefits. How are these payments reported on Paul's tax return?

A. 100% of the disability severance benefits may be excluded from income.
B. Up to 50% of the disability severance benefits may be excluded from income.
C. 100% of the disability severance benefits may be excluded from income tax, but is still subject to Social Security tax.
D. The disability severance benefits are taxable as ordinary income.

52. Stacy is unmarried and files head of household. She has four dependent children that live with her, all of whom are under 17 years of age. Stacy's mother, Racine, also lives with them. Racine has no income, and Stacy provides all of her mother's financial support. Based on this information, how many dependency exemptions may Stacy claim on her return?

A. Two.
B. Three.
C. Five.
D. Six.

53. Angelo is age 25 and unmarried. He does not have any dependents. In 2011, he earned $6,700 in wages and had no other income. He did not have to pay income tax because his gross income was less than the filing requirement. He filed a return only to have his withheld income tax refunded to him. In 2012, Angelo began work as a self-employed plumber. He expects to earn $30,000 in 2012. Based on his income, his tax for the year will be $3,684. Angelo made no estimated tax payments in 2012. Will he pay an underpayment penalty for failure to pay estimated tax?

A. He will pay an underpayment penalty.
B. He will not pay an underpayment penalty.
C. He will pay a failure-to-pay penalty, not an underpayment penalty.
D. In this case, assessment of the penalty will be at the IRS's discretion.

54. Joe has owned his home for ten years. Cristina is his girlfriend, and they have lived together in the home for three years. She was not an owner on the title. Joe and Cristina are married on January 1, 2012, but start having marital problems immediately, and Joe moves out. They divorce on June 1, 2012. As part of their divorce settlement, Joe transfers total ownership of the home to Cristina, who puts the house on the market and sells it for a $165,000 gain on November 30, 2012. How much of the gain is excludable on Cristina's individual tax return?

A. All the gain is excludable.
B. All the gain is taxable, because Cristina does not meet the ownership and use tests to exclude the gain.
C. A portion of the gain is taxable, because Cristina meets the ownership test but not the use test.
D. A portion of the gain is taxable and must be prorated by how long Cristina occupied and owned the property.

55. Gabriel has three dependent sons in college. He is unmarried and files head of household. Gabriel's AGI in 2012 is $61,000. All of Gabriel's' children are full-time students. Gabriel provides the majority of the financial support for his children, and he will claim all of them on his tax return. Here are the details regarding their education expenses:

- Jason, age 23, graduate student working on his master's degree, with $12,500 in qualifying higher education expenses. Jason had earned income from a part-time job totaling $4,200 in 2012.
- Marcus, age 21, a college senior working on his first undergraduate degree, with $9,100 in qualifying college expenses. Marcus has income of $5,700 from a part-time job in 2012.
- Billy, age 19, a college sophomore working on his first undergraduate degree. Billy had $4,400 in qualifying education expenses. He had no income during the year. Billy has a conviction for felony drug possession on his record.

Based on the facts above, which of the following statements is true?

A. Gabriel may take the Lifetime Learning Credit for Jason and the American Opportunity Credit for Marcus and Billy.
B. Gabriel may claim the American Opportunity Credit for all his sons.
C. Gabriel may claim the American Opportunity Credit for Marcus. He can take the Lifetime Learning Credit for Billy and Jason.
D. Gabriel may claim the American Opportunity Credit for Marcus. He can take the Lifetime Learning Credit for Jason. He cannot claim any education credits for Billy.

56. Mitch is a self-employed appliance repairman. His business has two employees. Which of the following insurance expenses is not deductible on Mitch's Schedule C?

A. Health insurance for Mitch.
B. Health insurance for Mitch's employees.
C. Liability insurance for Mitch's business.
D. Auto insurance on Mitch's work truck.

57. Jim and his wife Peggy are both attending graduate school. They file jointly, and their combined AGI is $45,000. In 2012, they had the following tuition expenses:

- Jim: $4,800 in tuition, books, and required materials
- Peggy: $6,900 in tuition, books, and required materials

Based on the information given, what is the amount of the education credits that will be shown on their joint return?

A. A $960 Lifetime Learning Credit for Jim, and a $1,380 Lifetime Learning Credit for Peggy.
B. Jim and Peggy are each eligible for a $2,500 AOC credit. The maximum credit on the return will be $5,000 ($2,500 X 2).
C. Jim and Peggy are limited to a $2,000 maximum Lifetime Learning Credit on their return.
D. Jim and Peggy are limited to a $4,000 maximum Lifetime Learning Credit on their return.

58. Ileana is a self-employed tax preparer who files a **Schedule C** to report her business income. In 2012, she has the following purchases, all of which are 100% business-use. She is on the cash basis. Ignoring any income limitations, what is her **section 179 deduction** for 2012?

1. New computer system: $4,600
2. New multi-line phone system: $3,600
3. Bathroom renovation for her business office $23,000
4. Phone bill charges: $1,300

A. $8,200.
B. $31,200.
C. $9,500.
D. $32,500.

59. Larissa has an 18-year-old dependent son named Braden. Larissa claims Braden on her return and files head of household. Braden has a part-time job, and he files his return on March 1, mistakenly claiming his own exemption on the return. Larissa tried e-filing her return and received an e-file rejection when she tried to claim her son. What should a tax preparer advise in this situation?

A. Advise Braden to amend his tax return using **Form 1040X**, removing his personal exemption from the return. Once the amended return is processed, Larissa may file her tax return normally, claiming her son as a dependent.
B. Larissa may not claim Braden, because he has already filed his own return claiming himself.
C. Larissa should use **Form 1040X** (instead of **Form 1040**), explaining the situation and reporting Braden's error.
D. Larissa may not claim her son Braden this year, but she is allowed to claim head of household on her tax return.

60. Rafael's 2009 tax return was due April 15, 2010. He filed it on March 20, 2010. Later, Rafael discovers that he is eligible for a tax credit that will result in a refund. He neglected to take this credit on his 2009 return. What is the latest date that Rafael can amend his 2009 tax return in order to receive a refund?

A. April 15, 2012.
B. April 15, 2013.
C. March 20, 2013.
D. April 15, 2011.

61. Polly is 72. She is required to take required minimum distributions (RMD) on her traditional IRA. She forgets to take the required minimum distribution in 2012. What is the amount of excise tax that will be assessed on the amount not withdrawn?

A. 6%.
B. 10%
C. 50%.
D. 100%.

62. When does the IRS require the owner of a Roth IRA to start taking withdrawals?

A. After the death of the IRA owner.
B. After age 59½.
C. After age 70½.
D. **Never**.

63. Daniela, 56, and Robert, 66, are married and file jointly in 2012. They do not itemize their deductions. Robert is blind. What is their standard deduction amount for 2012?

A. $11,900.
B. $13,050.
C. $7,600.
D. $14,200.

64. Which of the following taxpayers is the *most* likely to be required to pay estimated taxes?

A. A household employee.
B. A nonresident alien with U.S. investments, who is subject to backup withholding.
C. A statutory employee.
D. A statutory nonemployee.

65. Steven and Rita are married and file separately. Steven chooses to itemize deductions on his return. Rita does not have any itemized deductions to claim. What is the amount of Rita's standard deduction amount on her separate return?

A. $0.
B. $3,800.
C. $6,100.
D. $12,200.

66. Carlos is age 32 and single. His AGI for 2012 was $33,200. Of this amount, $3,000 was from gambling winnings. He had the following itemized deductions:

Medical expenses (gross amount)	$10,400
Mortgage interest on main home	$6,700
Property tax on main home	$2,300
Miscellaneous unreimbursed work expenses	$1,200
Charitable donation to his church	$1,600
Gambling losses	$4,600

After applying AGI limitations, what is the amount of his allowable itemized deductions on **Schedule A**?

A. $22,046.
B. $22,710.
C. $24,310.
D. $19,710.

67. When should a tax preparer calculate a taxpayer's itemized deductions on Schedule A?

A. After determining the taxpayer's gross income.
B. After determining the taxpayer's adjusted gross income.
C. Before determining the taxpayer's adjusted gross income.
D. Before determining the taxpayer's gross income.

68. Which of the following taxes is deductible on **Schedule A** as an itemized deduction?

A. State inheritance tax.
B. Qualified foreign income taxes.
C. Employment taxes.
D. Federal income taxes.

69. Kristin and Santiago file a joint return. Their adjusted gross income is $48,000. During the year, they paid the following medical expenses:

Copayments for prescription drugs:	$500
Dentist fees	$1,200
Medical insurance premiums	$300
Life insurance premiums	$500
Long-term care insurance premiums	$100
Vitamins	$90
Hospital bill	$3,000
Prescription eyeglasses	$350
Total costs	**$6,040**

The total of Kristin and Santiago's qualified medical expenses **after** the application of the 7.5% of AGI limit is $_____?

A. $3,600.
B. $1,850.
C. $453.
D. $4,190.

70. Penelope's home was damaged by a hurricane. She had $58,000 in damage and received $50,000 from her insurance company. In 2012, her AGI was $22,000. She had no other casualty losses during the year. What is her deductible casualty loss on Schedule A **after** applying the personal casualty loss deduction limits?

A. $8,000.
B. $7,900.
C. $2,200.
D. $5,700.

71. Suzy owns a residential rental property in addition to her primary residence. She pays mortgage interest and property taxes on both homes, and receives a separate **Form 1098** for each property. How should this mortgage interest be reported on her individual tax return?

A. The mortgage interest and taxes for both properties should be listed as an adjustment to income on **Form 1040**.

B. The mortgage interest and taxes for both properties should be listed as an itemized deduction on **Schedule A.**

C. The mortgage interest and taxes for the rental property should be listed as an expense on **Schedule E.** The mortgage interest and taxes for the primary residence should be listed on **Schedule A** as an itemized deduction.

D. The mortgage interest for the rental property should be listed on **Schedule E.** The mortgage interest for the primary residence and the property taxes for both properties should be listed on **Schedule A.**

72. In 2012, Astrid spent time searching for a new job as a dental assistant. She was a dental assistant in her previous job before being laid off. She also applied for several jobs in other industries. At the end of the year, she is still unemployed. Which of the following job search expenses are deductible on **Schedule A** as an itemized deduction?

A. Astrid cannot deduct her job search expenses because she is still unemployed. Once she gets a job, she will be allowed to deduct the accrued expenses.

B. Only job search expenses in Astrid's former occupation as a dental assistant are deductible.

C. All of Astrid's job search expenses are deductible, whether it is in her current occupation or in a new occupation.

D. None of the above. Job search expenses are never deductible, regardless of the situation or outcome.

73. Which of the following items will not increase a taxpayer's refund?

A. Refundable credits.

B. Excess Social Security tax withheld.

C. Withholding payments that exceed tax liability.

D. The alternative minimum tax.

74. Veronica is 26, single, and she purchased her first home in 2008. She applied for the $7,500 First Time Homebuyer Credit in 2008. Regarding this now-expired tax credit, how could it affect her individual tax return in 2012?

A. Expired credits have no effect on current-year returns.
B. In 2008, this credit took the form of a loan and must be repaid. Veronica must pay a portion of this loan back on her tax return in 2012.
C. This credit is a refundable credit, and does not need to be repaid unless Veronica sells or disposes of the property.
D. This past credit will only affect Veronica's current year return if she purchases a second home. In that case, the credit would be prorated.

75. Caitlyn is an unmarried U.S. citizen with a 26-year-old son, Javier, who is permanently disabled and lives with her. Caitlyn's son is employed under a special workshop program for individuals with disabilities. Javier makes $12,500 in wages from this workshop program. Since Javier is gainfully employed, is Caitlyn's son still considered a "qualifying child" for purposes of the EITC?

A. No. Since her son is gainfully employed, Caitlyn would not qualify.
B. No. Javier is not a qualifying child or a qualifying relative, because he exceeds the age and income limits for dependency. Therefore, Javier is no longer a qualifying child for EITC purposes.
C. Yes. Caitlyn's son is still considered a qualifying child for purposes of claiming the EITC.
D. None of the above.

76. In 2012, Phil's house was burglarized. His overall losses were $6,000. Phil's insurance company reimbursed him $4,000. Phil's adjusted gross income for the year is $20,500. What is Phil's theft loss deduction on **Schedule A,** after applying the $100 rule and the 10% rule?

A. $0.
B. $2,000.
C. $2,050.
D. $1,900.

77. Luke had the following items of income and loss in 2012:

Wages reported on Form W-2	$42,000
Gambling winnings	$2,000
Gambling losses	$4,000
Dependent care benefits (spent $3,200 on childcare)	$3,000
Capital loss carryover from prior year	$7,500

He does not itemize deductions. How much income must Luke report on his tax return?

A. $58,500.
B. $39,000.
C. $36,500.
D. $41,000.

78. In 2011, Harold loaned his neighbor, Trish, $10,000 in a bona-fide loan. In 2012, Trish files for bankruptcy, and she permanently settles her debt with Harold by paying $2,000. Which of the following statements is true?

A. Harold must report $2,000 in income, and Trish must report $8,000 in canceled debt.
B. Trish must report $10,000 in canceled debt. Harold is not required to report any income.
C. Trish must report $8,000 in canceled debt. Harold is not required to report any income.
D. Neither Harold nor Trish has taxable income from this exchange.

79. Jayden works for ABC Incorporated. In 2012, Jayden was granted 100 shares of ABC stock valued at $19,500, under the condition that he would be required to return the shares if he did not complete five years of service. ABC's basis in the stock was $14,000 in 2012. How much income must Jayden recognize on his 2012 tax return?

A. $19,500.
B. $14,000.
C. $3,900.
D. Jayden will not report any income until he completes five years of service.

80. Madison's uncle died two years ago. Her uncle had substantial assets and Madison is one of the beneficiaries of the estate. In 2012, Madison receives a distribution of nonpassive income from her uncle's estate. How will this distribution be reported to Madison, and how should she report the income on her own return?

A. The distribution from the estate would be reported to Madison on **Schedule K-1 (Form 1041)**. The amounts would be reported on **Schedule E (Form 1040)**.
B. The distribution from the estate would be reported to Madison on **Schedule K-1 (Form 1041)**. The amounts would be reported on page 1 of **Form 1040**.
C. The distribution from the estate would be reported to Madison on **Schedule K-1 (Form 1041)**. The amounts would be reported on **Schedule D (Form 1040)**.
D. The distribution from the estate is never taxable to the beneficiary, only to the estate.

81. Gerald dies in 2012, and his estate is formed. According to his will, $5,000 a year is to be paid to his widow, Abigail, and $2,500 a year is to be paid to his daughter out of the estate's income during the period of administration. For the year, the estate's distributable net income is $6,000. Based on this information, how much income is Abigail required to report on her individual tax return (**Form 1040**)?

A. $5,000.
B. $4,000.
C. $6,000.
D. Insufficient information to answer.

82. When are estate distributions taxable on the beneficiary's individual tax return (**Form 1040**)?

A. Income from an estate is only taxable to a beneficiary when it is distributed.
B. If income from an estate is credited or must be distributed to a taxpayer, the income must be reported in the year that the distribution is credited, even if the income is not distributed.
C. Income from an estate is only taxable to a taxpayer if he has physical possession of the funds.
D. Income to an estate is taxable to the beneficiary when the estate is created.

83. In 2012, an estate has distributable net income of $3,000, consisting of $1,800 in rents and $1,200 in taxable interest. The beneficiaries of the estate are Emily and Olivia, two sisters. The estate distributes the income equally (50/50) between the two beneficiaries. In 2012, the executor distributes $1,500 each to Emily and Olivia. How should they report this income on their individual tax returns?

A. Each will be treated as having received $900 in rents and $600 of taxable interest.
B. Each will be treated as having received $1,500 in ordinary income.
C. Each will be treated as having received $1,800 in rents and $1,200 of taxable interest.
D. This income does not need to be reported by the taxpayers, because it has already been taxed at the estate level.

84. For purposes of the Child Tax Credit, a *qualifying child* is a child who _____.

A. Is under the age of 18 and a full-time student (or disabled of any age).
B. Is under the age of 17 and claimed as a dependent on the taxpayer's return.
C. Lived with the taxpayer for the entire year, regardless of age.
D. Supplies more than half of his or her own support.

85. Shane sold 200 shares of Willitts Corporation stock on September 5, 2012. His basis in the shares was $5,500, and he sold the shares for $3,200. He paid a broker's fee of $80. On November 3, 2012, Shane repurchased 200 shares of Willitts Corporation stock for $3,100. What is his allowable loss on the sale of these securities?

A. $0.
B. $2,300.
C. $2,400.
D. $2,220.

86. During the year, Sophia paid $15,000 in mortgage interest on her primary residence. She also paid $3,900 in mortgage interest on her second home and $6,700 in loan interest on a recreational vehicle (RV) with sleeping, cooking, and toilet facilities. What is Sophia's maximum mortgage interest deduction on **Schedule A?**

A. $15,000.
B. $18,900.
C. $21,700
D. $25,600.

87. Tristan buys a residential rental for $35,000 cash and assumes a mortgage of $80,000 on the property. During the purchase, he also pays $2,300 in settlement fees to close the deal. Of those settlement fees, $800 was for title insurance on the property. Based on this information, what is Tristan's basis in the building?

A. $35,000.
B. $115,000.
C. $117,300.
D. $116,500.

88. Charlene is a tax preparer who reports her business income on **Schedule C**. She prepares the tax return for JMC corporation, and charges the company $1,200 for the tax return and bookkeeping. JMC corporation is having some financial difficulties, so it offers Charlene computer hardware worth $2,000 in lieu of paying the debt. Charlene agrees to the trade. Based on this information, how much business income would Charlene report on Schedule C as a result of this transaction?

A. $1,200.
B. $2,000.
C. $1,200 in business income, $800 in passive income.
D. $0, since the amount was not paid in cash.

89. Scott is a software programmer and computer repairman who reports his business income and loss on **Schedule C.** He creates a new software program for one of his clients, an auto dealership, to use at its business location. The cost of Scott's services is $14,000. Rather than paying the invoice, the dealership gives Scott a new van with an FMV of $14,500. Scott agrees to the trade and accepts the van in lieu of a cash payment. The dealership's basis in the van is $12,300. At the time he takes possession of the van, Scott is required to pay sales tax totaling $960. Scott plans to use the van for his computer business. Based on this information, what is Scott's depreciable basis in the van?

A. $12,300.
B. $14,000.
C. $14,500.
D. $14,960.

90. Mason is single and 32. He does not have any dependents. In 2012, Mason wins $12,000 at a casino. The casino withholds $1,300 in federal income taxes on the winnings. He also has $14,500 in gambling losses during the year. Mason itemizes deductions. How should this be reported on his return?

A. Mason must report $12,000 in gambling winnings. He should also report the $1,300 withholding on his return. He cannot deduct his gambling losses.

B. Mason must report $12,000 in gambling winnings. He should also report the $1,300 withholding on his return. Mason can deduct $14,500 in gambling losses as a miscellaneous itemized deduction.

C. Mason should report his net gambling losses of $2,500 ($14,500 - $12,000). He should also report the $1,300 withholding on his return.

D. Mason must report $12,000 in gambling winnings. He should also report the $1,300 withholding on his return. Mason can deduct up to $12,000 of gambling losses as an itemized deduction.

91. Zoe worked for two different employers during the year. As a result, she had excess Social Security tax withheld by her employer. How can Zoe receive a credit for these overpaid amounts?

A. She may claim the excess as a credit against her income tax.

B. Zoe must request a refund of her overpaid Social Security tax from her employer.

C. If Zoe had too much Social Security tax withheld, she may be able to claim the excess as a credit against next year's Social Security tax liability.

D. Zoe can claim the excess Social Security tax as a carryover against her tax liability in future years.

92. Colton is 22, a full-time student, and claimed as a dependent on his parent's tax return. He also has a part-time job at a local mall. Colton has $210 in dividend income in 2012. What is the maximum amount of wages that can be earned by Colton in 2012 without triggering the "kiddie tax"?

only on investment income

A. $5,950.
B. $950.
C. $1,900.
D. No maximum.

53

93. Isabelle was offered a new job in another state, and she incurred qualified moving expenses. Isabelle decided to drive her own car, and also hire a moving company to move all of her belongings. None of her moving expenses were reimbursed by her new employer. The expenses she incurred during the move were as follows:

Cost of shipping her horse	$450
Gasoline costs during the move	$120
Cost of packing and shipping household goods	$6,400
Hotel costs while in transit	$310
Meals while in transit	$120
Cost of breaking her lease at her old apartment	$520
Lost deposit on her old apartment	$440
Cost of connecting a phone line at her new home	$120

Based on the information above, what is the **total amount** of her qualified moving expenses for the moving expense deduction?

A. $8,480.
B. $7,400.
C. $7,840.
D. $8,360.

94. Mariah had income from a number of sources in 2012. During the year, she received $12,400 in Social Security benefits; $42,000 in wage income; and $31,000 in capital gains. Based on this information, what is the **maximum taxable amount** of Mariah's Social Security benefits?

A. $12,400.
B. $25,000.
C. $6,200.
D. $10,540.

95. A nonrefundable credit can reduce tax liability to _____.

A. Zero.
B. Below zero.
C. The next year.
D. None of the above.

96. In 2012, Vanessa adopts an eligible child. She has $11,000 in adoption expenses for the year. The adoption became final in December 2012. Her tax liability for the year is $9,500, and she applies the Adoption Credit, which reduces her tax to zero. What happens to the unused portion of the Adoption Credit?

A. In 2012, the Adoption Credit is refundable. Therefore, Vanessa will receive a refund of $1,500.
B. In 2012, the Adoption Credit is nonrefundable. Therefore, Vanessa will receive a carryover of $1,500 that she can use in the following year.
C. In 2012, the Adoption Credit is nonrefundable. Therefore, Vanessa will lose the remaining $1,500 in unused adoption expenses.
D. None of the above is correct.

97. Alton owns two residential rental properties. During the year, he purchased two stoves for his rental properties totaling $1,200. He replaced a broken window on one property at a cost of $350. He also replaced the roof on one property at a cost of $12,000. Alton wants to apply these expenses to offset his rental income, which is $16,000 for the year. Alton is not a real estate professional. Based on this information, what is his allowable section 179 deduction for the year? *does not apply to rental activity*

A. $0.
B. $1,200.
C. $1,550.
D. $13,200.

98. Kenneth, age 60, made an Individual Retirement Account (IRA) contribution of $6,000 on March 25, 2012. Two weeks later, Kenneth lost his job. His wages for 2012 were $4,500. His unemployment benefits totaled $12,600. He had no other items of income. Which of the following is true about Kenneth's traditional IRA contribution?

A. Kenneth has made a $1,500 excess contribution to his IRA. He must correct the excess contribution, or he will have to pay an excise tax.
B. Kenneth has made a $1,000 excess contribution to his IRA. He must correct the excess contribution, or he will have to pay an excise tax.
C. Kenneth has made a $6,000 excess contribution to his IRA. He must correct the excess contribution, or he will have to pay an excise tax.
D. Kenneth has not made an excess contribution to his IRA, because his overall compensation for the year exceeds his IRA contribution.

99. In the current year, Chester had a number of stock sales. His investment transactions this year were:

Activity	Bought	Sold
Sold 1400 shares of ABC stock for $3,000 (basis $1,400)	1/3/10	12/1/12
Sold 200 shares of Lemon stock for $500 (basis: $1,000)	1/3/09	12/25/12
Sold 50 shares of Harrington stock for $1,700 (basis: $1,500)	2/1/12	9/12/12

What is Chester's **net long-term** capital gain (or loss)?

A. $1,000 long-term capital loss.
B. $1,200 long-term capital loss.
C. $1,100 long-term capital gain.
D. $1,600 long-term capital gain.

100. Doris bought a new home during the year. The mortgage loan included charges for points, which were detailed on her closing statement (HUD-1). How would the charges for points be reported on her tax return?

A. The points are deductible mortgage interest on **Schedule A.**
B. The amounts for points would not be deductible currently. Instead, the amounts are added to the basis of the home.
C. Deductible as a miscellaneous expense, subject to the 2% floor on **Schedule A.**
D. This transaction does not affect a person's individual tax return.

Please review your answers with the answers in the back.

#2 Individuals Sample Exam

1. Jenni is legally separated from her husband and files MFS. They have not lived to-gether for three years. In 2012, Jenni has $48,000 in wages and $26,500 of passive losses from a rental real estate activity in which she actively participated. How much of her rental losses are allowable on her MFS return?

A. $0. All the losses must be carried forward.
B. $12,500.
C. $25,000.
D. $26,500.

2. Which of the following scenarios is considered a passive activity and subject to the passive activity rules?

A. Rental activity in which the taxpayer is a real estate professional.
B. Farming activity in which the taxpayer does not materially participate.
C. A general partner who earns income from the partnership.
D. Income earned from investments.

3. Felicia has a part-time nanny who works in her home. She pays the nanny $1,800 in wages during 2012. Which of the following statements is true? *answer is wrong*

A. Felicia does not have to report and pay Social Security and Medicare taxes on the nanny's 2012 wages.
B. The income is not taxable to the nanny.
C. No reporting is required by either party if the wages are paid in cash.
D. Felicia can deduct the nanny's wages on **Schedule C-EZ**.

4. Wesley has a great number of employee business expenses this year. In which scenario would he use **Form 2106** for his expenses?

A. When Wesley has no records of the expenses.
B. When Wesley's employer reimburses the full amount of Wesley's expenses.
C. When Wesley's expense reimbursements from his employer were included in his wage income.
D. When Wesley chooses not to deduct his employee business expenses.

5. Which of the following numbers is not a valid Taxpayer Identification Number (TIN)?

A. ATIN.
B. ITIN.
C. SSN.
D. PTIN.

6. Courtney is 18, single, and legally blind. She lives at home with her parents who claim her as a dependent on their joint tax return. Courtney received $1,950 of taxable interest and dividend income. She did not work during the year. Is she required to file a tax return?

A. Yes, she is required to file a return.
B. She is required to file a return, and her parents cannot claim her as a dependent.
C. No, she is not required to file a return.
D. Insufficient information to answer.

7. Patty has an HSA (health savings account). In 2012, Patty dies. She names her son Chase as the beneficiary for all her assets, including her HSA account. What will occur with the HSA Chase inherits?

A. Chase can choose to roll over the inherited HSA into his own HSA.
B. The account ceases to be an HSA, and the fair market value of the account is taxable to Chase in 2012.
C. The fair market value of the HSA is taxable to Patty on her final tax return (Form 1040). The amounts are not taxable to Chase.
D. The account continues to be an HSA, and the fair market value of the account is taxable to Chase in 2012.

8. How are gambling losses deducted on an individual tax return?

A. As an adjustment to income on **Form 1040**.
B. As an itemized deduction not subject to the 2% floor on **Schedule A**.
C. As an itemized deduction subject to the 2% floor on **Schedule A.**
D. Gambling losses are not deductible.

9. Jasmine is a self-employed enrolled agent, and she files a Schedule C. In which of the following instances would Jasmine not be required to obtain an Employer Identification Number (EIN)?

A. When she hires an employee.
B. When she forms a partnership with her husband.
C. When she operates multiple sole proprietorships.
D. When she files bankruptcy under Chapter 7.

10. Reggie is a U.S. Army veteran who recently returned to college for his first undergraduate degree. He is receiving educational assistance from the GI Bill. The GI Bill paid $4,750 toward his tuition, which was paid directly to the college. Reggie's total tuition cost for the year was $6,800. Reggie also paid the following additional educational costs during the year:

Required textbooks	$450
Mandatory student health fees	$186
Required lab equipment	$1,260

Reggie wants to claim the American Opportunity Credit (AOC) on his tax return. What are his qualifying educational expenses for purposes of the credit?

A. $3,946.
B. $3,760.
C. $8,510.
D. $2,050.

11. Tanner has a health FSA (flexible spending arrangement) through his employer. In 2012, he contributes $2,000 to his FSA in anticipation of his medical expenses. Which of the following statements is true?

A. Amounts contributed to an FSA must be reported on the taxpayer's individual return.
B. Amounts contributed to an FSA are not subject to federal income taxes, but are subject to Social Security tax.
C. Amounts contributed to an FSA are not subject to employment or federal income taxes.
D. Employers cannot contribute to an employee's FSA. The amounts must be fully funded by employee salary reduction in order to be qualifying contributions.

12. In 2012, Regina, who is single and lives alone, gives birth to a baby boy who only lives for two days. A Social Security Number was not issued for the child. Which of the following statements is true?

A. Regina may not claim the child as a dependent because he did not live with her for at least six months.
B. Regina may not claim the child as a dependent because he did not live with her for at least six months; however, Regina still qualifies for head of household filing status.
C. Regina may claim the child as a dependent and may file as head of household since she is unmarried.
D. Regina may claim the child as a dependent, but she may not file as head of household because she did not maintain a home for a qualifying dependent for at least six months.

13. Rodrigo provides all the financial support for his father, who is a citizen of Mexico. His father is not eligible for a Social Security Number. Rodrigo wants to claim his father as a dependent on his tax return. What must he do?

A. Nothing. Rodrigo cannot claim a citizen of Mexico on his tax return.
B. His father must apply for an Individual Taxpayer Identification Number (ITIN), and then Rodrigo can claim his father as a dependent.
C. Rodrigo can file a paper return and attach a copy of his father's identification in lieu of a Taxpayer Identification Number.
D. Rodrigo must apply for a Social Security Number on behalf of his father, before he can claim his father on a tax return.

14. Which of the following is true about Roth retirement accounts?

A. In 2012, anyone can make a qualified rollover contribution to a Roth IRA, regardless of the taxpayer's modified AGI.
B. In 2012, anyone can participate in and contribute to a Roth IRA, regardless of the amount of the taxpayer's modified AGI.
C. In 2012, anyone withdrawing funds from a Roth IRA will be subject to a withdrawal penalty, unless that person is over 59½ when the withdrawal is made.
D. In 2012, taxpayers can contribute to a traditional IRA as well as a Roth IRA, regardless of the taxpayer's modified AGI.

15. Adam's personal-use car was damaged in a flood in 2012. His loss after insurance reimbursement was $2,000. His adjusted gross income in 2012 is $29,500. Adam must first apply the $100 rule and then the 10% rule. What is his deductible casualty loss in 2012?

A. $0.
B. $1,900.
C. $2,000.
D. $2,950.

16. Brittany is 25 years old and unmarried. In 2012, she was covered by a retirement plan at work. Her wages for 2012 were $62,000 and her modified AGI was $69,000. Based on this information, is she allowed to make a traditional IRA contribution to her individual plan?

A. No, she is not allowed to make a traditional IRA contribution in 2012.
B. Yes, she is allowed to make a traditional IRA contribution in 2012, and it will be partially deductible.
C. Yes, she is allowed to make a traditional IRA contribution in 2012, and it will be fully deductible.
D. Yes, she is allowed to make a traditional IRA contribution in 2012, but she must designate the contribution as nondeductible.

17. John and Dianne are married, but have been legally separated since April 2012. They have one daughter, Simone, who lived with Dianne all year. Dianne provided over half of Simone's support. John does not want to file jointly with Dianne. What is the best filing status for Dianne?

A. Single.
B. Head of household.
C. Married filing separately.
D. Married filing jointly.

18. Each of the following individuals will automatically be taxed as a resident of the United States except:

A. A foreign-born individual physically present in the United States for 350 days.
B. A nonresident alien who marries a U.S. citizen in 2012.
C. A foreign-born person with a valid green card.
D. A foreign-born green card holder living outside the United States for one year.

19. Daniel and Maria are married and file jointly. They do not have any children. However, Daniel supports his 65-year-old stepmother who lives in an assisted living facility. Daniel's stepmother has interest income of $2,300 in 2012, and no other income. How many exemptions may Daniel and Maria claim on their tax return?

A. 0.
B. 1.
C. 2.
D. 3.

20. Odin and Hailey have been physically separated since September 2012, but they are not divorced. Their 14-year-old son, Sam, lived with Odin the entire year. Hailey moved out and is living in her own apartment, and she sees Sam on the weekends. Odin provided over half the cost of keeping up his home. Odin plans to file married filing separately, and he also plans to itemize his deductions. What are Hailey's options for filing her tax return?

A. Hailey can file head of household, so long as she does not take the dependency exemption for Sam.
B. Hailey must file MFS, and she may itemize or take the standard deduction.
C. Hailey can file head of household, so long as she lives with her husband the last six months of the year.
D. Hailey must file MFS, and she will also be forced to itemize. She cannot claim the dependency exemption for Sam.

21. Amber lives with her 16-year-old son Chad. She provided $5,100 toward Chad's support for the year. Chad also has a part-time job and provided $12,900 toward his own support. Can Amber claim her son as a dependent?

A. Yes, she can claim her son as a qualifying child, because he is a minor.
B. Yes, she can claim Chad as a qualifying relative.
C. No, Chad provided more than half of his own support for the year. Therefore, he is not Amber's qualifying child or her qualifying relative.
D. None of the above.

22. Greta has four dependents. Which of the following dependents would qualify for the Child Tax Credit?

A. Max, 21 years old and a full-time college student.
B. Becca, 18 years old and disabled.
C. Aaron, 16 years old and a full-time student.
D. Susannah, 65 years old, Greta's dependent parent.

23. For purposes of the Earned Income Credit, which is not a type of qualifying income for a taxpayer to claim the EIC?

A. Nontaxable combat pay.
B. Union strike benefits.
C. Tips.
D. Legal gambling income.

24. Desmond has a dependent child who is 15 years old. He is single and qualifies for head of household filing status. In 2012, his income was $22,000 in wages, and he also had investment income. What is the maximum amount of investment income that Desmond can have before he is disqualified from claiming the Earned Income Credit (EIC)?

A. $950.
B. $2,900.
C. $3,200.
D. $5,700.

25. Rayna pays $500 a month for after-school care for her daughter Melanie. On May 1, Melanie turned 13. How much of Rayna's expenses are qualifying expenses for purposes of the Child and Dependent Care Credit?

A. $2,000.
B. $3,000.
C. $6,000.
D. Some other amount.

26. Which of the following persons can claim the Earned Income Credit?

A. A taxpayer with a valid Social Security Number and a foster child.
B. A disabled taxpayer who is a dependent of another person.
C. A taxpayer with a qualifying child who files married filing separately.
D. A 66-year-old single taxpayer who meets the income thresholds but does not have a qualifying child.

27. Francesca and Bob were legally married for three years. In 2012, Francesca moves out and files for an annulment. However, the annulment is not final until February 10, 2013. They do not have any dependents. What is Francesca's filing status for 2012?

A. Single.
B. Married filing separately.
C. Married filing jointly.
D. Head of household.

28. Eligible educators can deduct a maximum of _____ in qualified expenses paid in 2012 as an adjustment to income.

A. $0.
B. $150.
C. $250.
D. $500.

29. Rebecca works as a real estate agent for Veranda Fine Realty. She visits Veranda's offices at least once a day to check her mail and her messages. She manages dozens of listings and splits her real estate commissions with Veranda. She does not work for any other real estate company. How must Rebecca be classified by her employer?

A. Employee.
B. Statutory employee.
C. Corporate shareholder.
D. Statutory nonemployee.

30. In 2012, what is the maximum amount of wages subject to Social Security tax?

A. There is no maximum.
B. $86,000.
C. $106,800.
D. $110,100.

31. Divorce decrees may define alimony payments. However, when may the IRS re-classify alimony payments as child support?

A. If the alimony payments are to a nonresident alien spouse.
B. If the alimony is decreased because of a contingency related to the child.
C. If one spouse refuses to cash the alimony checks.
D. If one spouse contests a prenuptial agreement.

32. Tamara and Bill are married and file jointly. In 2012, they decide to give Tama-ra's nephew, Jared, $25,000. What are the tax consequences of this gift?

A. The gift is taxable to Jared on his individual return.
B. The gift is taxable to Tamara and Bill on their joint return.
C. The gift is not taxable, but must be reported on Form 709.
D. The gift is neither taxable nor reportable.

33. Melissa had a difficult year financially. In 2012, she stopped paying her credit card bills and other obligations, and she received a 1099-C reporting canceled debt. In which case must canceled debt be included in Melissa's gross income?

A. If the debt was discharged before Melissa filed for bankruptcy.
B. If Melissa was insolvent at the time of cancellation.
C. If the cancellation is qualified principal residence debt.
D. If the canceled debt was forgiven as a gift from a family member.

34. Raul had the following income items in 2012. Which of the following amounts is not considered taxable income?

A. $20,000 in wages.
B. $12,000 inheritance.
C. $2,500 in traditional IRA distributions.
D. $3,000 in alimony.

35. Tina is unmarried. She and her five-year-old son, Bradley, lived all year with her mother, Marsha, who paid the entire cost of keeping up the home. Tina's AGI is $19,000. Marsha's AGI is $28,000. Tina and Marsha both attempt to claim Bradley as a qualifying child for the Earned Income Credit. What is the tie-breaker rule regarding this scenario?

A. **Neither** can claim Bradley as a qualifying child.
B. Marsha has the higher AGI and also paid the cost of keeping up the home, so she has the right to claim Bradley as her dependent, as well as to file as head of household.
C. Tina has the right to claim Bradley as her qualifying child, because she is the child's parent.
D. Tina has the right to file as head of household, as well as to claim Bradley as her qualifying child.

36. Emma and Steve are divorced. They have one child who is 13 years old. The child lives with Emma most of the time and stays with Steve on weekends. Emma has physical custody, but Steve provides more than half of the child's support. If Steve receives permission from Emma, the custodial parent, to claim the child on his tax return, is Steve eligible for the Earned Income Credit based on the dependent child?

A. Yes.
B. **No.**
C. Only if Steve provides over half of his child's overall support.
D. Only if Steve provides over half of his child's overall support and also obtains a signed **Form 8332,** *Release/Revocation of Release of Claim to Exemption for Child by Custodial Parent.*

37. Jamal received $1,600 in interest income in 2012. How should this income be reported on his tax return?

A. On page one of Form 1040.
B. On Schedule B.
C. On Schedule D.
D. On Form 1099-DIV.

38. Janice is the sole proprietor of a restaurant that had a net profit of $25,000 in 2012. Her husband, Marty, is also self-employed. Marty runs a carpentry business that had a net loss of $1,500 in 2012. Janice and Marty file jointly. How should this income and loss be reported?

A. Janice and Marty may file a single Schedule C netting the income and loss from both businesses. The Schedule SE will show total earnings subject to SE tax of $23,500.

B. Janice must file a Schedule C for the restaurant showing her net profit of $25,000, and Marty must file his own Schedule C for the carpentry business showing his net loss of $1,500. Their Schedule SE will show total earnings subject to SE tax of $23,500.

C. Janice must file a Schedule C for the restaurant showing her net profit of $25,000, and Marty must file his own Schedule C for the carpentry business showing his net loss of $1,500. Janice's Schedule SE will show total earnings subject to SE tax of $25,000.

D. Janice must file a Schedule C for the restaurant showing her net profit of $25,000, and Marty must file his own Schedule C for the carpentry business showing his net loss of $1,500. Janice's Schedule SE will show total earnings subject to SE tax of $25,000. Marty's Schedule SE will show a credit for $1,500 (the amount of his loss).

39. Felix and Samantha sold their home on May 7, 2012. Through April 30, 2012 they made home mortgage interest payments of $12,200. The settlement sheet (HUD-1) for the sale of the home showed an additional $50 in interest for the six-day period in May up to, but not including, the date of sale. They also had a mortgage prepayment penalty of $2,000. In March, they paid $120 in late payment fees to their mortgage lender due to a missed payment. How much is their allowable mortgage interest deduction in 2012?

A. $12,200.
B. $12,250.
C. $12,370.
D. $14,370.

40. Victoria and Pete divorced five years ago. Under her divorce settlement, she must pay her ex-husband $15,000 a year, which she has paid in equal installments each month. She is also required to pay his ongoing medical expenses for a condition he acquired during their marriage. In 2012, Pete's medical expenses were $11,400. She paid $10,000 of the medical expenses directly to the hospital. The other $1,400 she gave directly to Pete after getting a copy of the doctor's bill. How much of these payments can be properly deducted by Victoria as alimony?

A. Victoria may claim $15,000 in alimony as an adjustment to income.
B. Victoria may claim $15,000 in alimony paid as an adjustment to income, and $10,000 as a medical expense on **Schedule A** of her own return.
C. Victoria may claim $26,400 in alimony paid as an adjustment to income on her individual **Form 1040.**
D. Victoria may deduct $26,400 in alimony paid as a deduction on **Schedule A.**

41. In 2012 Laverne pays her attorney $8,000 for handling her divorce. After the divorce is final, Laverne's ex-husband refuses to pay the alimony. Laverne pays an additional fee of $4,500 for legal services to ensure the alimony is collected. How much of the legal fees are deductible on Laverne's individual tax return, and how should they be reported?

A. $0; none of the legal expenses are deductible.
B. Laverne can deduct $4,500, subject to the 2% limit, as a miscellaneous itemized deduction.
C. Laverne can deduct $4,500, not subject to the 2% limit, as a miscellaneous itemized deduction.
D. Laverne can deduct $12,500, subject to the 2% limit, as a miscellaneous itemized deduction.

42. Kayla, who is eight years old, has a small role in a television series. She made $65,000 during the tax year, but her parents put all the money in a trust fund to pay for college. Her parents have a joint AGI of $41,000. Kayla lived at home with her parents all year. Does she meet the support test in order for her parents to claim her as a dependent?

A. Yes, Kayla meets the support test, and her parents can claim her as a dependent.
B. No, Kayla does not meet the support test, and her parents cannot claim her as a dependent.
C. Since Kayla made the most money in the household, she can legally file her own tax return as single and claim her parents as dependents.
D. None of the above.

43. Which of the following would prevent a taxpayer from being eligible for the Earned Income Credit?

A. Being married to a resident alien with a valid Social Security Number.
B. Using the head of household filing status.
C. Correctly claiming the foreign earned income exclusion on Form 2555.
D. Filing a joint return with a spouse who died in 2012.

44. Patrick is 65, and he experiences age discrimination on the job. He decides to sue his company. After he files the lawsuit, he is attacked by the company owner, who breaks Patrick's arm when he pushes him. The court eventually awards Patrick the following amounts:
- $4,000 for emotional distress
- $10,000 for loss of wages
- $35,000 for physical injury related to the assault

How much of this award is taxable to Patrick as ordinary income?

A. $0.
B. $4,000.
C. $10,000.
D. $14,000.

45. Giselle's main home was destroyed by a tornado. The home was located in a federally declared disaster area. Giselle receives an insurance reimbursement that exceeds her basis in the home. How many years does Giselle have to replace the home before she will have to pay tax on the gain?

A. Two years.
B. Three years.
C. Four years.
D. There is no gain on the involuntary conversion of a primary residence.

46. Gabrielle adopted a child whose adoption was final in 2012. Gabrielle had $14,500 in out-of-pocket adoption expenses in 2012. Her tax liability for the year is $3,500. What is her maximum allowable Adoption Credit in 2012?

A. $0.
B. $3,500.
C. $13,360.
D. $14,500.

47. Terry is married filing separately. She has a dependent child in daycare. Terry has a flexible spending account at work and had $2,500 taken out of her wages for daycare costs. She paid $3,000 in daycare costs during the year. Which of the following statements is true?

A. Terry can exclude the $3,000 from her wages as part of the flexible spending account.
B. Terry can exclude $2,500 from income. She can take the Child and Dependent Care Credit for the remaining $500.
C. Terry can exclude a total of $2,500 from her gross income. She may not claim the Child and Dependent Care Credit for the remaining $500.
D. Terry cannot exclude any amount because she is married filing separately. All the benefits are therefore taxable to Terry as ordinary income.

48. Matt is an investor who subscribes to *Forbes* and *Kiplinger* magazines. He also pays for a safe deposit box where he holds his investments and stock certificates. Which of the following statements is true?

A. Matt may deduct these expenses on **Schedule A** as a miscellaneous itemized deduction, subject to the 2% floor.
B. Matt may deduct these expenses on **Schedule A** as a miscellaneous itemized deduction, not subject to the 2% floor.
C. Matt may not deduct these expenses.
D. Matt may deduct these expenses on **Schedule C** as a business expense.

49. Leigh is single, 58, and works for XYZ Corporation. She has a traditional IRA retirement plan with XYZ Corporation that is currently valued at $79,000. On December 1, 2012 Leigh dies. Her only son, Tom, age 27, inherits his mother's retirement plan. Which of the following statements is true?

A. Tom must start taking minimum distributions from the retirement plan, which will be subject to the 10% early withdrawal penalty, since Tom is not 59½.
B. Tom may roll over the inherited retirement plan into his own retirement plan, essentially treating it as his own.
C. Tom may choose to take a lump sum distribution or start taking minimum distributions from the retirement plan, which will not be subject to the 10% early withdrawal penalty. He cannot roll over the inherited retirement plan into his own plan.
D. Tom cannot start taking distributions from his inherited retirement plan until he reaches age 59½.

50. Benny and Arabella Smith are investors in a mutual fund. In 2012, the mutual fund notified the Smiths that they had $12,000 in capital gains. However, only $5,000 was actually distributed to the Smiths in 2012. What is the correct amount of capital gain the Smiths must report on their 2012 tax return?

A. $0.
B. $5,000.
C. $7,000.
D. $12,000.

51. Ellen started her own catering business in 2012. She paid $10,000 for a delivery van; contributed $20,000 of her own savings in cash to the business; and purchased $13,000 in equipment, glassware, and other tools on her personal credit cards. What is her at-risk amount for this business activity?

A. $0.
B. $10,000.
C. $30,000.
D. $43,000.

52. Pam owns a 50% interest in a residential rental house. Last year she paid $968 to repair a broken window. She replaced it with a premium energy-saving window. What is the correct treatment of this expense?

A. Pam cannot deduct the cost since it was an improvement (an upgrade); she must add it to the basis of the property.
B. Pam can deduct $484 (50% × $968) as a rental expense on **Schedule E.** She is entitled to reimbursement for the remaining half from the co-owner.
C. Pam can deduct $968 as a rental expense on **Schedule E.**
D. Pam can deduct $968 on **Schedule A** as an itemized deduction.

53. Clark received a scholarship to attend San Francisco State University. He decides to take three classes, but he is not a degree candidate. The scholarship is for $5,000. Clark's tuition was $3,000 and his books were $900. He had no other education expenses. How much of the scholarship is taxable to Clark?

A. $0.
B. $2,000.
C. $1,100.
D. $5,000.

54. Ursula is unmarried and has two qualifying children. They are both full-time students. Lila is 21 and a junior in college. Lila had $5,000 in tuition expenses in 2012. Lynette is 23 and attends graduate school for her master's degree. Lynette had $6,000 in tuition expenses in 2012. Assuming that Ursula meets all the other requirements for claiming the credit, what is the maximum American Opportunity Credit that Ursula can take on her 2012 tax return?

A. Ursula may take $2,500 as an American Opportunity Credit for Lila only.
B. Ursula may take $2,500 as an American Opportunity Credit for Lila, and another $2,500 for Lynette.
C. Ursula may claim a total of $8,000 ($4,000 for each student) as an American Opportunity Credit.
D. Ursula may take $4,000 as an American Opportunity Credit for Lila only.

55. David moved to a new home 40 miles from his former home because he changed job locations. His old job was three miles from his former home. His new job location is 60 miles from that home. David paid $3,000 to move his belongings to his new home. He also paid $150 in storage fees during the move and had $50 in meal expenses while moving. Which of the following statements is true?

A. David's moving expenses are not deductible because he does not meet the distance test.
B. David may deduct all his moving expenses ($3,000 + $150) except for the cost of his meals ($50).
C. David may deduct only the $3,000 in actual moving expenses. The cost of the meals and storage fees are not deductible.
D. David may deduct all the costs related to his move, including the cost of meals.

56. In order to meet the substantial presence test in determining residency for IRS purposes, an individual must be physically present in the United States for at least _____ days over a three-year period.

A. 214.
B. 183.
C. 120.
D. 365.

57. Ramon is a U.S. citizen serving in the Navy in Japan. His wife and children live with him, and he is able to claim the children as dependents. Ramon's wife, a citizen of Japan, chooses not to be treated as a resident alien for tax purposes. She does not want to file a joint return with him. Which of the following statements is true?

A. Ramon may not file a return until he comes back to the United States.

B. Ramon may file as head of household and claim his children as dependents.

C. Since Ramon is married and living with his spouse, he cannot claim head of household status. He must file married filing separately.

D. Ramon may still file jointly with his wife and sign on her behalf, since his wife is a nonresident alien.

58. Carol and Joaquin are married and plan to file a joint return. Carol is 66 and had gross income of $11,000 for the tax year. Joaquin is also 66. His gross income was $5,000 for the year. They have no dependents. Which of the following is the best answer?

A. They are required to file a tax return.

B. They are not required to file a return.

C. Carol is required to file a tax return.

D. They should file a tax return, because they qualify for the Earned Income Credit.

59. Which of the following individuals must file a tax return?

A. Rose, 68, who is widowed and supported by her son. She had $8,000 in Social Security income for 2012.

B. Frances, 70, whose only source of income in 2012 was her pension of $10,600.

C. Emmett, 64, a single taxpayer with $2,000 in self-employment income and $4,500 in Social Security income.

D. None of the above must file a tax return.

60. Who of the following is required to have an Individual Taxpayer Identification Number (ITIN)?

A. All nonresident aliens.

B. All nonresident and resident aliens.

C. Anyone who does not have a Social Security Number.

D. All nonresident and resident aliens who must file a return or who are claimed on someone else's return and are not eligible for a valid SSN.

61. Generally, how long should taxpayers keep the supporting documentation for their tax returns?

A. Four years from the due date.
B. Three years from the due date.
C. Two years from the due date.
D. At least one year after the due date.

62. Two years ago, Alice paid $1,050 for 100 shares of ABC, Inc. stock, plus a broker's commission of $50. Alice received ten additional shares of ABC stock as a nontaxable stock dividend. What is the current adjusted basis of Alice's stock?

A. $9 per share.
B. $10 per share.
C. $11 per share.
D. $25 per share.

63. Eric and Zelda are married but will not file a joint return together. Both are 40 years old. Eric's gross income from wages is $30,150, and Zelda's wage income is $3,800. Which of the following is true?

A. Only Eric is required to file.
B. Only Zelda is required to file.
C. Both Eric and Zelda are required to file.
D. Neither Eric nor Zelda must file.

64. Three years ago, Lenny bought 500 shares of XYZ Corporation stock for $1,500, including his broker's commission. On April 6, 2012, XYZ distributed a 2% nontaxable stock dividend (10 shares). Three months later, on July 6, 2012, Lenny sold all 510 shares of his XYZ stock for $2,030. What is the nature of Lenny's gain?

A. Lenny has a long-term capital gain.
B. Lenny has a short-term capital gain.
C. Lenny has an ordinary gain.
D. Lenny must prorate his gain between the short-term gains and long-term gains. Five hundred shares will have long-term capital gain treatment, and the remainder will have short-term capital gain treatment.

65. Nora has one **Form W-2** for $22,000 and one **Form 1099-INT** and no other income. Her **Form 1099-INT** shows both interest income of $2,000 and an early withdrawal penalty of $450. Nora will not itemize deductions, and she cannot claim any tax credits. Which of the following statements is true?

A. Since Nora does not itemize, she cannot deduct the early withdrawal penalty of $450.
B. Nora can claim an adjustment for the penalty on early withdrawal of savings on **Form 1040.**
C. Nora can claim the adjustment for the penalty on early withdrawal on **Form 1040-EZ**.
D. Nora is precluded from claiming the penalty for early withdrawal this year, but the amount can be treated as a carryover to a future year to offset investment income.

66. Mark and Carmen are divorced. Their daughter, Stephanie, lives with Carmen, who claims her as a dependent. Carmen paid for and deducted Stephanie's medical and dental bills. Mark also paid a $5,000 emergency medical bill when Stephanie broke her arm. Carmen will not release their child's dependency exemption to Mark. Which of the following is correct regarding the medical expense that Mark paid for his child?

A. Only a custodial parent can claim a deduction for a child's medical expenses.
B. Only the parent who claims the dependency exemption can claim medical expenses paid on behalf of the child.
C. Mark may deduct the emergency bill he paid, even if he does not claim Stephanie as his dependent.
D. None of the above is correct.

67. Harvey, 73, and Cindy, 66, are married and live together. They both work and each has a traditional IRA. In 2012, Harvey earned $2,000 in wages, and Cindy earned $30,000. If they file separate returns, what is the maximum that Harvey can contribute to his IRA?

A. $0.
B. $2,000.
C. $5,000.
D. $6,000.

68. In 2012, Jordan has unreimbursed medical costs of $6,600. Her AGI is $38,000 for the year. Jordan also paid $2,000 in medical costs for her 10-year-old son, but she does not claim him as a dependent because he lives with her ex-husband. What is the amount of her deductible medical expense on Schedule A *after* applying the 7.5% AGI limit?

A. $3,750.
B. $6,600.
C. $2,850.
D. $5,750.

69. Whitney refinanced her main home in 2012. As part of the refinance, she paid $1,800 in mortgage points, which was reflected on her closing statement. The new mortgage was a 30-year mortgage starting on November 1, 2012. How much of the points would be deductible as mortgage interest in 2012?

A. $10.
B. $12.
C. $60.
D. $1,800.

70. Olga paid the following taxes and fees in 2012: state income tax, $2,000; real estate taxes, $1,900; DMV fees, $100; homeowners' association fee, $250. What is Olga's total deduction for taxes on **Schedule A**?

A. $1,900.
B. $3,900.
C. $4,000.
D. $4,150.

71. Hana has contributed to a Roth IRA for the last four years. This year, she took the full amount of her Roth IRA as a distribution to help purchase her first home. Which of the following statements regarding this distribution is correct?

A. The entire distribution is excluded from her taxable income.
B. Only the return of her regular contributions is not included in her gross income. Any earnings are taxable.
C. The entire distribution is taxable.
D. The entire distribution is taxable, and is also subject to a 10% early withdrawal penalty.

72. Two years ago, Keith and Tiffany obtained home equity loans totaling $91,000. The couple used the loans to pay off gambling debts, overdue credit payments, and some other expenses. The current balance of their home equity loan is $72,000. The fair market value of their home is $230,000, and they carry $30,000 of outstanding acquisition debt on the home. If Keith and Tiffany file jointly, can they deduct the interest they pay on these loans?

A. Yes, they can deduct the interest on their loans.
B. No, they cannot deduct the interest on their loans.
C. The interest on the loans is only partially deductible and must be prorated to the amount of acquisition debt on their home.
D. None of the above.

73. Which of the following is a qualified charitable deduction?

A. The cost of a raffle ticket at a church fundraiser.
B. Blood donated to the Red Cross.
C. Out-of-pocket travel expenses for a volunteer to attend a church fundraiser.
D. Direct contributions to a homeless individual.

74. Luis is 16 years old and has a congenital heart condition. Luis and his mother Marie travel to another state so that he may receive specialized medical care. They had the following travel expenses related to the medical care:

Hotel costs for seven days (at $125 per night)	$875
Meals while traveling	$325
Cost of train tickets to the hospital	$220

Marie claims Luis as a dependent on her tax return. Based on this information, what is the amount of qualified medical expenses, before any AGI limitations?

A. $570.
B. $920.
C. $1,095.
D. $1,420.

75. Paloma bought her home two years ago. She started having difficulty making her mortgage payments. In 2012, Paloma's mortgage lender agreed to reduce the principal on her home loan and refinance it with a better interest rate and lower monthly payments. The principal balance before the refinance was $230,000, and the lender reduced the principal loan amount to $200,000. The home has never been used for business or as rental property, and Paloma has not filed for bankruptcy. She continued to live in the home as her primary residence. Based on this information, how should Paloma report this transaction?

A. Report the transaction as nontaxable canceled debt on **Form 982**.
B. Report the transaction as a reduction in the basis of the home on line 10b of **Form 982**.
C. Report the $30,000 as a loss on **Schedule D**.
D. Include $30,000 of debt cancellation in taxable income on **Form 1040**.

76. Mai Lin is single. In 2012, she has $120,000 in wage income. She also owns a residential rental property that has a $28,000 loss for the year. Mai Lin actively participated in the rental activity. How much of her rental loss is deductible in the current year?

A. $0.
B. $15,000.
C. $25,000.
D. $28,000.

77. Nikki is a bartender at a local sports arena. She usually receives cash tips. Occasionally, she receives movie tickets and concert tickets from some of her customers. How are these non-cash tips taxed?

A. Noncash tips are subject to income tax.
B. Noncash tips are subject to income tax and Social Security tax.
C. Noncash tips are subject to income tax and self-employment tax.
D. Noncash tips are not subject to tax.

78. Raymond has a traditional IRA. Rollover rules allow Raymond to do which one of the following without incurring any income tax or penalty?

A. Roll over funds from his traditional IRA plan to a Roth IRA account.
B. Roll over his traditional IRA into the IRA of a spouse.
C. Roll over funds into a government deferred-compensation plan.
D. Roll over into an educational savings plan.

79. Mike's cost basis was $2,400 for 900 shares of Deva Corporation stock he purchased in June 2004. Mike sold the 900 shares on December 12, 2012 for $4,400 and paid an additional $100 commission. The gross proceeds from the sale were $4,400 on **Form 1099-B.** What was the sales price for the shares and the amount of capital gain?

A. $4,400 sales price and $2,000 gain.
B. $4,400 sales price and $1,900 gain.
C. $4,500 sales price and $2,100 gain.
D. $4,300 sales price and $1,900 gain.

80. Carlos moves to another city in 2012, and he decides to convert his former home into a residential rental property. Three years ago, Carlos bought his home for $182,000. At the time of the purchase, the value of the land was assessed at $20,000. On the date the home was converted to a rental, Carlos's property had a fair market value of $168,000, of which $21,000 was allocated to the land value, and $147,000 was for the house. What is Carlos's basis of depreciation for the rental property?

A. $134,000.
B. $147,000.
C. $162,000.
D. $182,000.

81. Kyle sold all his shares in a mutual fund. The sale resulted in a capital loss of $7,000. Kyle has wages of $32,000 in 2012. He has no other income or losses. What is Kyle's adjusted gross income in 2012?

A. $25,000.
B. $29,000.
C. $32,000.
D. Some other amount.

82. Kevin is a member of the U.S. Army who has been serving in a combat zone since March 1. Is Kevin entitled to an extension of time for filing and paying his federal income taxes, and will penalties and interest be assessed on Kevin's delinquent tax return?

A. Kevin is granted an extension on his filing deadline, and he will not be charged interest or penalties attributable to the extension period.
B. Kevin is granted an extension on his filing deadline, but he will be charged interest attributable to the extension period.
C. Kevin is not granted an extension on his filing deadline, but he will not be charged interest or penalties attributable to the extension period.
D. Kevin is not granted an extension on his filing deadline.

83. In 2012, Elizabeth gave the following gifts:

- $13,000 to her sister Marjorie
- $16,000 for her grandson Tim's tuition, which was paid directly to the college
- $14,000 to her Uncle Frank
- $15,000 to the Democratic Party

How should these gifts be reported under the gift tax rules?

A. Marjorie and Frank are required to file gift tax returns and pay tax on the gifts.
B. Elizabeth must file a gift tax return only for the $14,000 gift to Frank.
C. Elizabeth must file a gift tax return for the gifts to Frank and Tim.
D. All of the gifts are reportable.

84. Josh, a full-time student with no compensation, marries Heather during the year. Both are age 27. For the year, Heather has taxable compensation of $50,000. She plans to contribute the maximum to her traditional IRA. If Josh and Heather file jointly, how much can each contribute to a traditional IRA?

A. Heather can contribute $5,000 to her traditional IRA.
B. Heather can contribute $5,000 to her traditional IRA, and also make a spousal contribution of $5,000 for Josh to his traditional IRA.
C. Heather and Josh can both contribute $6,000 to a traditional IRA.
D. None of the above.

85. Andy donated to his church several times during the year. Which of the following charitable gifts does not meet IRS substantiation (recordkeeping) requirements?

A. A $210 donation made with a check. Andy has a copy of the canceled check, but no receipt from the church.
B. A $340 donation made in cash. Andy has a contemporaneous receipt from the church.
C. A contribution of noncash property worth $5,200. Andy has a contemporaneous receipt from the church, but no appraisal.
D. Charitable mileage totaling $125 that was incurred while Andy was volunteering. Andy does not have a receipt, but he has a written mileage log.

86. In 2012, the maximum amount taxpayers may claim for the nonrefundable Child Tax Credit is _____ for each qualifying child.

A. $500.
B. $1,000.
C. $3,700.
D. Some other amount.

87. A fire destroyed Chelsea's home. The home had an adjusted basis of $80,000, and the insurance company paid her $130,000 for the loss. Chelsea bought a replacement home for $100,000. How much is her gain (if any), and her basis in her new home?

A. Chelsea does not have a taxable gain. Her basis in the new home is $130,000.
B. Chelsea has a taxable gain of $30,000. Her basis in the new home is $80,000.
C. Chelsea has a taxable gain of $50,000. Her basis in the new home is $80,000.
D. Chelsea has a taxable gain of $30,000. Her basis in the new home is $100,000.

88. Chuck purchased his main home five years ago. He sells his home in June 2012. Chuck marries Jayme in September 2012. For purposes of the section 121 exclusion, Chuck meets the ownership and use tests, but Jayme does not. On their jointly filed return, how would Chuck report the sale of his home?

A. Chuck cannot exclude any of the gain from the sale of his home, because Jayme does not meet the ownership and use tests.
B. Chuck and Jayme can exclude up to $500,000 of gain on their joint return for 2012.
C. Chuck can exclude up to $250,000 of gain on their joint return for 2012.
D. None of the above.

89. Kris owns a vacation home by the lake. In 2012, Kris rented the home for two weeks, earning $1,200. She also lived in the home for four months. Kris paid $5,000 in mortgage interest on the home in 2012. The remainder of the year the home was vacant. What is the proper treatment of this activity?

A. Kris does not have to report the rental income. The mortgage interest is deductible on Schedule A as an itemized deduction.
B. The rental income should be reported on Schedule E, and the mortgage interest is deductible on Schedule A as an itemized deduction.
C. The rental income and mortgage interest should be reported on Schedule E.
D. The rental income can be reported as "other income" on Form 1040. The mortgage interest is not deductible, since it is a vacation home.

90. Wilson rents a two bedroom apartment. He is a self-employed enrolled agent and works exclusively out of a home office. In 2012, Wilson paid $1,000 a month in rent for his apartment. He also paid $50 a month in utilities. His home office is 240 square feet (12 feet × 20 feet). The total square footage of his apartment is 1,200 square feet. Ignoring any income limitations, what is Wilson's allowable deduction for home office expense?

A. $1,050.
B. $1,200.
C. $2,520.
D. $12,600.

91. Angel is a nurse working for Mercy General Hospital. He attended a continuing education course in Los Angeles. His expenses related to the trip were as follows:

Lodging	$300
Airfare to the event	$245
Meals	$60
Fees for the course	$150

What is Angel's deductible educational expense (before the application of any AGI limits)?

A. $150.
B. $395.
C. $725.
D. $755.

92. Scott is a police officer. In 2012, he pays $450 for new uniforms and $300 for dry cleaning the uniforms. How much of this expense is deductible, and how would the expense be reported?

A. $0; the costs are not deductible.
B. $450 (the cost of the uniforms) is deductible as a miscellaneous itemized deduction, subject to the 2% floor.
C. $750 is deductible as a miscellaneous itemized deduction, not subject to the 2% floor.
D. $750 is deductible as a miscellaneous itemized deduction, subject to the 2% floor.

93. Jean owns a business office. She allows her church to use the building rent-free for six months. Jean normally rents the office for $600. However, other offices are renting for $700 in the same building, so the fair market value of the rental is $700 per month. How much can Jean deduct as a charitable deduction?

A. $0.
B. $3,600.
C. $4,200.
D. $7,200.

94. In 2012, Audrey discovers that her housekeeper stole personal property from her. The property had an adjusted basis of $4,000 and a fair market value of $10,000. Audrey's adjusted gross income in 2012 is $24,000. What is Audrey's casualty loss deduction (after applying the $100 and 10% limitations)?

A. $1,500.
B. $2,400.
C. $7,500.
D. $8,910.

95. In 2012, Liam installs $20,000 in qualifying energy-efficient exterior windows on his main home. What is the maximum amount of his Residential Energy Efficient Property Credit?

A. $200.
B. $1,500.
C. $5,000.
D. $20,000.

96. Which of the following statements regarding Roth retirement plans is false?

A. A Roth IRA requires minimum distributions at age 70½.
B. A Roth IRA does not permit a tax deduction at the time of contribution.
C. Married taxpayers who file separate returns (MFS) may contribute to a Roth IRA.
D. Compensation for purposes of a Roth IRA does not include earnings and profits from rental property.

97. Gregory and Flavia are married, but file separately (MFS). In 2012, Gregory sells 300 shares of ABC Company stock. The stock value had fallen, and he has a $4,000 long-term capital loss on the sale. He has no other capital gains or losses. Within 15 days after Gregory sells his stock, Flavia purchases 500 shares of stock in ABC Company. How should the stock sale be reported on Gregory's separate tax return?

A. Gregory may deduct the $4,000 on his tax return as a long-term capital loss.
B. Gregory may deduct $3,000 of the loss on his tax return, and the remaining $1,000 must be carried over to the next year.
C. Gregory can deduct the loss only if he files jointly with Flavia. Otherwise, the entire loss is treated as a carryover.
D. Gregory has a wash sale, and he may not deduct the loss.

98. Pastor Green is a full-time minister. The church allows him to use a parsonage that has an annual fair rental value of $24,000. The church also pays Pastor Green an annual salary of $67,000, of which $7,500 is designated for his home utility costs. Pastor Green's actual utility costs during the year were $7,000. What is Pastor Green's income for self-employment tax purposes?

A. $500.
B. $60,000.
C. $67,000.
D. $91,000.

99. A taxpayer is blind and has a service dog, a seeing-eye dog for the blind. The taxpayer works full-time and makes $50,000 per year. Which of the following statements is true?

A. The veterinary care for the service animal is deductible as a medical expense.
B. The veterinary care for the service animal is not deductible as a medical expense.
C. This blind person is able to work and is therefore not considered disabled for tax purposes, meaning he cannot claim medical expenses related to his condition.
D. Veterinary care is never deductible as a personal or medical expense.

100. Brock agrees to sell his vacation property to a buyer under an installment sale. He sells the property at a contract price of $120,000, and his gross profit is $15,000. Brock will receive four equal payments (one payment per year) until the note is paid off. He receives the first payment of $30,000 in 2012. The first payment does not include any interest. He wants to use the installment method to report income from the sale. What is the amount of installment sale income that Brock will report in 2012?

A. $0.
B. $3,750.
C. $7,500.
D. $15,000.

Please review your answers with the answers in the back.

Part 2: Businesses Practice Exams

Sample exam #1: page 89

Sample exam #2: page 115

#1 Businesses Sample Exam

1. Daley Company is a calendar-year corporation that uses the accrual method of accounting. On December 20, 2012, Daley was entitled to receive a $22,000 payment on a contract. Daley received half of the payment ($11,000) on December 29, 2012. However, Daley did not receive the remainder of the payment from the vendor until January 20, 2013. Daley did not cash either check until January 23, 2013. When should Daley report this revenue on its tax return?

A. $22,000 in 2012.
B. $22,000 in 2013
C. $11,000 in 2012 and $11,000 in 2013.
D. None of the above is correct.

2. Derrick is a 10% partner in Hartville Roads Partnership. According to the partnership agreement, Derrick is entitled to a fixed annual guaranteed payment of $5,000. During the year, Hartville Roads has $55,000 of ordinary income before deducting the guaranteed payment. How much partnership income should Derrick report on his individual return for this year?

A. $11,500.
B. $16,000.
C. $10,000.
D. $5,000.

3. During the year, Codex Corporation has $40,000 in capital losses and $32,000 in capital gains. How should this be reported on Codex's corporate tax return?

A. Codex will have an $8,000 capital loss carryover.
B. Codex will be allowed to claim $3,000 of the excess capital losses in the current year. The remaining losses will be carried over to future years.
C. A C corporation is only allowed to deduct its capital losses against its capital gains. Therefore, the $8,000 unused capital loss is disallowed.
D. Codex is allowed to carry back its excess capital loss up to three years, and forward up to five years. Codex should first carry back the $8,000 excess capital losses to a prior year, and carry forward any remaining amounts.

4. Gotay Corporation issued a dividend of $600 to each of its shareholders during the year. What form must the corporation use to report this distribution to its shareholders?

A. Form 1099-S.
B. Form 1099-DIV.
C. Form 1099-MISC
D. Form 1099-INT.

5. Which of the following is not indicative of a personal service corporation?

A. Its shareholders are also employee-owners that perform the personal services within the corporation.
B. Its principal business activity during the testing period is the performance of personal services.
C. The corporation is an S corporation.
D. The corporation's employee-shareholders own more than 10% of the FMV of the outstanding stock.

6. Pacific Property Corporation is a calendar-year, cash-basis C corporation. In 2012, Pacific has $100,000 in capital losses and $50,000 in capital gains. Their capital gains for the prior three years are:

- 2009: $0
- 2010: $24,000 capital gains
- 2011: $9,000 capital gains

Based on the following information, figure Pacific Property Corporation's capital loss *carryforward* for 2013.

A. $50,000.
B. $24,000.
C. $16,000.
D. $17,000.

7. Anthony transfers a large tract of unimproved land to Runway Corporation in exchange for stock. Immediately after the transfer, Anthony has majority control of the corporation and owns 85% of the outstanding stock. The remaining 15% is owned by another individual. Runway Corporation is an investment company. Is this a qualified section 351 exchange, and is the transfer a taxable event?

A. Yes, this is a qualified section 351 exchange. The exchange is not a taxable event.
B. No, it is not a qualified 351 exchange because Anthony does not own 90% of the outstanding stock.
C. No, it is not a qualified 351 exchange because Anthony does not own 100% of the outstanding stock
D. No, it is not a qualified 351 exchange because Runway Corporation is an investment company.

8. Trusted Brands Partnership has four employees. During the year, Trusted Brands pays its employee, Kelsey, the following amounts:

A. The aggregate cost of employer-sponsored medical coverage.
B. Payment for sick leave.
C. Payments made under an accountable plan.
D. The cost of group-term life insurance that exceeds the cost of $50,000 of coverage.
Which of these would not be reported on the Kelsey's Form W-2?

9. What is a closely held corporation?

A. A corporation with no more than 15 shareholders.
B. Another name for an S corporation.
C. A corporation with assets of less than $10 million.
D. A corporation with a small number of shareholders and no public market for its corporate stock.

10. Which of the following would be a qualified like-kind exchange of property under section 1031?

A. An exchange of an apartment building in Chicago with an apartment building in Mexico City, Mexico.
B. An exchange of a vacant lot for a factory building.
C. An exchange of a primary residence for a rental duplex.
D. An exchange of shares of stock for units of bonds.

11. Persil Corporation is a calendar-year C corporation that makes a $100,000 nonliquidating distribution to its two equal shareholders, April and Charles. Both shareholders received equal amounts. At the time of the distribution, Persil Corporation's current and accumulated earnings and profits were $90,000. Persil's paid-in capital for tax purposes was $390,000 at the time of the distribution. Based on this information, how would this transaction affect Charles's income and basis in his stock?

A. Charles would recognize a dividend of $45,000 and would reduce his stock basis by $5,000.
B. Charles would recognize a return of capital of $50,000.
C. Charles would reduce his stock basis by $90,000 and report a gain of $10,000.
D. Charles would reduce his stock basis by $45,000 and report a dividend of $5,000.

12. Pearly Corporation is an accrual-based C corporation. For the current year, the corporation has the following **book** income.

Net book income	$90,000
Capital losses	$8,000
Capital gains	$4,000
Tax exempt interest	$12,000
Accrued federal income tax	$22,000

Based on this information, reconcile the book income with tax differences, and calculate Pearly Corporation's **taxable** income, as would be reported on Schedule M-1 of Form 1120.

A. $116,000.
B. $64,000.
C. $104,000.
D. $128,000.

13. Contributions to the capital of a corporation, whether or not by shareholders, are considered "paid-in capital." The basis of property contributed to capital by a person other than a shareholder is _____?

A. The same in the corporation as the basis the donor had in the property.
B. Fair market value of the property.
C. The original cost basis of the property must be used.
D. Zero.

14. In February, Amy and Logan formed Security Systems Corporations. Amy contributed $500,000 in cash, and Logan contributed a building with a fair market value of $700,000 and an adjusted basis of $450,000. Logan also received $200,000 cash from the corporation when the land was contributed. Amy and Logan each receive 50% of the corporate stock after these contributions. What is the tax basis of the building to Security Systems Corporation?

A. $250,000.
B. $650,000.
C. $500,000.
D. $700,000.

15. Section 1245 generally does not apply to _____.

A. Depreciable personal property.
B. Fruit trees held for the production of income.
C. Pieces of machinery or equipment.
D. Real property.

16. A city charges a fee for installing curbing in front of a business. This is a type of _____:

A. Repair that can be deducted as a current expense.
B. Improvement that must be capitalized.
C. Assessment that is added to the property's basis.
D. Real estate tax that can be deducted.

17. Lori transfers machinery to Kirkus Calendars Corporation in exchange for 100% of the stock. At the time of the transfer, the machinery had a fair market value of $10,000. Lori's adjusted basis in the equipment before the transfer was $6,200, and the machinery was encumbered by an outstanding loan of $2,500, which was assumed by Kirkus Calendars. There was a bona-fide business reason for the transfer, and it qualifies for nonrecognition treatment under section 351. What is Lori's basis in her stock after the transfer?

A. $10,000.
B. $3,700.
C. $7,500.
D. $3,800.

18. The Golden Touch Partnership is formed by the following partners, two of which are corporate partners and one of whom is an individual. None of the partners are related persons or related entities.

Partner	Ownership stake	Tax Year End
Daisy Corporation (C Corp)	10%	30-Apr
Aster Corporation (C Corp)	45%	30-Apr
Shannon Jones (individual)	45%	31-Dec

What is the required tax year-end for Golden Touch Partnership?

A. A partnership with corporate partners may choose to use either a fiscal year-end or a calendar year-end. Golden Touch Partnership is allowed to select any tax year-end it chooses.
B. Golden Touch Partnership is required to use a calendar year-end.
C. Golden Touch Partnership is required to use April 30 as its tax year-end.
D. Insufficient information to answer.

19. Distributions of stock dividends are generally tax-free to shareholders except when:

A. The distribution is made at the end of the corporation's fiscal year.
B. The distribution gives cash or other property to some shareholders and an increase in the percentage interest in the corporation's assets or earnings and profits to other shareholders.
C. The distribution is only made to shareholders.
D. The distribution is made by a foreign corporation or by a member of a controlled group of corporations.

20. Zieser Corporation is a cash-basis C corporation. During the year, Zieser pays a salary to Thomas, the sole employee-shareholder. Later, the corporation is audited, and the salary is deemed excessive. If a corporation pays an employee-shareholder a salary that is unreasonably high considering the services actually performed, the excessive part of the salary will be treated as a _____.

A. Constructive distribution.
B. Liquidating distribution.
C. Ordinary dividend.
D. Nontaxable distribution.

21. At the beginning of the year, Clipper Sails Corporation has accumulated earnings and profits of $150,000. Christopher is the sole shareholder of Clipper Sales, a calendar-year C corporation. On September 1, the corporation distributes $200,000 to Christopher in a nonliquidating distribution. At the time of the distribution, Christopher's stock basis is $30,000. Clipper Corporation had no additional earnings and profits during the year. How should Christopher recognize this $200,000 distribution on his return?

A. Christopher must recognize dividend income of $150,000 and a taxable gain of $20,000. He must also reduce his stock basis to zero.
B. Christopher must recognize dividend income of $170,000 and reduce his stock basis to zero.
C. Christopher must recognize dividend income of $200,000. His stock basis remains the same.
D. Christopher must recognize dividend income of $150,000 and wage income of $20,000. He must also reduce his stock basis to zero.

22. Jerry transfers a building to Core Corporation in exchange for 70% of its outstanding stock. The building had an adjusted basis of $125,000 to Jerry, and a fair market value of $300,000. The stock that Jerry receives in the transfer has a fair market value of $300,000. How much gain (or loss) would Jerry recognize in this transfer?

A. A taxable gain of $175,000.
B. A deductible loss of $175,000.
C. A taxable gain of $300,000. Jerry's stock basis would be $125,000.
D. No gain or loss would be recognized by either the shareholder or the corporation in this transfer.

23. During the year, Grange Partnership distributes $6,000 in cash and factory machinery with an adjusted basis of $15,000 (FMV $23,000) to Susan, one of the general partners. Immediately before the distribution, Susan's adjusted basis in her partnership interest is $18,000. This was a nonliquidating distribution. What is Susan's basis in the factory machinery that was distributed, and what is her remaining partnership basis after the distribution?

A. $23,000 basis in machinery, $12,000 remaining partnership basis.
B. $12,000 basis in machinery, $0 partnership basis.
C. $15,000 basis in machinery, $12,000 remaining partnership basis.
D. $5,000 basis in machinery, $9,000 remaining partnership basis.

24. The domestic production activities deduction (DPAD) cannot exceed _____ of W-2 wages paid?

A. 20%.
B. 50%.
C. 60%.
D. 100%.

25. Which of the following types of fringe benefits would be deductible by an employer but not taxable to the employee?

A. *De minimis* fringe benefit.
B. Use of an employer's apartment, vacation home, or boat.
C. Membership in a country club or athletic facility.
D. A gift card.

26. Which of the following events would not cause an automatic termination of an S-election?

A. One shareholder dies and the shares are now owned by the deceased shareholder's estate.
B. A nonresident alien inherits 5% of the shares.
C. The S corporation was previously a C corporation, and it has passive investment income that exceeds 25% of its gross receipts for three consecutive tax years.
D. The shareholder limit of 100 is reached.

27. Travis is a self-employed farmer who reports income and loss on Schedule F. On February 1, 2012, a vandal destroyed a large tractor on Travis's farm. The tractor was not repairable. After a period of negotiations, Travis's insurance company compensated him for the full amount of the loss. He received the insurance check on December 2, 2012. How long does Travis have to replace the tractor, and when does he have to report the insurance proceeds on his return?

A. December 2, 2015.
B. December 31, 2014.
C. December 31, 2015.
D. April 15, 2014.

96

28. When calculating the ordinary income of a partnership, which of the following is allowed as a deduction from ordinary income?

A. Delinquent federal taxes.
B. Short-term capital losses.
C. Guaranteed payments.
D. Charitable contributions to exempt entities.

29. Brandon and Kerry form the B&K Partnership during the year. Brandon contributes $32,000 in cash. Kerry contributes $10,000 in cash and a delivery truck with an FMV of $40,000 and an adjusted basis of $18,000. Brandon and Kerry are equal partners. What is Kerry's partnership basis after her contribution?

A. $10,000.
B. $50,000.
C. $28,000.
D. $32,000.

30. Unlike limited partners, general partners have _____ in a partnership's debt obligations.

A. Joint and several liability.
B. Limited responsibility.
C. Legal absolution.
D. Nonrecourse.

31. Christian is a 50% partner in Kilduff Enterprises Partnership. On January 1, Christian's starting partnership basis was $1,000. Kilduff Partnership had the following items of income, calculated at the end of the year:

Ordinary income	$40,000
Tax exempt income	$20,000
Rental income	$4,000

There were no distributions to any of the partners during the year. Based on this information, what is Christian's partnership basis on December 31?

A. $33,000.
B. $23,000.
C. $21,000.
D. $22,000.

32. In general, a partnership terminates when:

A. All its operations are discontinued or at least 50% of the total interest in partnership capital and profits is sold or exchanged within a 12-month period, including a sale or exchange to another partner.
B. A partner sells his partnership interest to a corporate entity.
C. The death of a general partner occurs.
D. An ownership transfer occurs that is at least 40% interest in capital and a 60% interest in profits.

33. Holly contributed an office building to the Naples Partnership in exchange for a 30% partnership interest. The fair market value of the building was $180,000, and Holly's adjusted basis in the building was $60,000. The building was encumbered by a $30,000 mortgage, which the partnership assumed. Based on this information, what is Holly's partnership basis on the date of the contribution?

A. $40,000.
B. $150,000.
C. $30,000.
D. $20,000.

34. What does an S corporation's accumulated adjustment account include?

A. All items of income and expenses of the S corporation.
B. All items of income and expenses of the S corporation with the exception of portfolio income (and expenses related to portfolio income).
C. All items of income and expenses of the S corporation with the exception of tax-exempt income (and expenses related to tax-exempt income).
D. An accounting of each shareholder's stock basis in the corporation and related adjustments of foreign shareholders.

35. What is the dividends received deduction when the receiving corporation owns less than 20% of the stock?

A. Zero.
B. 50%.
C. 70%.
D. 80%.

36. Passive loss limits do not apply to:

A. C corporations.
B. Partnerships.
C. Estates.
D. Individuals.

37. Corporations generally are allowed to choose a fiscal year-end unless:

A. The corporation is a personal service corporation.
B. The corporation is an S corporation.
C. Both A and B are correct.
D. Any corporation may choose a fiscal year-end, regardless of structure or type.

38. Allay Corporation is an accrual-based, calendar-year C corporation. At the end of the year, Allay reported book income of $380,000. The calculation of book income included the following items:

Municipal bond interest income	$60,000
Federal income tax	$120,000
Municipal bond interest expense	$4,300

Based on this information, reconcile the book income with tax differences, and calculate Allay Corporation's **taxable** income, as would be reported on **Schedule M-1** of **Form 1120**.

A. $440,000.
B. $500,000.
C. $324,300.
D. $444,300.

39. Which of the following best describes a controlled group?

A. A privately-held corporation that does not publicly list its financial statements or other records.
B. A type of partnership controlled by fewer than five individuals.
C. A corporation or partnership that is owned by family members.
D. A group of corporations that are related through common ownership and are subject to rules regarding related party transactions.

40. Alpine Ski Corporation is a cash-basis C corporation. During the year, Alpine Ski distributed property with a fair market value of $260,000 and an adjusted basis of $40,000 to one of its shareholders, Misty. The property was subject to a $100,000 outstanding loan, which Misty assumed. This was not a liquidating distribution. What is the amount of income that Misty would report from this transaction, and what is her basis in the property distributed?

A. Misty must report a taxable dividend of $220,000. Her basis in the property is $260,000.
B. Misty must report a taxable dividend of $220,000. Her basis in the property is $160,000.
C. Misty must report a taxable dividend of $160,000. Her basis in the property is $260,000.
D. Misty does not have to report any taxable dividends. Her basis in the property is $220,000.

41. Hudson River Corporation has $260,000 in current and accumulated earnings and profits. The company distributes a parcel of land with a fair market value of $200,000 and a basis of $90,000 to one of its shareholders, Samuel. This is not a liquidating distribution. How much gain (or loss) would Hudson River Corporation realize in this transaction, and how much dividend income would Samuel report on his individual return?

A. Hudson would report a $110,000 gain. Samuel would report a $200,000 dividend.
B. Hudson would report a $200,000 gain. Samuel would report a $110,000 dividend.
C. Hudson would report a $110,000 gain. Samuel would report a $90,000 dividend.
D. Hudson would report a $200,000 gain. Samuel would report a $170,000 dividend.

42. At the beginning of 2012, Fitzmorris-Jones Corporation has $120,000 in accumulated earning and profits. During the year, Fitzmorris-Jones has current earnings of $90,000. On December 31, 2012, Fitzmorris-Jones distributes $220,000 to Leah, one of its shareholders. At the time of the distribution, Leah's stock basis was zero. How does this distribution affect the corporation's earnings and profits, and how would Leah report this distribution?

A. The distribution reduces Fitzmorris-Jones's E&P to zero. Leah must report a dividend of $210,000 and a capital gain of $10,000.
B. The distribution reduces Fitzmorris-Jones's E&P to zero. Leah must report a dividend of $220,000.
C. The distribution reduces Fitzmorris-Jones's E&P to $120,000. Leah must report ordinary income of $210,000 and a capital gain of $10,000.
D. The distribution reduces Fitzmorris-Jones's E&P to ($10,000). Leah must report dividend income of $210,000 and a capital gain of $10,000.

43. Alta Hills Partnership is a calendar-year, accrual basis entity. Alta Hills filed an extension this year. When is the *extended* due date for Alta Hill's tax return?

A. March 15.
B. April 15.
C. October 15.
D. September 15.

44. Tara paid $30,000 to acquire a 30% stake in the Harvest Breads Partnership, a new partnership she formed with two of her friends. Harvest Breads is a calendar-year, cash-basis partnership. She is a general partner and her 30% stake allows her to share in capital and profits according to her ownership percentage. In its first year, Harvest Breads earns ordinary income of $40,000. All of the profits are reinvested, so no distributions are made to any of the partners during the year. How much income should Tara report on her return, and what is her partnership basis at the end of the year?

Income to report	Year-end basis
A. $0	$42,000
B. $10,000	$36,000
C. $12,000	$42,000
D. $0	$30,000

45. Patricia is a sole proprietor with six employees. She reports her business income on Schedule C. She wants to set up a new SIMPLE IRA for herself and her employees. She has never had any type of retirement plan for her business. What is the final deadline for her to set up a SIMPLE IRA for the 2012 tax year?

A. October 1, 2013.
B. April 15, 2013.
C. December 31, 2012.
D. January 1, 2012.

46. Feral Feline Rescue is a 501(c)3 exempt entity that is organized as a calendar-year corporation. What is the normal (unextended) due date of Feral Feline Rescue's tax return, and which form number is it required to file?

Form Number	Due Date
A. Form 990	March 15
B. Form 990	May 15
C. Form 1120	March 15
D. Form 990	April 15

47. Which of the following would not be considered section 1245 property?

A. A grain silo.
B. A barn housing goats, sheep, and farming supplies.
C. Fencing to contain hogs.
D. A well to provide water to livestock.

48. Victor is a managing partner of RealTime Partnership. He has a 50% partnership interest and shares profits and losses based on his partnership interest percentage. At the beginning of the year, the basis of Victor's partnership interest is $35,000. RealTime Partnership has an $82,000 net operating loss for the year. How would RealTime Partnership report this loss on Schedule K-1, and how would this loss be reported on Victor's individual return?

A. Victor would report $35,000 in partnership losses and have a $6,000 loss carryforward.
B. Victor would report $41,000 in partnership losses and have a $5,000 loss carryforward.
C. Victor would report $41,000 in partnership losses.
D. Victor would report $6,000 in partnership losses.

49. Apple Valley Partnership has two general partners, Douglas and Craig, who share income and losses equally. In 2012, Apple Valley had $110,000 in net ordinary income in 2012. Craig received a cash distribution of $31,000 on September 12, 2012. Douglas received a distribution of $42,000 on May 1, 2012. Apple Valley is a cash-basis, calendar year partnership. How much taxable income will Apple Valley report on Craig's Schedule K-1 and on Douglas's Schedule K-1?

A. Craig: $31,000, Douglas: $42,000.
B. Craig: $55,000, Douglas: $55,000.
C. Craig: $24,000, Douglas: $13,000.
D. Craig: $79,000, Douglas: $68,000.

50. On which form are separately stated items of an S corporation reported?

A. Schedule K-1, Form 1120S.
B. Schedule M-1, Form 1120S.
C. Schedule K-1, Form 1120.
D. Schedule L, Form 1120S.

51. Partnerships are subject to the passive activity loss rules. In the case of a partnership with suspended passive activity losses, in which instance would those passive losses become deductible immediately?

A. In any year there is ordinary income to offset the passive losses.
B. The suspended losses would be immediately deductible in a taxable disposition of the entire interest of the passive activity.
C. In a like-kind exchange.
D. None of the above.

52. Zabrocki Corporation is a calendar-year C corporation. The three shareholders decide unanimously to elect S corporation status starting January 1, 2013. When can Zabrocki make this election and still be considered timely?

A. Anytime during 2012 or by April 15, 2013.
B. Anytime during 2012 or by March 15, 2013.
C. Anytime during 2013.
D. Anytime during 2012, as long as the election request is postmarked before January 1, 2013.

53. The Reading Exchange is a qualified 501(c)(3) organization with a fiscal year that ends on June 30, 2012. What is the normal (not extended) due date for its 2012 tax return?

A. May 15, 2013.
B. October 15, 2012.
C. November 15, 2012.
D. December 15, 2012.

54. Which of the following entities do not require any type of formal agreement or state filing in order to create their entity?

A. An LLC and a sole proprietorship.
B. A general partnership and a sole proprietorship.
C. An S corporation and a sole proprietorship.
D. A general partnership, a sole proprietorship, and an LLC.

55. Flooding destroys a warehouse owned by Telecast Corporation, and the company receives $45,000 in insurance reimbursement. The adjusted basis of the property was $20,000, and the FMV of the property at the time of the flood was $50,000. Telecast spends $41,000 of the insurance proceeds on qualifying replacement property. What is Telecast's taxable gain (or loss) from this involuntary conversion?

A. $4,000 gain.
B. $5,000 loss.
C. $9,000 gain.
D. No gain or loss is recognized in this conversion

56. Helvetica Corporation liquidated during the year by distributing assets with a fair market value of $200,000 to its shareholders. The assets had an adjusted basis of $62,000. How would this transaction be treated for tax purposes?

A. The distribution is not deductible by Helvetica. No gain or loss would be recognized on the distribution.
B. The distribution is treated as a sale. Helvetica would recognize income of $138,000 on the distribution.
C. The distribution is treated as an exchange. Helvetica would recognize a loss of $138,000 on the distribution.
D. The distribution is treated as a sale. Helvetica would recognize income of $200,000 on the distribution.

57. Ellington Corporation is a new C corporation with two equal shareholders. The corporation reports income and loss on a calendar year basis. Valerie owns 50% of the stock, and her beginning stock basis is $50,000. During the year, Ellington has $64,000 in current earnings and profits. The corporation allocates its profits based on stock ownership. On December 31, Ellington distributes $40,000 to both shareholders. How much gain (or loss) must Valerie recognize on this distribution, and how does the distribution affect her stock basis?

Income	Ending stock basis
A. $40,000 dividend	$10,000
B. $32,000 dividend	$10,000
C. $40,000 ordinary income	$50,000
D. $32,000 dividend	$42,000

104

58. What is the tax rate applicable to built-in gains for an S corporation?

A. 15%.

B. 25%.

C. 30%.

D. The highest corporate tax rate.

59. If an S corporation distributes appreciated property (rather than money) to a shareholder, what is the income effect on the corporation?

A. Gains or losses are not recognized because an S Corporation is a pass-through entity.

B. Gains are recognized for distributions of appreciated property, but losses are not.

C. Gains are not recognized for distributions of appreciated property, but losses are recognized.

D. Gains and losses are both recognized for distributions of appreciated property.

60. What will increase a shareholder's stock basis in an S corporation?

A. The shareholder's share of nondeductible expenses.

B. Contributions to capital.

C. The shareholder's share of corporate and exempt income.

D. Both B and C.

61. Rosas Fine Stationery is a cash-basis C corporation. During the year, Rosas received $140,000 in dividends from a domestic corporation in which it owns less than 20% of the stock. Rosas has taxable income of $180,000 during the year, before figuring the dividends-received-deduction. Based on this information, what is the dividends-received-deduction for Rosas Fine Stationery?

A. $126,000.

B. $70,000.

C. $98,000.

D. $100,000.

62. Which of the following would make a corporation ineligible to elect S corporation status?

A. A shareholder is a partnership.

B. A shareholder is a bankruptcy estate.

C. The corporation has both voting and nonvoting stock.

D. The corporation has 100 shareholders.

63. Parcel Express Corporation is a calendar-year C corporation. In 2012, Parcel Express had taxable income of $125,000 before figuring the dividends-received deduction. Parcel Express is entitled to a $40,000 dividends-received-deduction in 2012. In 2012, Parcel Express donated $30,000 to a qualified 501(c)(3) charity. What is Parcel Express's allowable deduction for charitable contributions on Form 1120?

A. $30,000.
B. $10,000.
C. $12,500.
D. $8,500.

64. In 2012, an S corporation's S-election for S-status was revoked, and the corporation reverted back to a C corporation. How long must the corporation wait before attempting to elect S status again?

A. 12 months.
B. Two years.
C. Five years.
D. A corporation cannot elect S status again after it has been revoked.

65. Troy is a 100% shareholder in Whitlock Corporation, a calendar-year S corporation. On January 1, Troy's stock basis in Whitlock was $95,000. Whitlock reported the following income and loss during the year:

Ordinary losses	$15,000
Long-term capital gains	$4,000
Short-term capital losses	$9,000
Municipal bond interest income	$2,000

What was Troy's basis in Whitlock Corporation at the end of the year?

A. $77,000.
B. $73,000.
C. $95,000.
D. $87,000.

66. If a fisherman elects income averaging, which schedule should he use?

A. Schedule K-1.
B. Schedule E.
C. Schedule J.
D. Schedule L.

67. Brett is the sole shareholder in Mussen Corporation, a calendar-year S corporation. Brett's stock basis at the end of the year is $24,000. Mussen Corporation makes a nondividend distribution of $30,000 to Brett at the end of the year. How would the distribution in excess of Brett's stock basis ($30,000 - $24,000 = $6,000) be taxed?

A. Brett must report a capital gain of $6,000 on his personal return.
B. Brett must report an ordinary dividend of $6,000 on his personal return.
C. Brett must report a capital loss of $6,000 on his personal return.
D. This transaction would not be reported. Instead, it would reduce Brett's stock basis to ($6,000).

68. Linden Financial Corporation is a calendar-year S corporation. At the beginning of the year, Roger was a 50% shareholder in Linden Financial. His stock basis was $16,000 on January 1. At the end of the year, Linden Financial had the following income and distributions:

Ordinary income	$80,000
Municipal bond interest income	$6,000
Year-end nondividend distribution to Roger	$50,000

What is Roger's stock basis in Linden Financial at the end of the year after the nondividend distribution?

A. $30,000.
B. $88,000.
C. $12,000.
D. $9,000.

69. What does the term "inside basis" mean in reference to a partner or partnership?

A. The partnership's basis in its assets.
B. A partner's basis in his partnership interest.
C. The basis of a general partner who signs a partnership's tax returns.
D. The basis of a limited partner who is an investor only in a partnership.

70. Justine and Richard are equal partners in the Bhada Partnership. At the end of the year, the adjusted basis of Justine's partnership interest was $60,000. She received a year-end distribution of $31,000 in cash, plus property with a fair market value of $38,000 and an adjusted basis to the partnership of $46,000. This was a nonliquidating distribution. What is Justine's basis in the property that was distributed?

A. $46,000.
B. $38,000.
C. $29,000.
D. $9,000.

71. With S Corporations, which of the following is a shareholder loss limitation?

A. Debt basis limitation.
B. At-risk limitation.
C. Passive activity loss limitation.
D. Casualty loss limitation.

72. What is required before the IRS will grant an organization 501(c)(3) status?

A. Donations of at least $1,000 as start-up funds for the charity.
B. An organizing document that specifies the permanent charitable purpose of the organization and a provision for distributing funds if it dissolves.
C. The establishment of bylaws and a board of directors.
D. All of the above.

73. Nicholas is a 50% partner in Lightning Partnership. According to the partnership agreement, Nicholas is contracted to receive a $10,000 guaranteed payment every year. At the end of 2012, Lightning Partnership has ordinary income of $42,000. Based on this information, how much partnership income will Nicholas report on his individual for the year?

A. $10,000.
B. $42,000.
C. $21,000.
D. $31,000.

74. At the partnership level, how are guaranteed payments made to individual partners generally treated?

A. As a distribution.
B. As a business expense.
C. As a nonrecourse loan.
D. As business income.

108

75. Section 280F of the Internal Revenue Code sets forth rules that limit the amount of depreciation for the following types of property:

A. Cell phones.
B. Passenger cars weighing less than 6,000 pounds.
C. Rental real property.
D. Boats.

76. Under the accrual method of accounting, income is realized when it is _____.

A. Received.
B. Earned.
C. Anticipated.
D. Capitalized.

77. Which of the following businesses would not be subject to the uniform capitalization rules?

A. A business that produces real or tangible personal property.
B. A business that produces inventory for resale.
C. A business that acquires inventory for resale to others.
D. Self-employed authors, photographers, and artists.

78. Randy is a partner in the Mango Fruits Partnership, which was newly formed in 2012. On December 31, Mango Fruits reports Randy's allocable share of ordinary income as $10,000. Randy also has an allocable share of $1,500 of municipal bond interest from the partnership. No distributions were made to Randy in 2012. On January 15, 2013, Mango Partnership distributes $11,000 to Randy. What is the effect of these transactions on Randy's partnership basis? How much taxable income must Randy report, and in which year is the income taxable?

A. Randy must report $10,000 in partnership income in 2012. After the distribution, his remaining partnership basis would be $500.
B. Randy must report $11,500 in partnership income in 2012. After the distribution, his remaining partnership basis would be $500.
C. Randy must report $11,000 in partnership income in 2013. After the distribution, his remaining partnership basis would be $500.
D. Randy must report $11,000 in partnership income in 2013. After the distribution, his remaining partnership basis would be $0.

79. Which of the following would not be section 1250 property?

A. A rental duplex.
B. A greenhouse to grow orchids.
C. A factory that manufactures premium jeans.
D. An office building.

80. The Lawton Industries Partnership has three partners: Carl, Diana, and Sherry. During the year, Carl wishes to liquidate his partnership interest. Diana and Sherry agree, and Carl receives a cash distribution of $20,000 in exchange for his entire partnership interest. Carl's partnership basis at the time of the distribution was $12,000. How would this transaction be reported by Carl?

A. Carl has an $8,000 capital gain.
B. Carl has a $20,000 capital gain.
C. Carl has an $8,000 ordinary gain.
D. No gain or loss is recognized in this transaction.

81. What is a disregarded entity?

A. A C corporation that is disregarded for federal tax purposes.
B. A C corporation that has chosen to elect S-status.
C. A single-member LLC that is disregarded for federal tax purposes.
D. A multi-member LLC that is disregarded for federal tax purposes.

82. A two-member LLC is formed during the year. How can this entity elect to be taxed?

A. As a corporation.
B. As a partnership.
C. As an estate.
D. Both A and B.

83. Which of the following exempt organizations is required to file an annual information return?

A. A church.
B. A governmental unit.
C. A private foundation.
D. A church mission society.

84. Cheryl is a 100% shareholder in Waterton Sundries Corporation, a cash basis C corporation. At the end of the year, Waterton Sundries has $20,000 in current and accumulated earnings and profits. Waterton Sundries makes a $30,000 cash distribution to Cheryl. At the time of the distribution, Cheryl's stock basis in the corporation was $0. What is the effect of this distribution?

A. Cheryl has a $20,000 taxable dividend and a $10,000 capital gain.
B. Cheryl has a $30,000 taxable dividend.
C. Cheryl has a $20,000 taxable dividend and a $10,000 capital loss.
D. Cheryl has a $30,000 capital gain.

85. When can the expenses incurred during a complete liquidation of a corporation be deducted?

A. In the year they are incurred.
B. On the final corporate return.
C. In the year in which the expenses are accrued.
D. Never. Liquidation expenses of a corporation are not a deductible business expense.

86. Which of the following is not a flow-through entity?

A. Partnership.
B. S corporation.
C. C corporation.
D. Sole proprietorship

87. Kathryn and Allison join together to form Orchard Farms Partnership. Allison contributes $100,000 in cash. Kathryn contributes farmland with an FMV of $90,000 and a tax basis of $10,000. Kathryn also contributes depreciable equipment that has an FMV of $50,000 and a tax basis of $75,000. Kathryn and Allison both acquire a 50% interest in the partnership after their contributions. Upon contributing the land and the equipment, what is Orchard Farms' tax basis in the equipment and the land?

Tax Basis

	Land	Equipment
A.	$90,000	$75,000
B.	$90,000	$50,000
C.	$10,000	$50,000
D.	$10,000	$75,000

88. Mark, Tom, Jessica, and Shannon are all equal partners in the Light Source Partnership. During the year, Light Source Partnership borrows $100,000 for the construction of a storage facility for its products. The partnership borrows the money from a bank and immediately has the facility constructed. All the partners are equally liable for the debt. Before borrowing the money, Mark's partnership basis was $46,000. What effect does the construction loan have on Mark's basis, if any?

A. Mark's partnership basis is increased to $71,000.
B. Mark's partnership basis is decreased to $21,000.
C. Mark's partnership basis is increased to $146,000.
D. This transaction has no effect on partnership basis.

89. Sydney is a general partner in the Yolo Davis Partnership. The adjusted basis of her partnership interest is $165,000. During the year, she receives a cash distribution of $80,000 and property with an adjusted basis of $28,000 and a fair market value of $30,000. This is a nonliquidating distribution. What is the basis of Sydney's partnership interest after this distribution?

A. $55,000.
B. $57,000.
C. $85,000.
D. $113,000.

90. Quicker Relay Corporation is going through a final liquidation and distributes property with a fair market value of $500,000 and an adjusted basis of $190,000. The property is encumbered by an existing mortgage of $620,000. How much gain (or loss) would Quicker Relay recognize in this distribution?

A. $430,000 gain.
B. $120,000 loss.
C. $310,000 gain.
D. $180,000 loss.

91. In the case of S corporations, any suspended losses in excess of stock basis are carried forward _____.

A. 20 years.
B. 5 years.
C. 10 years.
D. Indefinitely.

92. If a shareholder receives a nondividend distribution from an S corporation, the distribution is tax-free to the extent it does not exceed _____.

A. Ordinary income of the S corporation.
B. The shareholder's stock basis.
C. The shareholder's debt basis.
D. The fair market value of the shareholder's stock.

93. What is the latest that a partnership agreement can be modified during a taxable year?

A. Up until the close of the taxable year.
B. No later than the date for filing the partnership return.
C. Up until the first day of the taxable year.
D. No later than the extended due date for filing the partnership return.

94. Green Mountain Corporation is a calendar-year C corporation that was dissolved on July 12, 2012. When is the final tax return due for Green Mountain?

A. March 15, 2013.
B. September 15, 2012.
C. October 15, 2012.
D. September 12, 2012.

95. Which of the following is not a benefit of electing S-corporation status?

A. Avoiding double taxation on distributions.
B. Allowing corporate losses to flow through to shareholders.
C. Up to 10% of charitable contributions are deductible.
D. Corporate liability protection.

96. What is the replacement period for the sale or exchange of livestock in an area eligible for federal disaster assistance?

A. One year after the close of the first tax year in which the taxpayer realizes any part of his gain from the sale or exchange of livestock.
B. Two years after the close of the first tax year in which the taxpayer realizes any part of his gain from the sale or exchange of livestock.
C. Three years after the close of the first tax year in which the taxpayer realizes any part of his gain from the sale or exchange of livestock.
D. Four years after the close of the first tax year in which the taxpayer realizes any part of his gain from the sale or exchange of livestock.

97. Gram Brothers Partnership has two general partners that manage the day-to-day operations. Gram Brothers also has two employees, a receptionist and a paid intern. Which of the following taxes would not be applicable to Gram Brothers?

A. Federal income tax.
B. Excise taxes.
C. Federal unemployment (FUTA) tax.
D. Social security and Medicare taxes (for employee's wages).

98. Which type of entity is required to file a Schedule M-3 with its tax return?

A. A partnership.
B. An LLC.
C. A corporation with less than $10 million in assets.
D. A corporation with more than $10 million in assets.

99. A C corporation has a net operating loss in the current year. What is the carryback and carryforward period for corporation NOLs?

A. Two year carry back, twenty year carryforward.
B. Five year carry back, twenty year carryforward.
C. Two year carry back, carried forward indefinitely.
D. Three year carry back, five year carryforward.

100. During the year, APX Corporation has a $30,000 loss from business operations. APX Corporation receives $100,000 in dividends from a 20%-owned corporation. What is the amount of APX Corporation's dividends-received deduction and its net operating loss (if any)?

Dividends-Received Deduction	NOL
A. $80,000	$5,000
B. $70,000	$10,000
C. $80,000	$10,000
D. $70,000	$0

Please review your answers with the answers in the back.

#2 Businesses Sample Exam

1. Tony is a partner in the Care Heart Partnership. At the end of the year, his adjusted basis in Care Heart was $65,000. Tony received a nonliquidating distribution of land from Care Heart, as well as $15,000 in cash. The land had an adjusted basis of $65,000 to Care Heart and a fair market value of $54,000 immediately before the distribution. What is Tony's basis in the land after the distribution?

A. $50,000.
B. $54,000.
C. $44,000.
D. $65,000.

2. What is the accumulated earnings tax?

A. A 15% tax that is assessed on S corporation and partnership profits.
B. A 15% tax that is assessed on the accumulated earnings and profits of a C corporation.
C. A 20% tax that is imposed upon estates.
D. A 15% payroll tax that is imposed in addition to the trust fund recovery penalty.

3. Terries Corporation offers fringe benefits to its employees. Which of the following benefits is partially taxable to the employee?

A. Health insurance provided to an employee by the employer.
B. The value of $100,000 in life insurance coverage provided to an employee.
C. Employer-provided parking passes.
D. Employee discounts on merchandise.

4. The Darby Corporation was organized on May 15. It elected the calendar year as its accounting period. When is the tax return due for this corporation?

A. October 15.
B. April 15.
C. March 15.
D. May 31.

5. Most entities may choose whether to be taxed as a partnership or a corporation. All of the following statements are correct except:

A. Any eligible entity with two or more members may be classified as a partnership.

B. Any domestic LLC with a single member is disregarded as an entity by the IRS. Any income or losses are then taxable to the owner, just like a sole proprietorship.

C. Partnerships file Form 1065 to report income and losses.

D. A nonprofit entity that is classified as a corporation must file Form 1120 for tax purposes.

6. Rick wants to transfer assets to a corporation in exchange for a controlling interest in the corporation's stock. Which of the following transfers would create a taxable event under IRC section 351 for Rick?

A. Rick exchanges property in exchange for 100% of the corporation's stock.

B. The corporation assumes liabilities in excess of the basis of the assets transferred.

C. Cash is exchanged for 100% of the corporate stock.

D. Rick will not be required to recognize any gain in a transfer, so long as he has a controlling interest (over 80%) in the corporation's stock after the transfer.

7. All of the following entities are required to use the accrual method of accounting except:

A. A family farming corporation with gross receipts of $24 million.

B. A C corporation with gross receipts of $50 million.

C. A tax shelter with $30,000 in gross receipts.

D. A corporation with $50,000 in gross income and long-term contracts.

8. Paul and his sister, Susan, have formed a limited liability company (LLC). If they do not file Form 8832, *Entity Classification Election*, how will the IRS classify their business entity?

A. As a qualified family joint venture, with two separate sole proprietorships.

B. As a partnership.

C. As a C corporation.

D. As an S corporation.

9. In 2012, the Morrison Bioresearch Corporation purchases a number of assets, which all qualify for section 179 treatment:

- Equipment: $100,000 ✓
- New computer: $5,000 ✓
- Qualified leasehold improvements: $350,000   *250,000*

Morrison Bioresearch is not subject to any income limitations. What is the company's maximum *allowable* section 179 deduction in 2012?

A. $105,000.
B. $250,000.
C. $355,000.
D. $455,000.

10. Backup taxes are generally withheld at a rate of _____ for U.S. citizens and resident aliens.

A. 39%.
B. 35%.
C. 28%.
D. 15%.

11. Sunway Partnership is a calendar-year, cash-basis entity. In 2012, Sunway provided services to a client, and in exchange the partnership received a used car with a fair market value of $8,000 and an adjusted basis of $7,500. The partnership also received design services with a value of $3,000. How much of this must the Sunway Partnership report as income in 2012?

A. $3,000.
B. $8,500.
C. $10,500.
D. $11,000.

12. Gulls Seafood Corporation is a calendar-year corporation that completely dissolved on July 22, 2012. When is Gulls Seafood's final tax return due?

A. October 15, 2012.
B. April 15, 2013.
C. March 15, 2012.
D. October 15, 2013.

13. Jessie and Trevor are general partners in the Midway Beer Distributorship. In 2012, they drove the company van 7,000 business-related miles out of a total of 10,000 miles and had $5,500 in total gasoline expenses. They also had to pay $25 for the annual state license tags, $20 for their city registration sticker, and $235 in DMV fees. They are claiming actual car expenses, rather than the standard mileage rate. What is their allowable business deduction for automobile expenses?

A. $3,500.

B. $4,046.

C. $5,780.

D. $8,137.

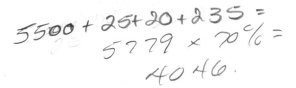

14. The filing of a bankruptcy petition creates a _____.

A. Bankruptcy estate.

B. An excise tax.

C. Gift tax liability.

D. Debtor trust.

15. Which of the following entities is not required to e-file their business return?

A. A partnership with 200 partners (Schedules K-1).

B. A corporation with assets of $10 million that files at least 250 returns annually.

C. A sole proprietorship with 100 employees.

D. A small tax-exempt organization that wishes to file Form 990-N.

16. When are expenses related to a cell phone deductible to an employer and non-taxable to an employee?

A. Always.

B. Never.

C. When the phone is provided only to a non-highly compensated employee.

D. When the phone is provided primarily for noncompensatory purposes.

17. Aaron is a sole proprietor who uses the cash method. He pays $3,000 in 2012 for a business insurance policy that is effective for three years, beginning on July 1, 2012. How much of the insurance policy is deductible on Aaron's 2012 tax return?

A. $250.

B. $500.

C. $1,750.

D. $3,000.

18. Dwight died in April 2012. At the time of his death and settling his estate, none of his basic exclusion amount was used to reduce or eliminate payment of gift or estate taxes. Form 706 was filed in November 2012 and the full amount of deceased spousal unused exclusion (DSUE) was reported thereon. His wife Monica died in December 2012. As was the case with Dwight, none of her basic exclusion amount had been previously been used to offset gift taxes that would otherwise have been payable. What amount must Monica's taxable estate exceed in order to be subject to estate tax?

A. $5,120,000. – *each*
B. $1,772,800.
C. $5,000,000.
D. $10,240,000. – *for both, if neither has been used.*

19. The IRS is implementing new rules related to when a property is properly classified as an improvement rather than a repair. All of the following are correct statements regarding the changes except:

A. The new rules should make it easier for taxpayers to deduct rather than capitalize certain costs.
B. The new standards refer to the *betterment, restoration,* and *adaptation to new use* of units of property.
C. Taxpayers have the choice whether or not to adapt the new standards in tax year 2012.
D. The new improvement standards apply to the building structure and to each of the building's major component systems separately.

20. Carson Corporation sets up an IRA for its employees. The IRA is a payroll-deduction retirement account, where the amounts are taken from an employee's wages and deposited directly into each employee's individual IRA. Regarding this type of employer retirement arrangement, which of the following is false?

A. Participants are always 100% vested in all of the funds in their IRAs.
B. Participant loans are permitted.
C. IRA withdrawals are permitted at any time.
D. An employee may move the IRA assets from one IRA provider to another.

21. Janelle owns a bookstore. She recently signed a contract with a vendor, which was finalized over dinner. The total cost of the dinner was $250. Janelle's own dinner was $50. The vendor ate an expensive meal and also drank liquor, so his portion of the meal was $170. The remainder of the bill was for the tip and tax. Janelle also spent $10 in taxi fare to get to the meal. How much of this expense is actually deductible by Janelle as a business expense?

A. $25.
B. $110.
C. $135.
D. $250.

22. Manny is an attorney. He transfers property worth $150,000 and renders legal services valued at $13,000 to the Beltway Corporation in exchange for stock valued at $138,000. Right after the exchange, Manny owns 85% of the outstanding corporate stock. How much gain or loss does Manny recognize in this transaction?

A. $1,000 in capital loss.
B. $13,000 in ordinary income.
C. $12,000 in capital loss and $13,000 in ordinary income.
D. No gain or loss is recognized in this transaction.

23. Alex sold his office building to Cassandra, a real estate investor, who plans to use it as a business rental property. Alex was liable for $2,000 in delinquent real estate taxes on the property, which Cassandra agreed to pay. Which of the following statements is true?

A. Cassandra can deduct these taxes as a business expense.
B. Cassandra cannot deduct these taxes as a current expense, but should instead add the amount to her basis of the property.
C. Alex can deduct these taxes as an expense because he was the legal owner of the property.
D. The expense must be divided equally between Alex and Cassandra in order to be deductible.

24. Harrington Corporation does a section 1031 exchange of an airplane (adjusted basis $30,000) for another airplane (FMV $75,000). Harrington also pays an additional $40,000 in cash to complete the exchange. What is Harrington's basis in the new plane?

A. $70,000.
B. $75,000.
C. $105,000.
D. $115,000.

25. A calendar-year C corporation would like to change to a fiscal year end. How can the corporation change its tax year?

A. A C corporation may file a short period return and elect a fiscal year at any time during its existence without IRS consent.
B. The C corporation may switch to a fiscal year so long as it has not changed its annual accounting period at any time within the last 12 months.
C. The C corporation may request a change in its tax year by filing Form 1128.
D. The C corporation must dissolve before changing its tax year.

26. Which of the following is not included in the cost of goods sold calculation?

A. The cost of products or raw materials, including freight.
B. Storage costs for finished products.
C. Contributions to pension or annuity plans for workers who produce the products.
D. The cost of shipping finished products to customers.

27. U.S. tax law requires businesses to submit a Form 1099-MISC for every contractor paid at least _____ for services during a year.

A. $400.
B. $600.
C. $850.
D. $1,000.

28. Mario and Juan decide to form an equal partnership. Mario contributes $30,000, and Juan contributes property with an FMV of $40,000 and an adjusted basis of $25,000. What is the basis of each partner?

A. Mario has a $30,000 basis, and Juan has a $25,000 basis.
B. Mario has a $30,000 basis, and Juan has a $40,000 basis.
C. Mario has a $25,000 basis, and Juan has a $25,000 basis.
D. None of the above.

29. Which of the following cannot be a shareholder in an S Corporation?

A. An estate.
B. A nonresident alien.
C. A U.S. resident who is not an American citizen.
D. A 501(c)(3) corporation.

30. Which of the following would be classified as a "guaranteed payment" to a partner in a partnership?

A. A partner only receives the payment if the partnership earns a profit.
B. A payment that was contractually obligated but remained unpaid at the end of the partnership's taxable year.
C. A payment that a partner constructively received during the partnership's taxable year.
D. Both B and C.

31. Doreen acquires a 20% interest in a partnership by contributing a building that had an adjusted basis to her of $800,000 and is encumbered by a $400,000 mortgage. The partnership assumes payment of the mortgage. The basis of Doreen's partnership interest is:

A. $400,000.
B. $480,000.
C. $640,000.
D. $800,000.

32. The Kendall Entertainment Corporation is a calendar-year C corporation. Kendall Entertainment has net income of $600,000 before its charitable contribution of $65,000. The company also has a net operating loss carryover of $200,000 from the prior year. What is Kendall Entertainment's allowable charitable contribution in 2012?

A. $0.
B. $6,500.
C. $60,000.
D. $40,000.

33. Amino Corporation trades old manufacturing equipment for new equipment in a qualified section 1031 exchange. The cost basis of the old equipment was $50,000. The old equipment had $26,000 in accumulated depreciation. Amino also paid an additional $12,000 in cash to obtain the new equipment. The new equipment has a fair market value of $48,000. What is Amino's adjusted basis in the new equipment after the 1031 exchange?

A. $24,000.
B. $36,000.
C. $50,000.
D. $62,000.

34. What penalty is assessed if the IRS determines that a prohibited transaction has occurred that relates to a taxpayer's 401(k) plan?

A. 6% tax.
B. 10% tax.
C. 15% tax.
D. Liquidation of the taxpayer's 401(k) fund.

35. Corporations generally must make estimated tax payments if they expect to owe tax of _____ or more.

A. $100.
B. $500.
C. $1,000.
D. $5,000.

36. ABC Corporation owns 85% of the outstanding stock in S&V Corporation. In 2012, ABC Corporation receives $250,000 in dividends from S&V Corporation. What percentage of the dividends does ABC Corporation have to pay taxes on?

A. 0%.
B. 10%.
C. 20%.
D. 30%.

37. Which of the following vehicles is not an "excepted vehicle" for purposes of the listed property rules?

A. An ambulance.
B. A hearse.
C. A taxi.
D. All of the above are excepted vehicles.

38. Which of the following property is eligible for the section 179 deduction?

A. Inventory.
B. Section 197 intangibles.
C. A patent.
D. Livestock.

39. Which of the following statements about a corporate stock distribution is correct?

A. A stock distribution must be treated as a property distribution that is taxable to the shareholder.
B. A stock distribution is taxable to the corporation when the stock is distributed to shareholders.
C. A stock distribution is deductible by the corporation as an expense.
D. A stock distribution is not taxable to shareholders and not deductible by the corporation.

40. Lorna is the sole owner and shareholder in Mechanics Corporation, a cash-basis S corporation. In 2012, Mechanics had the following activity:

- Gross income from operations: $50,000
- Tax exempt interest: $1,000
- Residential rental income: $5,000
- Charitable contribution: $2,000
- Deductible business expenses: $20,000

How much **ordinary income** must Mechanics Corporation report?

A. $28,000.
B. $30,000.
C. $35,000.
D. $55,000.

41. Which of the following items is not factored into the calculation for ordinary income of a partnership?

A. Cost of goods sold.
B. Partnership contributions to a partner's IRA account. —Treated as a distribution item - Separately Stated
C. Partnership contributions to an employee's IRA account.
D. Section 179 deduction.

42. Which of the following is not a pass-through entity?

A. Sole proprietorship.
B. S corporation.
C. C corporation.
D. Partnership.

43. Jorge is a 10% shareholder in Octavia Corporation with an outstanding $10,000 loan from the corporation. He files for bankruptcy and defaults on the loan. Octavia cancels Jorge's debt in 2012. How should this cancellation of debt be reported?

A. Treat the debt cancellation as a $10,000 taxable distribution to Jorge.
B. Treat the debt cancellation as a liquidation of stock.
C. Treat the debt cancellation as wages to Jorge.
D. Treat the debt cancellation as a $10,000 return of capital.

44. Gracie Development Corporation owes one of its vendors $250,000 for a delinquent invoice. The vendor threatens to sue to recover the debt. Gracie Development agrees to transfer a commercial building to the vendor in order to satisfy the debt. Gracie Development purchased the building seven years ago for $190,000. How must this transaction be reported?

A. Gracie Development must recognize a taxable gain of $60,000.
B. Gracie Development must recognize forgiven debt of $250,000.
C. Gracie Development must recognize a taxable gain of $250,000.
D. Gracie Development can recognize a loss of $60,000 on the sale of the commercial building.

45. Build Rite Architects is a cash-basis C corporation and also a personal service corporation. The corporation's net income in 2012 is $68,000 before applying a net operating loss carryover of $22,000 from the previous year. What amount of corporate tax does Build Rite owe in 2012?

A. $10,200.
B. $23,800.
C. $46,000.
D. $16,100.

46. In which of the following instances would Gabe be treated as having constructive ownership of more than 50% of the partnership?

Ownership Percentages
A. Gabe 20%; Gabe's son 20%; Gabe's brother 60%.
B. Gabe 25%; Gabe's wife 10%; Gabe's aunt 75%.
C. Gabe 45%; Gabe's cousin 51%; Gabe's son 4%.
D. Gabe 45%; Gabe's cousin 55%.

47. Oliviera Meatpackers Corporation is having financial trouble and liquidates in 2012. In the course of liquidation, Oliviera distributes $10,000 in cash and a machine with a fair market value of $12,000 and an adjusted basis of $8,000 to Gordon, a 10% shareholder. Gordon's basis in his stock is $17,000. How much gain will Gordon recognize in this transaction?

A. $2,000.
B. $5,000.
D. $3,000.
E. $18,000.

48. Quigley Corporation rents office space from its only employee-shareholder. The fair rental value of the office space is $4,500 per month, but the corporation pays the shareholder $6,000 per month, and the corporation deducts the full amount as rent expense. Which of the following statements is true?

A. The IRS may reclassify the excess $1,500 per month in rental payments as a constructive dividend, and the corporation would lose that amount as a deduction.
B. The IRS may reclassify the entire $4,500 per month in rental payments as a constructive dividend.
C. The IRS may reclassify the entire $6,000 per month in rental payments as a constructive dividend.
D. The IRS may reclassify the excess $1,500 per month in rental payments as a stock dividend.

49. Grassroots Corporation repurchased all of its outstanding bonds in 2012 for $580,000. The bonds were originally issued two years ago for a face value of $550,000. How should this transaction be reported by Grassroots?

A. Grassroots has a $30,000 capital loss.
B. Grassroots has a $30,000 interest expense.
C. No gain or loss is recognized on a repurchase of a corporation's own securities.
D. Grassroots has a $30,000 ordinary gain.

50. Which of the following statements is true regarding a husband and wife who own and run a business together?

A. A husband and wife may jointly operate as a sole proprietorship and file a Schedule E for both taxpayers.
B. A married couple who jointly operate a business may choose for each spouse to be treated as a sole proprietor by electing to file as a "qualified joint venture."
C. A husband and wife may not operate a partnership together because of the related party transaction rules.
D. A husband and wife may elect to be treated as a single individual for Social Security tax purposes.

51. Which form is used by a C corporation to report income and losses?

A. Form 1120.
B. Form 1120-W.
C. Form 1065.
D. Form 8832.

52. A few years ago, Starlite Music Corporation purchased land at a cost of $90,000. In 2012, the land is condemned by the federal government for development of a railway. Starlite Music receives a $160,000 condemnation award for the land. Within the same year, Starlite Music purchases replacement land for $80,000. How much gain (if any) should the company recognize on this transaction?

A. $10,000.
B. $20,000.
C. $70,000.
D. $160,000.

53. Wendy runs a sole proprietorship. She hires her 15-year-old daughter, Kylie, to answer phones part-time and do filing and other office tasks. Wendy pays her daughter a reasonable wage of $5,000 for the year. Which of the following statements about the wages for Kylie is correct?

A. Kylie's wages are subject to the "kiddie tax."
B. Wendy cannot deduct her daughter's wages because of related party transaction rules.
C. Kylie's wages are deductible, and the amounts are not subject to Social Security and Medicare taxes.
D. Kylie's wages are subject to backup withholding.

54. Jaime is the single owner shareholder of XYZ Corporation, which is a calendar-year, accrual-basis C corporation. On December 31, 2012, XYZ had accrued a $20,000 bonus for Jaime and $32,000 in wage expenses for other employees. The wages and the bonus were not actually paid until January 15, 2013. How much of the wage expense (if any) can XYZ deduct on its 2012 tax return?

A. $0.
B. $20,000.
C. $32,000.
D. $52,000.

55. Andrew owns and operates a restaurant. He has ten servers working for him. Which of the following is not a requirement for employers who have tipped employees?

A. Tips are considered taxable income and are subject to federal income taxes.
B. Tips that an employee receives from customers are subject to withholding.
C. The employer must collect income tax, employee Social Security tax, and employee Medicare tax on the employee's tips.
D. All of the above are correct.

56. Blair forms an LLC in 2012. She wants her business to be classified as a corporation for tax purposes. What form must Blair file in order to elect this treatment?

A. Form 4898.
B. Form 8832.
C. Form 7006.
D. Form 8821.

57. An interest in a partnership is treated as a _____ when it is sold.

A. Loss.
B. Capital asset.
C. Section 1231 asset.
C. Section 197 intangible asset.

58. The Brookshire Partnership is having financial difficulties in 2012. The partners decide to file for bankruptcy. In this case, the debt cancellation income and tax attribute reduction occurs where?

A. At the partnership level. Tax attribute reduction is reported on the partnership return and reduces the income of the partnership.
B. Each partner's share of debt cancellation income must be reported on the partner's individual return.
C. The debt cancellation is not reported on the partnership return or on the partner's individual return.
D. A partnership cannot legally declare bankruptcy; the partners must declare bankruptcy individually.

59. Doezie Pharmaceuticals is a C corporation with a fiscal year-end of June 30, 2012. Doezie files an extension. What is Doezie's extended due date?

A. September 15, 2012.
B. October 15, 2013.
C. March 15, 2013.
D. April 15, 2013.

60. The Lento Corporation is a cash-basis C corporation. Lento has $190,000 in taxable income in 2012. It also has a $21,000 capital loss from the prior year and a net operating loss of $35,000 from a prior year. The corporation did not have any capital gains income. Assuming a corporate tax rate of 39% for all income, what is Lento's income tax liability for the year?

A. $74,100.
B. $52,260.
C. $60,450.
D. $65,910.

61. In 2012, Exposition Convention Corporation distributed a nondividend distribution of $800 to its sole shareholder, Ned. Ned's stock basis before the distribution is $1,000. What is the effect of this transaction?

A. Ned must report a $1,000 capital gain.
B. Ned must report a $200 capital loss.
C. Ned must reduce his stock basis by $800.
D. Ned must report $800 in capital gain.

62. A tax exempt 501 (c)(3) corporation has $1,200 in unrelated business income in 2012. How should this income be reported?

A. The entity should report the unrelated business income on Form 1120.
B. The IRS will revoke the exempt status of the organization if it has business income.
C. The entity should report the unrelated business income on Form 990-T.
D. The entity should report the income on Form 990.

63. Renee is a general partner in Brown Bonnets Partnership. Renee receives a parcel of land from the partnership that has a fair market value of $50,000 but a basis of $40,000. Her outside basis in the partnership is $32,000. How must Renee recognize this transaction?

A. Renee must reduce her partnership basis to zero, and her basis in the land is $32,000.
B. Renee must reduce her partnership basis to zero, and her basis in the land is $40,000.
C. Renee must recognize a capital gain of $8,000, and her basis in the land is $50,000.
D. Renee must recognize a capital gain of $10,000, and her basis in the land is $50,000.

64. Conrad Surfwear Corporation is a new company that elects to amortize its organizational costs. Which of the following is considered a qualifying organizational cost?

A. State incorporation fees.
B. Costs for issuing and selling stock or securities.
C. The cost of transferring assets to the corporation.
D. All of the costs are qualifying organizational costs.

65. Jack is a self-employed plumber. He purchased the following equipment in 2012:

Video recorder	$195
Laptop	$450
Digital camera	$123
Desk chair	$53
Cellular phone	$75
Work tools	$178
Tool belt	$95
Total	**$1,169**

Of the overall equipment purchases, how much is considered *listed property* for depreciation purposes?

A. $0.
B. $768.
C. $843.
D. $1,041.

66. Which of the following business-related meal expenses would not be subject to the 50% rule?

A. A meal incurred while entertaining a business client.
B. A meal while attending a business convention.
C. A meal fully reimbursed to an employee under an accountable plan..
D. A business meal that qualifies as a *de minimis* fringe benefit.

67. Jacob is a 10% partner in Texas Tumbleweed Partnership. In 2012, his beginning partnership basis was $7,000. He received a distribution of $10,000 in cash, plus a car with a partnership basis of $3,000 and a fair market value of $4,500. What is the result of this transaction to Jacob, and how must he recognize the distributions?

A. $3,000 in capital gain; his partnership basis is zero, and his basis in the car is zero.
B. $6,000 in capital gain; his partnership basis is zero, and his basis in the car is $3,000.
C. Zero in capital gain; his partnership basis is (-$3,000), and his basis in the car is $3,000.
D. $4,500 in capital gain; his partnership basis is zero, and his basis in the car is $4,500.

68. When a partnership decides to go out of business and stops all operations and distributes the remaining assets and cash to the partners, this process is called:

A. Consolidation.
B. Liquidation.
C. Closure.
D. Redistribution.

69. On October 1, 2012 Spillway Corporation, a cash-basis, calendar-year corporation, purchases a building, with a $20,000 cash down payment and a mortgage of $30,000. Spillway also pays attorneys' fees of $2,300 to complete the sale. Spillway promptly demolishes the existing building in order to start construction on a new building. The demolition costs are $12,000. What is the basis of the land, and how much can be taken as a current expense in 2012?

A. $50,000 land basis, $14,300 current expense.
B. $52,300 land basis, $12,000 current expense.
C. $62,000 land basis, $2,300 current expense.
D. $64,300 land basis, $0 current expense.

70. Lynden Corporation gives its traveling salespeople $1,000 a month ($12,000 a year) as a car allowance. The salespeople do not have to provide any proof of their car expenses to Lynden Corp. How should these payments be treated?

A. The car allowances are deductible as contractor payments, and they are not taxable to the employees.
B. Lynden must include the $12,000 on each salesperson's Form W-2. The amounts are not subject to Social Security or Medicare tax.
C. Lynden must include the $12,000 on each salesperson's Form W-2. The amounts are subject to withholding, as well as to Social Security and Medicare tax.
D. The payments can be treated as a gift.

71. The death of a partner has what effect on the partnership?

A. The death of a partner closes the partnership's tax year for that partner.
B. The death of a partner closes the partnership's tax year for the remaining partners.
C. The death of a partner causes an immediate liquidation of partnership assets.
D. The death of a partner is treated as a distribution.

72. Which of the following activities qualifies for the domestic production activities deduction?

A. Selling food or beverages prepared at restaurants or dining establishments.
B. Software development in the United States.
C. Leasing items to a related party.
D. Customer service businesses.

73. All of the following qualify for a deduction for depletion, except:

A. Patents.
B. Timber.
C. Gas wells.
D. Mines and natural deposits.

74. The uniform capitalization rules do not apply to any of the following except:

A. Property produced under a long-term contract.
B. Research and experimental expenditures.
C. Loan originations.
D. The production of property for sale to customers.

75. Which form is used to file an estate tax return?

A. Form 1041.
B. Form 706.
C. Form 911.
D. Form 709.

76. Chris became a limited partner in the Dubishar Partnership by contributing $12,000 in cash on the formation of the partnership. The adjusted basis of his partnership interest at the end of the current year is $21,000, which includes his $15,000 share of partnership liabilities. At the end of the year, Chris sells his partnership interest for $10,000 in cash. How must Chris report this transaction?

A. He must report $4,000 as a capital gain.
B. He must report $2,000 as a capital loss.
C. He must report $15,000 as a capital gain.
D. He must report $6,000 as a capital gain.

77. During the year, Diamondback Corporation had a $20,000 net operating loss from operations. It also received $100,000 in dividends from a domestic corporation, in which Diamondback holds a 15% stock ownership. There were no other items of income or loss during the year. What is Diamondback's dividends-received deduction?

A. $56,000.
B. $80,000.
C. $64,000.
D. $70,000.

78. Which of the following items does not decrease an asset's tax basis?

A. The cost of defending a title to the property.
B. A casualty loss.
C. Section 179 accelerated depreciation.
D. A manufacturer's rebate.

79. The Binary Trust is required to distribute all of its income annually. The income and expenses of the trust are shown below. Five hundred dollars of the fiduciary fee is allocated to the tax-exempt interest. How much taxable income will pass through to the trust beneficiaries?

1.	Interest from a certificate of deposit	$4,000
2.	Tax-exempt interest	$2,000
3.	Fiduciary fee	$1,000

A. $3,500.
B. $2,500.
C. $1,500.
D. $5,000.

80. In 2012, Trinity Church had the following activity. What tax return, if any, is Trinity Church required to file?
- Paid $30,000 in wages to three church employees
- Had $800 in unrelated business income
- Received $300,000 in donations from parishioners

A. A church is not required to file a tax return.
B. Trinity must file payroll tax returns and **Form 990-T.**
C. Trinity must file payroll tax returns.
D. Trinity must file **Form 990, Form 941,** and **Form 990-T.**

81. The Las Vegas Rottweiler Rescue qualifies for exempt status as an animal rescue organization. Which form is used by the organization to apply for exemption under IRC section 501(c)(3)?

A. Form 990.
B. Form 1023.
C. Form 1024.
D. Form 2106.

82. All of the following assets are business related. Which of the following does not qualify for a nontaxable 1031 exchange?

A. The exchange of an empty apartment building for farmland.
B. The exchange of partnership interests.
C. The exchange of investment property in one state for the exchange of investment property in another state.
D. The exchange of farm animals of the same sex.

83. Section 1245 property includes all of the following depreciable properties except:

A. Buildings and their structural components.
B. Tangible personal property.
C. A single purpose agricultural structure.
D. Intangible personal property.

84. Philip is the sole shareholder of Leisure Crafts Corporation. In 2012, Leisure Crafts sells a utility van with an adjusted basis of $12,000 and a fair market value of $22,000 to Philip's sister, Gayle, for $11,500. Gayle plans to use the utility van in her business. How must this transaction be reported?

A. Leisure Crafts may take a deductible loss of $500 on the sale of the asset.
B. Leisure Crafts must recognize gain of $500 on the sale of the asset.
C. Leisure Crafts will recognize neither gain nor loss on the sale of the asset.
D. Leisure Crafts. may take a deductible loss of $10,500 on the sale of the asset.

85. Dermahydrate Corporation is an accrual-basis, calendar-year C corporation. On December 15, 2012, the board of directors authorizes a charitable contribution of $3,000 to a qualified charity. What is the last day that Dermahydrate can make this charitable contribution and still take the expense on its **2012** tax return?

A. December 15, 2012.
B. December 31, 2012.
C. January 15, 2013.
D. March 15, 2013.

86. Cameo Films Corporation owned a building that burned down in 2012. The basis of the building before the fire was $240,000. The insurance company reimbursed Cameo Films $500,000. How long does Cameo Films have to reinvest the insurance proceeds in order to receive nonrecognition treatment for this involuntary conversion?

A. One year from the date of the involuntary conversion.
B. Three years after the close of the year that the involuntary conversion occurred.
C. Two years after the date the involuntary conversion occurred.
D. Three years from the date of the insurance reimbursement.

87. Kristy is a 10% shareholder in Jungle Parties Corporation, a C corporation. She is not an employee of Jungle Parties. The C corporation loans Kristy $40,000 interest-free for one year. The applicable federal rate at the time of the loan is 7% ($40,000 X 7% = $2,800). How will this transaction be reported, and will Kristy have to recognize any income?

A. Kristy will be forced to recognize $2,800 in imputed interest as dividend income. Jungle Parties is not allowed a deduction for the dividend paid.
B. Kristy will not be required to recognize any dividend income so long as she repays the loan within the year.
C. Kristy will be forced to recognize $2,800 in imputed interest as dividend income, and Jungle Parties will be allowed a tax deduction for the dividend paid.
D. Kristy will be forced to recognize $2,800 as taxable wages. Jungle Parties is not allowed a deduction for the wages paid.

88. What is the maximum amount of start-up costs that a business can deduct as a current expense in 2012?

A. $1,000.
B. $5,000.
C. $10,000.
D. $50,000.

89. Which of the following is allowable as a business expense?

A. A political contribution.
B. Lobbying expenses.
C. Repairs to equipment that increase the useful life of an asset.
D. Prepayment penalty on a mortgage.

90. Sam owns Sammy's Sausage Palace. He bought his store building ten years ago, making a down payment of $30,000 and a mortgage of $110,000. Sam paid off the mortgage in six years. He sold the building for $205,000 in 2012. Straight-line depreciation on the building on the date of sale was $22,000. What is the nature and the amount of the gain on the sale of the building?

A. $43,000.
B. $95,000.
C. $87,000.
D. $153,000.

91. What is the maximum amount of time allowed for an exempt entity to submit its application for exemption, starting with the date of its creation?

A. Four months.
B. Six months.
C. Nine months.
D. Fifteen months.

92. Shania owns a small hair salon as a sole proprietor. During the year she has the following income and expenses:

- Gross receipts $42,000
- Supplies expense $3,500
- Wages for part-time employee $5,000
- Utility expenses $800
- Section 1231 gain $800
- Charitable contribution $1,200

How much business income should Shania report on her **Schedule C?**

A. $53,300.
B. $32,700.
C. $33,500.
D. $32,300.

93. Angie owns a 30% interest in the Günter Partnership. All the general partners share profit and loss according to their ownership stake. There are no limited partners. The partnership reports $90,000 in income for 2012 and distributes $23,000 to Angie. How much income will Angie recognize on her individual return, and what is the character of the income?

A. $23,000 income, subject to self-employment tax.
B. $23,000 income, not subject to self-employment tax.
C. $27,000 income, subject to self-employment tax.
D. $27,000 income, not subject to self-employment tax.
E. $30,000 income, subject to self-employment tax.

94. Davenport Inc. is a fiscal year C corporation that reports income and loss on the accrual basis. Which of the following is required for Davenport to accrue and deduct an expense?

A. Davenport must first pay the expense in order to accrue and deduct it.
B. Davenport must receive an invoice or other bill in order to accrue and deduct it.
C. Davenport must meet the all events test and have economic performance in order to deduct the expense.
D. Davenport must have received a bill for the expense and paid it before the end of its fiscal year.

95. Which of the following applies only to partnerships?

A. Estimated tax payments.
B. Involuntary conversions.
C. Capital gains.
D. Guaranteed payments.

96. During 2012, the Premium Pet Food Corporation had the following items of income and expense:

Income from operations	$50,000
Expenses from operations	$40,000
Dividends-received from TAM Corp (a 20% owned corporation)	$120,000

Based on the information above, what is Premium Pet Food Corporation's dividends-received deduction?

A. $10,000.
B. $96,000.
C. $104,000.
D. $84,000.

97. Temple Corporation is a fiscal year-end, cash-basis corporation. Temple's tax year ends June 30. When are its estimated taxes due?

A. October 15, December 15, March 15, and June 15.
B. April 15, June 15, September 15, and December 15.
C. March 15, June 15, September 15, and December 15.
D. April 15, June 15, September 15, and January 15.

98. What is the dollar limit of section 179 depreciation in 2012?

A. $250,000.
B. $350,000.
C. $500,000.
D. $2 million.

99. Driveline Corporation is a calendar-year S corporation. It has four shareholders. The corporation has 10,000 shares outstanding. The shareholders have the following ownership:

Shareholder	Ownership
1. Thomas	4,500 shares
2. Ashley	2,000 shares 4000 6000
3. Simon	2,000 shares
4. Charlotte	1,500 shares
Total	**10,000 shares**

Charlotte and Thomas wish to terminate Driveline's S-election, but Ashley and Simon do not. Which of the following statements is true?

A. Charlotte and Thomas do not have enough stock ownership to terminate the election.

B. All of the shareholders must agree to terminate an S-election.

C. Charlotte and Thomas do have enough stock ownership to terminate the election.

D. At least 75% of the shareholders with active ownership must agree to the termination.

100. Gloss Photos Corporation is a C corporation. Gloss Photos has a net short-term capital gain of $3,000 and a net long-term capital loss of $9,000. The short-term gain offsets some of the long-term loss, leaving a net capital loss of $6,000. The corporation also has $50,000 in ordinary income. Which of the following statements is true regarding this corporation's capital loss?

A. The corporation can use $3,000 of this $6,000 loss to offset ordinary income. The remainder must be carried forward.

B. The corporation treats this $6,000 as a long-term loss that must be carried back for one year and carried forward for up to five years.

C. The corporation treats this $6,000 as a short-term loss that must be carried back for three years and carried forward for up to five years.

D. The corporation treats this $6,000 as a long-term loss that must be carried back for two years and carried forward for up to 20 years.

Please review your answers with the answers in the back.

Part 3: Representation Practice Exams

#1 Representation Sample Exam

1. Which of the following statements is true regarding tax practitioners?

A. A tax practitioner is prohibited from charging contingent fees.
B. A tax practitioner may notarize documents for the clients that he represents before the IRS.
C. A tax practitioner may represent two clients when there is a clear conflict of interest, as long as the clients sign a disclosure agreement.
D. A tax practitioner is allowed to endorse a client's refund check, but only if the client signs a power of attorney.

2. Lacey wants to designate her tax preparer as the Third Party Designee on her individual tax return. Based solely on the Third Party Authorization, which of the following will her preparer not be able to do on Lacey's behalf?

A. Call the IRS for information about the processing of her return.
B. Receive copies of notices or transcripts related to her return.
C. Respond to IRS notices about math errors on her return.
D. Designate her preparer to receive (but not cash) her tax refund check on her behalf.

3. Why is it important for paid preparers to compare prior year returns with the current year information?

A. In order to bill the client correctly.
B. In order to review significant changes and to avoid potential math errors from one year to another.
C. In order to protect themselves from lawsuits.
D. None of the above.

4. What is the penalty for a preparer who negotiates a taxpayer's refund check?

A. No penalty.
B. $500 per occurrence.
C. $500 per year.
D. $1,000 per occurrence.

5. For businesses that have employees and are on a fiscal year, what are the tax periods for Forms 941?

A. The tax period is the first, second, third, or fourth quarter of the fiscal year.
B. The tax period is the first, second, third, or fourth quarter of the calendar year.
C. The due date for Form 941 is April 15.
D. None of the above is correct.

6. Kimberly is a bookkeeper who also prepares a limited number of tax forms. She is subject to the e-file mandate. Kimberly has a client that refuses to e-file his tax return. What is the proper procedure for this scenario?

A. Kimberly must refuse the engagement.
B. Kimberly must fire the client.
C. Kimberly can prepare the client's return on paper and attach Form 8948.
D. Kimberly should encourage the taxpayer to file electronically. If the client refuses, then Kimberly does not need to sign the return as a paid preparer.

7. Enrolled agents are allowed to assert a limited tax practitioner confidentiality privilege relating to _____.

A. Noncriminal tax matters brought before the IRS or noncriminal tax proceedings brought in federal court.
B. Noncriminal tax matters, including communications regarding tax shelters.
C. Communications in furtherance of a crime or fraud.
D. Criminal tax matters brought before the IRS.

8. Marion is a tax preparer. She has a client named Leo who has several unpaid invoices. Marion prepared Leo's tax return, and called him to pick it up. Later that week, Leo comes to Marion's office and demands return of his records. Leo refuses to pay for any outstanding invoices. What is Marion required to do in this case?

A. Marion must promptly return any and all records belonging to the client that are necessary for him to comply with his federal tax obligations.
B. Marion must promptly return any and all records, including the return that she prepared, regardless of any fee dispute.
C. Marion is not required to return the client's records while there is an ongoing fee dispute.
D. Marion is only required to return the client's records if the client pays in full.

9. On a jointly filed return (MFJ) both spouses are _____ for all the tax due even if one spouse earned all the income.

A. Independently liable.
B. Jointly and severally liable.
C. Partially liable.
D. Not responsible.

10. Which of the following enrolled practitioners has the most limited areas of practice before the IRS?

A. Enrolled agent.
B. Certified public accountant.
C. Attorney.
D. Enrolled actuary.

11. What practice rights do enrolled agents have?

A. Unlimited practice rights before the IRS.
B. Unlimited practice rights before the IRS and the U.S. Tax Court.
C. Limited practice rights.
D. None of the above.

12. Which IRS office is responsible for matters relating to practitioner conduct and discipline, including disciplinary proceedings and sanctions?

A. Return Preparer Office.
B. Department of the Treasury
C. Office of Professional Responsibility.
D. State Board of Accountancy

13. Which IRS office is responsible for processing enrollment applications and administering competency testing?

A. Office of Chief Council.
B. Return Preparer Office.
C. Office of Professional Responsibility.
D. The Office of the IRS Commissioner.

14. An enrolled agent is able to represent tax clients before all of the following except:

A. The IRS Appeals division.
B. Revenue agents.
C. A U.S. District Court.
D. IRS Collections division.

15. If an enrolled agent is disbarred from practice, the IRS _____.

A. Will still allow the practitioner to represent clients before the IRS examination division.
B. Will not recognize a power of attorney that names the individual as a representative.
C. Will retain limited practice rights for representation of past clients.
D. None of the above.

16. If a disbarred practitioner seeks reinstatement, he or she may still practice before the IRS _____.

A. While the reinstatement proceedings are pending.
B. While the appeals process takes place.
C. After an appeals petition is filed with the Office of Professional Responsibility.
D. Under no circumstances. A disbarred practitioner may not practice before the IRS.

17. Lester was disbarred from practice by the IRS. How many years must he wait before he can petition the IRS for reinstatement?

A. One year.
B. Five years.
C. Ten years.
D. Disbarment is always permanent.

18. Which of the following type of IRS guidance has the highest authority in establishing precedence?

A. Revenue ruling.
B. Private letter ruling.
C. Technical advice memorandum.
D. Information letter.

19. Which of the following is not a requirement when a taxpayer requests "innocent spouse relief"?

A. The taxpayer filed a joint return that has an understatement of tax (deficiency) that is solely attributable to a spouse's erroneous item.
B. When the taxpayer signed the joint return he or she did not know, and had no reason to know, that there was an understatement of tax on the return.
C. Taking into account all the facts and circumstances, it would be unfair to hold the taxpayer liable for the understatement of tax.
D. The taxpayer must have already filed for divorce or legal separation when the "innocent spouse relief" is requested.

20. In serving a complaint against an enrolled practitioner, the Office of Professional Responsibility may use all of the methods listed below except:

A. Private delivery service.
B. E-mail.
C. First class mail.
D. In person.

21. Tax practitioners should use "best practices" when representing a client before the IRS. All of the following are considered examples of "best practices" except:

A. Advising the client regarding any potential penalties.
B. Acting fairly and with integrity in dealings with the IRS.
C. Establishing relevant facts, evaluating reasonableness of assumptions or representations, applying relevant legal authorities in arriving at a conclusion supported by the client's information.
D. Clearly communicating with clients and the IRS.

22. The IRS requires tax preparers to take appropriate steps to safeguard taxpayers' private information. Which of the following is not an IRS recommendation for keeping information secure?

A. Assess the risks in his own office to taxpayer information.
B. Write a plan of how the business will safeguard taxpayer information, and put appropriate safeguards in place.
C. Use only service providers who have policies in place to also maintain an adequate level of information protection.
D. Store all client information electronically rather than retain hard copies of information.

23. Which of the following is considered a "tax preparer" for purposes of Circular 230?

A. A person who prepares returns for VITA, Volunteer Income Tax Assistance.
B. A retired CPA who prepares tax returns for friends without accepting any payment.
C. A person who prepares returns for TCE, Tax Counseling for the Elderly.
D. A non-signing tax return preparer who prepares all or a substantial portion of a return or claim for refund.

24. There is a _____ statute of limitation period for the criminal offense of willfully attempting to evade or defeat any tax.

A. Three year.
B. Six year.
C. Ten year.
D. No limit.

25. Which of the following may be grounds for denial of enrollment?

A. Failure to have a valid Social Security number.
B. Failure to have valid U.S. citizenship.
C. Failure to timely pay personal income taxes.
D. When the EA candidate is insolvent or going through bankruptcy proceedings.

26. Which of the following actions would cause the IRS 10-year collection period to be suspended?

A. A request for a CDP hearing.
B. An installment agreement.
C. The filing of delinquent returns.
D. The filing of a Tax Court petition.

27. What is a federal tax lien?

A. A preliminary assessment of tax.
B. A legal seizure of the taxpayer's property to satisfy a tax debt.
C. A legal claim to the property of the taxpayer as security for a tax debt.
D. A collection action by the courts.

28. A taxpayer's return fraudulently contains the Earned Income Credit (EIC). The taxpayer already received and spent his $3,000 refund when an audit notice is issued. During the examination, the taxpayer cannot provide documentation to support his EIC claim. What is likely to happen in this case?

A. The EIC will be disallowed, and the taxpayer will have a balance due, including penalties.
B. The EIC will be disallowed, and the taxpayer will have a balance due, including penalties and interest. In addition, the taxpayer may be disallowed from claiming EIC in future years.
C. The EIC will be disallowed, but the taxpayer will not owe any additional penalties.
D. The EIC will not be disallowed for the current year return, but it may be disallowed in future years.

29. Herbert is a tax preparer. When preparing a return for his client, Amelia, Herbert learns that she does not have a bank account to receive a direct deposit of her tax refund. Herbert offers to use his account to receive the direct deposit, and says he will turn the money over to Amelia once the refund is deposited. Is this an acceptable action?

A. Yes.
B. No.
C. Only if Amelia signs Form 2848, *Power of Attorney and Declaration of Representative*, giving Herbert the right to receive her refund.
D. Only if Herbert receives prior written consent from both Amelia and the IRS.

30. Disbarred individuals are still allowed to:

A. File powers of attorney with the IRS.
B. State that they are eligible to practice before the IRS.
C. Prepare or file documents (including tax returns) or other correspondence with the IRS.
D. Appear before the IRS as a trustee, receiver, guardian, administrator, executor, or other fiduciary if duly qualified/authorized under the law of the relevant jurisdiction.

31. In which situation may the IRS contact the taxpayer directly, even if a recognized representative is in place?

A. When the taxpayer is outside the United States.
B. When the taxpayer is an estate.
C. When a recognized representative has unreasonably delayed or hindered an examination.
D. When the recognized representative is not an enrolled practitioner.

32. Zena is an enrolled agent. She represents Phillip, her client. Phillip's 2011 tax return is under examination by the IRS. Phillip's tax return was jointly filed with his wife, but they have since divorced. Philip does not know the whereabouts of his ex-wife. Phillip still wants Zena to represent him before the IRS. What is the proper course of action in this case?

A. Zena cannot represent Phillip during the examination of his previously filed joint return, because she does not have authorization from his ex-wife (who was listed on the return).
B. Zena is allowed to represent Phillip during the examination of his joint return, but only if he agrees to amend his filing status to married filing separately.
C. Zena is allowed to represent Phillip during the examination of his joint return, as long as Phillip signs a valid power of attorney (Form 2848).
D. Phillip must represent himself during the examination of his joint return.

33. In which of the following cases is a power of attorney (Form 2848) not required?

A. When an enrolled agent represents a taxpayer before the IRS appeals division.
B. When a taxpayer wishes to be represented during a collection due process hearing.
C. A power of attorney is not required to be submitted by an attorney of record in a case that is docketed in the Tax Court.
D. A power of attorney is required in all the cases listed above.

34. The IRS will release an existing tax lien in all of the following cases except:

A. When the tax debt is fully paid.
B. When the taxpayer requests an offer in compromise.
C. When payment of the debt is guaranteed by a bond.
D. When the statute period for collection has ended.

35. You are an enrolled agent. You have a new client named Roxanne who received a bill from the IRS regarding a joint return she filed with her ex-husband, Steve. During the course of your interview, you learn that Steve was a gambling addict. Upon further examination of the client's IRS transcripts, you discover several items of income that were left off the original return, and all of them were related to Steve's gambling habit. Roxanne had no idea that the return she filed had underreported income. Does your client have any recourse in this case?

A. No, Roxanne and her ex-husband are both jointly and severally liable for the tax on the return, and she has no recourse in this case.
B. Roxanne may be able to qualify for relief as an innocent spouse.
C. Roxanne may be able to qualify as an injured spouse.
D. Roxanne should request a Tax Court appearance at this time

36. Which of the following disclosures of taxpayer information is not allowable without a taxpayer's written consent?

A. When there is a disclosure of taxpayer information for preparation of state or local tax returns.
B. When a tax preparation firm discloses return information to others in the firm for purposes of assisting in the preparation of the tax return.
C. When a disclosure is made to a taxpayer's fiduciary.
D. When a disclosure solicits additional business from an existing client and the business is not related to the IRS.

37. All of the following persons may practice before the IRS except:

A. Certified public accountants.
B. Certified financial planners.
C. Enrolled actuaries.
D. Enrolled retirement plan agents.

38. In which of the following cases is the IRS not allowed to seize a taxpayer's property in order to satisfy a tax debt?

A. When the taxpayer has a current installment agreement.
B. When the taxpayer has a pending offer in compromise.
C. When the taxpayer is in a provable economic hardship and would not be able to meet basic living expenses.
D. All of the above.

39. The Tax Equity and Fiscal Responsibility Act of 1982 (TEFRA) requires that all partnerships not meeting the definition of a "small partnership" be examined _____.

A. At the partnership level.
B. At the partner level.
C. At the general partner level only.
D. None of the above.

40. Esther is an enrolled agent. She has a former client named Kent. During the year, Esther receives an IRS summons relating to Kent, with an order for her to appear before the IRS. What must Esther do about the summons?

A. Esther must respond to the summons.
B. Esther is not required to respond to the summons, but she must attempt to notify the IRS by mail that Kent is no longer her client.
C. Esther is required to forward the summons to Kent, but she is not required to respond to it since Kent is no longer her client.
D. Esther is not required to respond to the summons or notify her former client of the summons.

41. Who is responsible for paying the trust fund recovery penalty?

A. Any person with authority and control over funds to direct their disbursement.
B. Any employee within an organization who has the duty to perform and the power to direct the collecting, accounting, and paying employment (trust fund) taxes.
C. A member of a board of trustees for a nonprofit charity.
D. All of the above may be responsible for paying the trust fund recovery penalty.

42. If the IRS discovers an understatement of a taxpayer's liability due to an unreasonable position taken by tax return preparer, what is the applicable penalty?

A. There is no preparer penalty in this case. The penalty would be assessed against the taxpayer.
B. The greater of $1,000 or 50% of the income derived by the tax return preparer related to the return or claim for refund.
C. The lesser of $1,000 or 50% of the income derived by the tax return preparer related to the return or claim for refund.
D. The greater of $5,000 or 100% of the income derived by the tax return preparer related to the return or claim for refund.

43. What is the preparer penalty for failure to comply with EIC due diligence requirements?

A. $100 for each failure.
B. $500 for each failure.
C. $1,000 for each failure.
D. There is no preparer penalty in this case. The penalty would be assessed against the taxpayer.

44. When a question arises about the accuracy of a partnership return, it may be impractical for the IRS to audit each individual partner's return. Under the Tax Equity and Fiscal Responsibility Act of 1982 (TEFRA), the IRS will first audit the partnership as a single entity, with a _____ serving as the main contact.

A. Limited partner.
B. Tax matters partner.
C. General partner.
D. Independent mediator.

45. All of the following are examples of disreputable conduct that can lead to suspension or disbarment for an enrolled agent except:

A. Failing to include a valid PTIN on tax returns.
B. Willfully failing to e-file returns electronically if the preparer falls under the e-filing mandate.
C. Solicitation of former clients using direct mail.
D. Maintaining an active partnership with a practitioner who has been disbarred (but does not sign returns).

46. Nellie is an enrolled agent who received a complaint from the Office of Professional Responsibility. The formal complaint from the OPR is not required to disclose:

A. The nature of the complaint.
B. The deadline for response to the complaint.
C. The identity of the employee who drafted the complaint.
D. The specific sanctions recommended against the practitioner.

47. Cora is an enrolled agent, and she is cleaning up her office. When is the earliest she may shred the records related to her continuing professional education?

A. Three years after the date of the EA renewal for which the CPE is credited.
B. Six years after the date of the EA renewal for which the CPE is credited.
C. Immediately after the date of the EA renewal for which the CPE is credited
D. Cora should not destroy her CPE records as long as she is in active status.

48. The Billiard Partnership is under examination by the IRS. The partnership has nine general partners and one passive partner who is an investor only. Will the Billiard Partnership be subject to the TEFRA audit rules?

A. Yes, the partnership is considered a TEFRA partnership and will be subject to TEFRA audit rules.
B. No, the partnership is not a TEFRA partnership and will not be subject to TEFRA audit rules.
C. There is not enough information to answer whether this partnership is a TEFRA partnership.
D. Only partnerships with assets of $1 million or more are subject to TEFRA audit rules.

49. For Circular 230 purposes, the definition of *tax return* includes:

A. A claim for a refund.
B. An amended return.
C. A Tax Court petition.
D. Both A and B are correct.

50. Mattie is a new client. She owns her own home and pays mortgage interest. She claims to have paid $10,500 in mortgage interest during the year, but she does not have Form 1098. How may the tax preparer claim the mortgage interest deduction in this case?

A. A tax practitioner may not take a deduction for mortgage interest if a Form 1098 is not present.
B. If Mattie provides the name, address, and TIN of the lender, the mortgage interest may be entered on Schedule A.
C. Mattie is required to obtain a Form 1098. If she does, the mortgage interest can be claimed on an amended return.
D. Mattie can take the mortgage interest deduction with no further information, other than the amount.

51. Eva is an enrolled agent, and the Vecchione Corporation is her client. The corporation wishes to take an aggressive tax position on a particular tax credit. Eva does some research and discovers that this issue is currently being litigated in the courts, and the IRS is appealing the issue in several pending cases. It is possible that the issue will continue to be litigated for years. Based on the individual circumstances of her client's case, Eva determines that Vecchione has a good argument for its position. What is Eva's responsibility in this case?

A. Eva cannot file the return or recommend a position that is contrary to a current IRS position.
B. Eva should request a private letter ruling for her client. Otherwise, she may not take the position on the return.
C. Eva may claim the credit on her client's tax return so long as the position is not incorrect, inconsistent, or incomplete; is not frivolous; and is adequately disclosed.
D. Eva may claim the credit on her client's tax return so long as the position is not incorrect, inconsistent, or incomplete, and is not frivolous. Additional disclosure is not required.

52. Which of the following tax practitioners would be allowed to use the term "enrolled agent" to describe their status?

A. A person who has passed all three parts of the EA exam but who has not received his or her confirmation of enrollment yet.
B. An enrolled agent who has been placed on inactive status.
C. An enrolled agent who is currently appealing an official OPR censure.
D. An enrolled agent who has let his license lapse.

53. Benjamin Jones is an enrolled agent. He wants to print up new business cards for his office. Which of the following descriptions would be prohibited by Circular 230?

A. Benjamin Jones, enrolled agent, certified to practice before the Internal Revenue Service.
B. Benjamin Jones, enrolled agent, enrolled to practice before the Internal Revenue Service.
C. Benjamin Jones, enrolled agent, authorized to practice before the Internal Revenue Service.
D. Benjamin Jones, EA, enrolled to practice before the IRS.

54. Elmer is an enrolled agent. He sends out a targeted mail advertisement during the year. How long must he retain a copy of the advertisement?

A. 12 months.
B. 24 months.
C. 36 months.
D. Targeted mail solicitation is prohibited by Circular 230.

55. In which of the following situations does the confidentiality privilege for enrolled practitioners apply?

A. Communications in a criminal tax matter.
B. Noncriminal tax proceedings brought in federal court.
C. Noncriminal communications regarding tax shelters.
D. The confidentiality privilege is guaranteed in all tax matters.

56. Clarence is an enrolled agent. His client wants to know if their discussions during normal tax preparation are privileged. Which statement is correct?

A. Per Circular 230, discussions surrounding the preparation of a tax return are privileged if the preparer is an enrolled practitioner.
B. Discussions surrounding the preparation of a tax return are not privileged, regardless of whether the preparer is an enrolled practitioner or not.
C. Discussions surrounding the preparation of a tax return are always privileged, even if the practitioner is an unenrolled preparer.
D. None of the above is true.

57. Sam is an enrolled agent. During the year, he purposely neglected to sign several tax returns that he prepared for compensation. What is the penalty for a paid preparer who fails to sign a return?

A. No penalty.
B. $50 per failure.
C. $100 per failure.
D. $500 per failure.

58. When is a paid preparer required to sign a tax return?

A. Paid preparers are required to sign each return they prepare after presenting it to the taxpayer for signature.
B. Paid preparers are required to sign before the return is completed.
C. Paid preparers are required to sign each return they prepare after it is completed but before presenting it to the taxpayer for signature.
D. Paid preparers are required to sign each return they prepare after it is completed but before it is readied for mailing or e-filing.

59. What is the minimum number of CPE hours that an enrolled agent must take each year of his or her renewal cycle?

A. A minimum of 16 hours, two of which must be ethics hours.
B. A minimum of 18 hours, two of which must be ethics hours.
C. A minimum of 72 hours, two of which must be ethics hours.
D. A minimum of 16 hours.

60. If an e-filed return is rejected, what is the preparer required to do?

A. The preparer must take reasonable steps to inform the taxpayer within 72 hours of the rejection.
B. The preparer must take reasonable steps to inform the taxpayer within 48 hours of the rejection.
C. The preparer must take reasonable steps to inform the taxpayer within 24 hours of the rejection.
D. It is the taxpayer's responsibility to ensure that his or her e-filed return is correctly submitted.

61. Which of the following returns can be e-filed?

A. Prior year returns.
B. Tax returns with fiscal year tax periods.
C. Amended tax returns.
D. Tax returns with Adopted Taxpayer Identification Numbers (ATIN).

62. Luther is an enrolled agent who was subject to a disbarment proceeding. The administrative law judge upheld the OPR's decision to disbar him from practice. Does Luther have any appeal rights at this point?

A. Within 60 days after the administrative law judge makes a decision on a complaint filed by the OPR, the practitioner may appeal the decision to the Secretary of the Treasury.
B. Within 60 days after the administrative law judge makes a decision on a complaint filed by the OPR, the practitioner may appeal the decision to the Commissioner of the IRS.
C. Within 30 days after the administrative law judge makes a decision on a complaint filed by the OPR, the practitioner may appeal the decision to the Secretary of the Treasury.
D. No, Luther does not have any appeal rights after the administrative law judge makes his decision.

63. Based on Circular 230, in which of the following cases may the IRS suspend a certified public accountant from practice before the IRS?

A. If a CPA moves outside the U.S. and attempts to represent overseas taxpayers.
B. If a CPA is suspended from practice by a state board of accountancy for a matter unrelated to taxation.
C. If a CPA takes an aggressive position on a tax return.
D. If a CPA hires unenrolled preparers to work in his office.

64. Etta is an enrolled agent, and she employs several return preparers in her firm. One of Etta's employees prepares a return for a client. The return is later selected for examination, and one of the larger deductions is disallowed. Etta will not be subject to a preparer penalty if: _____.

A. She does not sign the return, and instead directs her employee to sign it.
B. There was a reasonable basis and substantial authority for the position, and the preparer acted in good faith.
C. She warned the preparer that the deduction was an aggressive position to take.
D. If the preparer based the return on the information provided by the client.

65. Which of the following practitioners would not be eligible for inactive status?

A. An enrolled agent who no longer wishes to represent taxpayers before the Internal Revenue Service.
B. An enrolled agent going through disbarment proceedings.
C. An enrolled agent who has retired from the profession.
D. An enrolled agent who does not wish to fulfill his ongoing CPE requirement.

66. Daisy is a tax preparer who plans to retire this year. She sells her practice to Agnes, who is a CPA. What must occur when a tax business is sold?

A. Agnes is required to submit a new e-file application and request her own EFIN.
B. Daisy may transfer her EFIN to Agnes, as long as the physical location of the practice does not change.
C. Agnes is not required to submit a new e-file application as long as Daisy gives her written permission to use the existing one. A formal transfer is not required.
D. The IRS will issue a new EFIN automatically when the preparer's PTIN information changes on the submitted returns.

67. What is the minimum time that Raymond should retain records relating to the purchase of a home?

A. Three years.
B. Six years.
C. Seven years.
D. Until the period of limitations expires for the year in which the taxpayer disposes of the property.

68. How long is an employer required to retain records relating to employment taxes?

A. Two years.
B. Three years.
C. Four years.
D. Ten years.

69. All of the following may cause a tax preparer to face disciplinary action from the Office of Professional Responsibility except:

A. A misdemeanor conviction for public drunkenness.
B. Misconduct while representing a taxpayer.
C. A felony drug possession conviction.
D. Giving a false opinion through gross incompetence.

70. If a taxpayer fails to file a return, and the failure is due to fraud, the penalty is

_____.

A. 15% for each month or part of a month that the return is late, up to a maximum of 50%.

B. 15% for each month or part of a month that the return is late, up to a maximum of 25%.

C. 5% for each month or part of a month that the return is late, up to a maximum of 50%.

D. 15% for each month or part of a month that the return is late, up to a maximum of 75%.

71. What is a "reportable transaction"?

A. A reportable transaction is a transaction of a type that the IRS has determined as having the potential for tax avoidance or evasion.

B. A reportable transaction is a court decision to which the IRS has officially nonac-quiesced.

C. A reportable transaction is another name for a private letter ruling.

D. A reportable transaction is a transaction of a type that the IRS has determined will benefit the public interest.

72. Mollie filed her individual tax return more than 60 days late. When she filed her return, she was owed a refund of $200. What is her tax penalty for filing late?

A. $200.

B. $135.

C. $0.

D. Insufficient information to answer.

73. During the IRS examination process, taxpayers have the right to:

A. Request that an enrolled practitioner represent them during the examination process.

B. Appeal any determination made by the IRS examination division.

C. Decline an IRS summons.

D. Both A and B are correct.

74. How long must a paid preparer retain a copy of a client's tax return?

A. Three years.
B. Four years.
C. Six years.
D. Indefinitely.

75. When it comes to possible preparer penalties, the *reasonable cause* and *good faith* exceptions do not apply to an understatement of income that is a result of _____.

A. A taxpayer who misrepresents information to the preparer.
B. An unreasonable position.
C. A preparer's mathematical error.
D. None of the above.

76. If a taxpayer files a claim for a refund and the refund claim is deemed to be erroneous, the penalty is _____.

A. 20% of the disallowed amount of the claim.
B. 50% of the tax shown on the return.
C. 100% of the disallowed amount of the claim.
D. $135 or the disallowed amount of the claim, whichever is smaller.

77. Fraud is distinguished from negligence, because fraud is always _____.

A. More complex.
B. Intentional.
C. Harder to detect.
D. More difficult to prosecute.

78. On a joint return, if it is deemed that one spouse committed fraud but the other did not:

A. The fraud penalty on a joint return applies to both spouses, regardless of the situation.
B. The fraud penalty on a joint return does not automatically apply to a spouse unless some part of the underpayment is due to the fraud of that spouse.
C. The fraud penalty on a joint return does not automatically apply to a spouse unless both spouses continue to file jointly.
D. The fraud penalty on a joint return does not automatically apply to a spouse if the spouses have divorced at a later date.

79. In both criminal and civil fraud, the burden of proof rests with the _____.

A. Taxpayer.
B. Tax preparer.
C. Government.
D. Tax Court

80. Edgar and Mae are married and have always filed jointly. In 2012, Mae dies and her daughter from her first marriage is named as the executor of Mae's estate. In this case, who should file the joint return for 2012?

A. Edgar should sign for himself, and the executor of Mae's estate should sign on Mae's behalf.
B. Edgar should sign for himself, and also sign on Mae's behalf as the surviving spouse
C. Edgar should not file a joint return because he is not the executor of his wife's estate. He should file a separate return, and Mae's executor should file a separate one for Mae.
D. Edgar is allowed to sign for his wife, Mae, as long as the executor gives Edgar verbal permission.

81. Katherine and Michael are married. Michael is currently serving in a combat zone, and Katherine has no way to contact her husband for several months. When one spouse is serving in a combat zone, what is required in order to file a joint return?

A. Both spouses must sign the return, so Katherine must appeal to the IRS for a special filing exemption.
B. Katherine may sign the joint return on her husband's behalf, but only if she secured a power of attorney in advance.
C. Katherine may sign on behalf of her husband, whether or not she has a signed power of attorney.
D. Katherine may delay filing the tax return until Michael has returned to the United States and can sign the return.

82. How can a taxpayer change his filing status on a return that has already been processed?

A. By filing an amended return using Form 1040X.
B. By petitioning the U.S. Tax Court.
C. By refiling another original return on Form 1040.
D. A taxpayer cannot change his or her filing status without prior IRS permission.

83. During the examination of a taxpayer's Form 1040, the IRS examiner found numerous errors resulting in additional tax. One of the adjustments was a large amount of unreported income discovered in a concealed bank account. Some deductions were supported with altered or defaced documents. The taxpayer gave false information and misrepresented the facts throughout the examination. All of the acts of the taxpayer, when seen as a whole, indicate _____.

A. Negligence.
B. Fraud.
C. Noncompliance.
D. A tax protester argument.

84. If a tax preparer is assessed a penalty under IRC 6694, how many days does the preparer have to file an appeal before the penalty is assessed?

A. 10 days.
B. 30 days.
C. 45 days.
D. The penalty is assessed immediately.

85. When filing a taxpayer's return with an ITIN: _____.

A. If a primary taxpayer, spouse, or both have ITINs, they are ineligible to receive the Earned Income Credit, even if their dependents have valid SSNs.
B. If a primary taxpayer, spouse, or both have ITINs, they are eligible to receive the Earned Income Credit, but only if their dependents have valid SSNs.
C. If a taxpayer and spouse (if filing jointly) have valid SSNs, only dependents with valid SSNs will qualify to receive the Earned Income Credit.
D. Both A and C are correct.

86. In 2012, Alex plans to submit a Form W-7 for his client, Anne, who needs to request an ITIN in order to file her return. What type of identifying documents must accompany the ITIN application?

A. Form W-7 must include photocopies of supporting documentation, such as a passport or birth certificate.
B. Form W-7 must include original supporting documentation, such as a passport or birth certificate. Photocopies and notarized copies are no longer sufficient.
C. Form W-7 must include original or notarized copies of supporting documentation, such as a passport or birth certificate. Photocopies are not sufficient.
D. Form W-7 does not require any additional documentation as long as it is filed with an original return.

87. An official IRS censure _____:

A. Prohibits an enrolled practitioner from practicing before the IRS.
B. Prohibits an enrolled practitioner from filing tax returns.
C. Prohibits an enrolled practitioner from practicing before the IRS and from filing tax returns.
D. A censure does not prevent an enrolled practitioner from filing returns or representing taxpayers before the IRS.

88. Which of the following situations represents a conflict of interest?

A. When the representation of a taxpayer would be in conflict with the tax preparer's personal interests.
B. When the preparer provides tax planning services for one spouse, when the other spouse may have opposing interests.
C. When the preparer provides tax planning services for a married couple in the midst of a divorce proceeding.
D. All of the above.

89. Sophia applied for equitable relief last year, but it was denied because her request was filed after the two-year limit. Now that the two-year limit has been lifted, what is the correct course of action for Sophia to reapply for equitable relief?

A. Sophia may reapply by using IRS Form 8857, *Request for Innocent Spouse Relief*, if the collection statute of limitations for the tax years involved has not expired.
B. Sophia may reapply by filing a case request with the U.S. Tax Court.
C. Sophia may reapply for equitable relief by submitting her application request directly to the Secretary of the Treasury.
D. Sophia will automatically be granted equitable relief based on her past application status. There is no need to reapply.

90. If a tax preparer is deemed to have stated a position on a tax return that was due to "willful and reckless" conduct, what is the preparer penalty in this case?

A. $500, or 10% of the income derived by the position.
B. $1,000 per occurrence.
C. $5,000 or 50% of the income derived, whichever is *greater*.
D. $1,000 or 50% of the income derived, whichever is *smaller*.

91. Russell is an enrolled agent. In 2012, he was deemed to have knowingly disclosed confidential taxpayer information to a third party for profit. This was biographical information that Russell had collected from his clients when he was preparing their tax returns. What is the preparer penalty for unauthorized disclosure of taxpayer information?

A. $250 for each unauthorized disclosure.
B. $500 for each unauthorized disclosure.
C. $1,000 for each unauthorized disclosure.
D. 30 days incarceration and a $10,000 fine.

92. The Office of Professional Responsibility has disciplinary authority over:

A. Enrolled preparers only.
B. Unenrolled preparers only.
C. All paid preparers.
D. None of the above. The disciplinary authority over preparers is held by the Secretary of the Treasury.

93. Circular 230 is found in _____ of the U.S. Code, which governs practice before the Internal Revenue Service.

A. Title 31.
B. Title 26.
C. The Uniform Commercial Code.
D. None of the above.

94. Which of the following preparers is not covered by the authority of Circular 230?

A. A financial professional who gives tax advice for compensation, but does not prepare returns.
B. A reporting agent that occasionally provides consulting on the issue of employee classification issues.
C. An enrolled practitioner that does representation before the IRS, but does not prepare tax returns.
D. An employee of a tax preparation firm who collects receipts, organizes records, and gathers information for an enrolled practitioner.

95. How can a preparer apply for a PTIN?

A. A preparer may request a PTIN by mail using form W-12.
B. A preparer may request a PTIN online at the IRS website.
C. A preparer may request a PTIN by phone by calling the Practitioner Priority Line.
D. Both A and B are correct.

96. Which of the following IRS guidance holds the most weight?

A. Proposed regulations.
B. Temporary regulations.
C. Final regulations.
D. U.S. Tax Court memorandum decisions.

97. Enrolled practitioners are required to be in compliance with all their existing tax obligations in order to maintain their licensing. For Circular 230 purposes, what is the definition of "tax compliance?"

A. A preparer is in tax compliance if all returns that are due have been filed.
B. A preparer is in tax compliance if all returns that are due have been filed and all taxes that are due have been paid (or acceptable payment arrangements have been established).
C. A preparer is in tax compliance if all returns that are due have been filed and all taxes that are due have been paid (a payment arrangement is not sufficient—the taxes must be paid in order to be "in compliance").
D. A preparer is in tax compliance if all taxes that are due have been paid (or acceptable payment arrangements have been established), even if there are unfiled returns.

98. When multiple paid preparers are involved in preparation of a return, who is required to sign the return?

A. Any preparer that has the proper licensing to sign the return.
B. Any of the preparers involved in the task of preparation may sign.
C. The signing tax preparer should be the individual preparer who has the primary responsibility for the overall accuracy of the return.
D. Multiple preparers may sign in the preparer section of the return, because all the preparers have joint and several liability for the return's accuracy.

99. Beatrice is a full-time accountant for Ortega Brothers Partnership. As part of her job duties, she prepares the partnership return for Ortega Brothers, including the Schedule K-1 for all the individual partners. Beatrice does not prepare any other returns for compensation. Is Beatrice required to obtain a PTIN?

A. Yes, Beatrice is a preparer and must obtain a PTIN.
B. No, Beatrice is not a preparer and she is not required to obtain a PTIN.
C. Only if the IRS gives her a written waiver is Beatrice allowed to forgo obtaining a PTIN.
D. Beatrice is not required to obtain a PTIN in 2012, but she will be required to do so in 2013.

100. Are all ERPAs (enrolled retirement plan agents) required to obtain a PTIN?

A. Yes, all enrolled practitioners are required to have a PTIN.
B. No. ERPAs that prepare only Form 5300 or Form 5500 series returns are not required to obtain a PTIN.
C. ERPAs are not considered enrolled practitioners for purposes of the PTIN requirement.
D. None of the above is correct.

Please review your answers with the answers in the back.

#2 Representation Sample Exam

1. Cyril is an enrolled agent, and he has a PTIN. Cyril's tax firm employs a bookkeeper named Tania. She gathers client receipts and invoices, and organizes records for Cyril. Cyril prepares all the clients' tax returns and makes all substantive determinations that go into computing the tax liability. Does Tania need a PTIN?

A. No, she is not a tax return preparer and is not required to have a PTIN.
B. Yes, Tania is required to have a PTIN.
C. Tania is a return preparer, but she is not required to have a PTIN because she is an employee.
D. None of the above.

2. Most paid preparers are now required to e-file tax returns. If a paid preparer is required to e-file a return, which form is required in order for the tax return to be filed on paper?

A. No additional forms are necessary in order for a paid preparer to file a tax return on paper.
B. Tax returns prepared by a paid preparer but filed on paper must be submitted with Form 8948. A reason must be provided for each return that is not e-filed.
C. Tax returns prepared by a paid preparer but filed on paper must be submitted with Form 2848. A reason must be provided for each return that is not e-filed.
D. Circular 230 regulations mandate that tax returns prepared by a paid preparer must be e-filed in all circumstances.

3. Which of the following professional designations is not always required to obtain a PTIN?

A. CPAs.
B. Attorneys.
C. Enrolled agents.
D. Both A and B.

4. In the licensing of enrolled agents, an enrollment cycle refers to _____?

A. The enrollment year preceding the effective date of renewal.
B. The three successive enrollment years preceding the effective date of renewal.
C. The year in which the enrolled agent receives his or her initial enrollment.
D. The amount of continuing professional education required each year of enrollment.

5. Which of the following individuals qualifies as an enrolled practitioner under Circular 230?

A. Certified public accountant.
B. Enrolled actuary.
C. Attorney.
D. Unenrolled student volunteers at a VITA site.
E. All of the above.

6. Ethan claimed the Earned Income Credit in 2010, 2011, and 2012. He was audited, and the EIC was disallowed in 2012. The IRS also found that Ethan claimed the EIC due to reckless disregard of the EIC rules. Ethan cannot claim the EIC for _____

A. One tax year.
B. Two tax years.
C. Three tax years.
D. Ethan can never claim the EIC again.

7. What is an IP PIN?

A. A new preparer identification number for a registered tax return preparer.
B. An identifying number that a paid preparer must use in order to e-file returns.
C. A unique tax number issued to an individual taxpayer who has been the victim of identity fraud.
D. Another name for a PTIN.

8. Randall is an accounting student and works for a CPA firm, but he is not a CPA. Randall assists with tax returns but a CPA signs them. Randall is supervised by a licensed CPA. Is Randall required to obtain a PTIN and pass a competency test?

A. Randall needs a PTIN, and he must pass a competency test.
B. Randall needs a PTIN, but he does not need to pass a competency test.
C. Randall does not need a PTIN, and he does not need to pass a competency test.
D. Randall does not need a PTIN and he may sign the returns, so long as he is supervised by a licensed CPA, enrolled agent, or attorney.

9. Which form is used to apply for initial enrollment?

A. Form 23.
B. Form 8826.
C. Form 32.
D. Form 5500.

10. What form is used to request innocent spouse relief?

A. Form 8857.
B. Form 2110.
C. Form 8379.
D. Form 8832.

11. Doug Jones recently received his enrollment card, and he wants to purchase new business cards. Which of the following presentations would be acceptable under Circular 230 guidelines?

A. Doug Jones, certified Enrolled Agent.
B. Doug Jones, certified to practice before the Internal Revenue Service.
C. Doug Jones, licensed agent.
D. Doug Jones, enrolled to practice before the Internal Revenue Service.

12. Can multiple individuals in one office share a single PTIN?

A. Yes, multiple preparers may share a single PTIN.
B. Yes, multiple preparers may share one PTIN, but only at the same office location.
C. Yes, multiple preparers may share one PTIN, but only if the principal preparer continues to sign the tax returns.
D. No, each preparer must obtain his or her own PTIN.

13. Which IRS insignia may a tax practitioner use in his or her advertising?

A. The official IRS e-file logo.
B. The U.S. Treasury seal.
C. The IRS eagle insignia.
D. The FMS insignia.

14. What is not considered earned income for purposes of the Earned Income Credit?

A. Nontaxable combat pay.
B. Union strike benefits.
C. Long-term disability benefits received prior to minimum retirement age.
D. Alimony.

15. Which of the following best describes an IRS levy?

A. A levy is not a legal seizure of property.
B. A levy on salary or wages will end when the time expires for legally collecting the tax.
C. A levy can only be released by the filing of a lien.
D. A levy does not apply to the taxpayer's clothing and undelivered mail.

16. Which of the following taxpayer number is valid for claiming the Earned Income Credit?

A. Social Security Number.
B. Adoption Taxpayer Identification Number.
C. Individual Tax Identification Number.
D. Employer Identification Number.

17. Which of the following statements regarding e-file is true?

A. E-file providers may charge contingent fees based on a percentage of the refund.
B. Separate fees may be charged for Direct Deposited refunds, so long as the fee is not contingent on the refund amount.
C. E-file providers may charge contingent fees for e-file, but not for paper returns.
D. An e-file provider is required to sign an e-filed return.

18. Which of the following actions is not considered "practice before the IRS"?

A. Appearing as a taxpayer's witness before the IRS.
B. Corresponding with the IRS on behalf of a taxpayer.
C. Communicating with the IRS for a taxpayer regarding the taxpayer's rights.
D. Representing the taxpayer at an examination.

19. Which form is used to apply for renewal of enrollment?

A. Form 23.
B. Form 2587.
C. Form 2550.
D. Form 8554.

20. In which of the following situations is an IRS power of attorney required?

A. Allowing the IRS to discuss return information with a third party designee.
B. Allowing a tax matters partner to perform acts for the partnership.
C. Allowing the IRS to discuss return information with a fiduciary.
D. Allowing the tax practitioner to receive, but not cash, taxpayer refund checks.

21. A third-party designee has the right to do which of the following tasks?

A. Sign a binding agreement for the taxpayer.
B. Respond to IRS notices about math errors, offsets, and return preparation.
C. Represent the taxpayer before the IRS.
D. Receive refund checks.

22. The IRS may accept an offer in compromise based on three grounds. Which of the following is not a valid basis for submitting an offer in compromise to the IRS?

A. Doubt as to collectability.
B. Effective tax administration.
C. Doubt as to liability.
D. Legitimate hardship argument.

23. Which of the following is considered the most important source of tax law?

A. The United States Code.
B. The Internal Revenue Code.
C. The U.S. Commercial Code.
D. The Congressional Record.

24. Lloyd is an enrolled agent. He has a new client, Kelly, who has self-prepared her own returns in the past. Lloyd notices that Kelly has been claiming head of household on her tax returns, but she does not qualify for this status, because she does not have a qualifying person. What is Lloyd required to do?

A. Amend the incorrect returns.
B. Refuse any future engagement with this client unless she corrects the prior year returns.
C. Notify Kelly of the error and tell her the consequences of not correcting the error.
D. Notify Kelly of the error and correct the error.

25. Which type of practitioner fee is prohibited by Circular 230?

A. Charging a fee for Direct Deposit.
B. Fixed fees for bookkeeping services.
C. Hourly fee rates for tax consulting
D. Charging a fee for e-filing a return.

26. Which is not a requirement to be approved for enrollment as an enrolled agent?

A. Pass a tax compliance and suitability check.
B. Be age 21 or older.
C. Pass all three parts of the Special Enrollment Exam (SEE).
D. File Form 23 to apply for enrollment within one year of the date of passing the exam.

27. Erin files jointly with her husband, who has delinquent student loans. Their tax refund check is applied against his past due amount. Erin would like to claim her portion of their tax refund, so she files for _____ relief.

A. Innocent spouse.
B. Equitable.
C. Injured spouse.
D. Separation of liability.

28. For the 2012 tax filing season, which one of the following tax preparers is required to e-file his clients' returns?

A. A paid preparer who anticipates filing 11 or more Forms 1120.
B. A paid preparer who anticipates filing 11 or more Forms 1040.
C. A paid preparer who anticipates filing 11 or more Forms 1065.
D. All of the preparers listed above are subject to the e-file mandate.

29. A tax preparer must complete the paid preparer section of the tax return in which of the following scenarios?

A. An employee preparer who completes employment tax returns for his employer.
B. An enrolled agent who prepares her own tax return.
C. A tax professional who prepares a return for her brother and charges him only $30.
D. An enrolled agent who prepares his neighbor's return for free.

30. Some returns cannot be e-filed. Of the following, which return may be e-filed?

A. A return that is two years delinquent.
B. An amended return.
C. A tax return where the taxpayer has an ITIN.
D. A tax return where the taxpayer has adopted a child and the child has an ATIN.

31. Under Internal Revenue Code §7216, a tax preparer who violates certain privacy rules by knowingly or recklessly disclosing or using tax return information faces what specific penalty?

A. $500 fine for each violation of section 7216.
B. $1,000 fine for each violation of section 7216.
C. $1,000 for all violations of section 7216.
D. $1,000 fine and imprisonment up to one year, or both, for each violation of section 7216.

32. Which of the following is an example of an individual filing a fraudulent or frivolous tax return?

A. A taxpayer who incorrectly claims the Earned Income Credit when he is not eligible for it because he did not read the instructions.
B. A taxpayer who files a return and strikes out the jurat.
C. A preparer who files a return five years late because the taxpayer refused to file.
D. A fiduciary who files an incorrect return and later amends it.

33. Morgan owns a business with five employees. How long is she required to keep employment tax records?

A. Three years.
B. Six years.
C. Five years.
D. Four years.

34. Which of the following disciplinary actions will not prevent an enrolled agent from practicing before the IRS?

A. Censure.
B. Disbarment.
C. Suspension.
D. None of the above.

35. All of the following statements about the Office of Professional Responsibility are correct except:

A. The OPR has exclusive authority to institute disciplinary procedures against enrolled agents.
B. The OPR is independent and separate from IRS offices enforcing the Internal Revenue Code.
C. The OPR processes and reviews all new PTIN applications.
D. The OPR makes final determinations on appeal from return preparer eligibility or suitability decisions.

36. Which of the following statements is true?

A. The IRS is not required to notify the taxpayer of an audit.
B. In certain circumstances, the IRS may audit tax returns for up to six years after the filing date.
C. Tax returns can only be audited for up to two years after filing.
D. An original tax return that is filed late does not extend the statute of limitations for an audit on the return.

37. How long is an IRS power of attorney authorization valid?

A. A power of attorney is valid until the taxpayer's retirement.
B. A power of attorney is valid for three years.
C. A power of attorney is valid until the close of the taxable year for which it was filed.
D. A power of attorney is valid until revoked.

38. Taxpayers must sign their returns _____.

A. Under penalty of perjury.
B. With a physical signature.
C. Before the return has been prepared.
D. Before paying their tax preparer.

39. Tracy is an enrolled agent, and she prepares approximately 300 returns for compensation during the year. Which of the following numbers is required in order for her to prepare tax returns for compensation?

A. An Electronic Filing Identification Number (EFIN).
B. A Preparer Tax Identification Number (PTIN).
C. Both A and B.
D. An Employer Identification Number (EIN).

40. Which of the following actions is not considered "disreputable conduct" by the IRS?

A. Willfully failing to e-file returns electronically if they fall under the e-filing mandate.
B. Failing to include a valid PTIN on tax returns.
C. Performance as a notary by an enrolled practitioner.
D. Willfully failing to file a tax return.

41. Which of the following statements is true regarding tax practitioners?

A. A tax practitioner is prohibited from charging contingent fees in all cases.
B. A tax practitioner may not notarize documents for the clients that they represent before the IRS.
C. A tax practitioner may not represent two clients when there is a clear conflict of interest.
D. A tax practitioner is forbidden from discussing tax shelters with a client.

42. Rachel is a CPA. She is taking an aggressive position on a tax return, which requires disclosure. Which form is used to disclose a position on a tax return?

A. Form 8275.
B. Form 8823.
C. Form 656.
D. Form 1040X.

43. Judith, an enrolled agent, prepares William's income tax return. William gives Judith power of attorney, including the authorization to receive his federal income tax refund check. Accordingly, the IRS sends William's $1,000 refund check to Judith's office. William is very slow in paying his bills and owes Judith $500 for tax services. Judith should:

A. Use William's check as collateral for a loan to tide her over until William pays her.
B. Refuse to give William the check until he pays her the $500.
C. Get William's written authorization to endorse the check, cash the check, and reduce the amount William owes her.
D. Turn the check directly over to William.

44. Craig is an enrolled agent. He wants to request a hardship waiver for an exemption from the electronic filing requirements. Which one of the following statements is true?

A. There is no option for a hardship waiver for paid preparers with the electronic filing requirements.
B. There is an option for administrative appeal if the IRS denies an e-file hardship waiver request.
C. An e-file waiver will usually be granted automatically, and will be valid until revoked.
D. An e-file waiver may only be requested by paid preparers who can prove financial hardship.

45. Shari is an enrolled agent. A client comes in and wants to use Direct Deposit. Which of the following statements is false?

A. Shari must accept any Direct Deposit election to any eligible financial institution designated by the client.
B. Shari may designate refunds for Direct Deposit to up to three qualified accounts.
C. Taxpayers should not request a deposit of their refund to an account that is not in their own name.
D. The taxpayer may designate refunds for Direct Deposit to credit card accounts.

46. What is the penalty for preparers who violate due diligence rules related to the EIC?

A. Any tax return preparer who fails to comply with due diligence requirements for the EIC can be liable for a penalty of $1,000 for each failure.
B. Any tax return preparer who fails to comply with due diligence requirements for the EIC can be liable for a penalty of $500 for each failure.
C. There is no preparer penalty, but there is a taxpayer penalty for fraud.
D. Any tax return preparer who fails to comply with due diligence requirements for the EIC can be formally reprimanded, suspended, or disbarred by the OPR, but there is no monetary penalty.

47. A tax preparer is required to provide a copy of the return to a client. Which of the following statements is false?

A. The preparer must provide a complete copy of the return to the taxpayer.
B. A scanned copy of the tax return is sufficient to meet this requirement.
C. The IRS requires that the client receive a paper copy of the tax return.
D. The client copy does not need to contain the Social Security Number of the paid preparer.

48. What is a private letter ruling?

A. It is a private letter that a taxpayer writes to the IRS and that becomes public once tax court litigation begins.
B. It is a private letter issued by the U.S. Tax Court.
C. Private letter rulings are written decisions by the Internal Revenue Service in response to a taxpayer's written request for guidance on a particular tax issue.
D. The Commissioner of the IRS may request a private letter ruling from Congress, in order to clarify Congressional action on a particular tax issue.

49. What is the penalty for filing a frivolous argument with the U.S. Tax Court?

A. Up to $1,000.
B. $5,000 or more.
C. $25,000.
D. Up to $200,000.

50. What is the dollar limit for the U.S. Tax Court small case division?

A. $50,000 or less.
B. $50,000 or more.
C. $15,000 or less.
D. $100,000 or less.

51. Which of the following is not a type of Treasury regulation?

A. Legislative regulations.
B. Interpretative regulations.
C. Congressional regulations.
D. Procedural regulations.

52. If an Authorized IRS e-file Provider uses radio, television, Internet, signage, or other advertising methods, which of the following statements is true?

A. The practitioner must keep a copy of the advertising for a minimum of 30 days after the last transmission or use.
B. The practitioner must keep a copy of the advertising until the end of the calendar year following the last transmission or use.
C. The practitioner must keep a copy of the advertising for at least three years following the last transmission or use.
D. The practitioner is not required to keep a copy of advertising.

53. A rejected electronic individual income tax return can be corrected and re-transmitted without new signatures if changes do not differ from the amount on the original electronic return by more than:

A. $50 to total income or AGI.
B. $100 of tax due.
C. $50 of tax due.
D. A rejected e-file return cannot be retransmitted without new signatures.

54. In which of the following cases would a taxpayer's federal refund not be delayed?

A. Errors in Direct Deposit information.
B. A financial institution refusal of Direct Deposit.
C. Bankruptcy.
D. All of the above may delay a taxpayer's refund.

55. Megan is a CPA, and Alfred is her client. Alfred's e-file return was rejected by the IRS, and Megan is unable to clear the e-file rejection. What is Megan's responsibility, if any?

A. Megan must mail a paper copy of the tax return to Alfred.
B. Megan must take reasonable steps to inform Alfred of the rejection within 24 hours.
C. Megan must take reasonable steps to inform Alfred of the rejection within 48 hours.
D. Megan is not required to notify Alfred of the rejection.

56. What happens when a taxpayer has a late payment on an installment agreement?

A. The late payment will generate an automatic 30-day notice.
B. The late payment will extend the statute of limitations for collecting the tax.
C. The late payment will cause the installment agreement to default.
D. The IRS will file a Notice of Deficiency.

57. The following individuals are all enrolled agents. At the end of 2012, they totaled up their CPE, and this is how many hours each preparer took during the year. Which of them has not met the minimum yearly educational requirements for license renewal?

Preparer	Regular CPE	Ethics CPE
Francisco	24 hours	1 hour
Gloria	16 hours	2 hours
Mona	14 hours	4 hours

A. Francisco.
B. Gloria.
C. Mona.
D. None of these preparers have met their minimum yearly CPE requirement.

58. A Refund Anticipation Loan (RAL) is a loan between:

A. A taxpayer and a lender.
B. A taxpayer and the IRS.
C. A tax practitioner and the IRS.
D. A lender and the IRS.

59. Natalie became a new enrolled agent two years ago. For renewal purposes, which of the following statements is false?

A. Natalie is required to take a minimum of 16 hours of CPE each year.
B. Natalie is required to take a minimum of two hours of ethics CPE per year.
C. Natalie must still fulfill the overall CPE requirement of 72 hours, even though she has only been an EA for two years of the enrollment cycle.
D. For renewal purposes, the annual CPE requirements only apply for the years in which Natalie was an enrolled agent.

60. What is the penalty for a preparer who endorses or otherwise cashes a taxpayer's refund check?

A. $100 per occurrence.
B. $500 per occurrence.
C. $1,000 per occurrence.
D. $25,000 per occurrence.

61. Under IRS regulations, which of the following does not constitute an "understatement of liability"?

A. Taking a tax protester position on a return.
B. Understating net tax payable.
C. Overstating the net amount creditable or refundable.
D. Taking a position with no realistic possibility of success.

62. Which of the following statements is false regarding Refund Anticipation Loans?

A. A tax preparer may charge a fee based on the percentage of the refund in exchange for preparing a Refund Anticipation Loan application.
B. The IRS has no responsibility for the payment of any fees associated with the preparation of a return.
C. Tax practitioners must advise taxpayers that RALs are interest-bearing loans.
D. The advertisement on an RAL or other financial product must be in large, readable print.

63. Cherie has a 21-year-old daughter named Abby. Abby's tax return was chosen for examination by the IRS. Cherie is not an enrolled agent, attorney, or CPA. Which of the following statements is true?

A. Cherie may represent her daughter before all levels of the IRS if Abby signs a Form 2848.
B. Cherie may not represent her daughter before the IRS because Abby is no longer a minor and Cherie is not enrolled to practice before the IRS.
C. Cherie may not represent her daughter because she is not a trained tax accountant.
D. A parent may not represent a child because of privacy regulations.

64. The "Statutory Notice of Deficiency" is also known as:

A. A 30-day letter because the taxpayer generally has 30 days from the date of the letter to file a petition with the Tax Court.
B. A 90-day letter because the taxpayer generally has 90 days from the date of the letter to file a petition with the Tax Court.
C. An Information Document Request (IDR) because the taxpayer is asked for information to support its position regarding liability for tax.
D. A federal tax lien.

65. Enrolled agents have a limited confidentiality privilege for communications with their clients. Which of the following statements is false regarding the confidentiality protection between an EA and his tax client?

A. The confidentiality protection for certain communications between a taxpayer and an attorney applies to similar communications between a taxpayer and any federally authorized tax practitioner.
B. The confidentiality protection applies to all noncriminal tax matters before the IRS.
C. The confidentiality privilege extends to any administrative proceeding with any other federal agency.
D. The confidentiality privilege does not apply to the promotion of the direct or indirect participation of a corporation in a tax shelter.

66. What is the penalty a taxpayer faces for filing a return more than 60 days late?

A. $500.
B. $1,000.
C. 50% of his unpaid taxes.
D. The smaller of $135 or 100% of the unpaid tax.

67. What is the penalty a taxpayer faces for failing to pay his taxes on time?

A. 5% of the unpaid taxes for each month or part of a month after the due date that the taxes are not paid.
B. ½ of 1% (0.5%) of unpaid taxes for each month or part of a month after the due date that the taxes are not paid.
C. A minimum of $500.
D. A minimum of $1,000.

68. Tax practitioners may not base their fees on _____.

A. Time spent on preparing individual returns.
B. A percentage of the refund amount.
C. A set fee for preparation of an individual form.
D. A flat fee for certain types of returns.

69. The Director of the Office of Professional Responsibility has instituted a disciplinary proceeding against Barbara, an enrolled agent. Barbara fails to respond to the complaint. Which of the following statements is false?

A. The failure to respond constitutes an admission of guilt and a waiver of the hearing.
B. The administrative law judge may make a decision on the case by default without a hearing or further procedure.
C. Barbara does not have the right to appeal the administrative law judge's decision if she fails to appear or respond to the complaint.
D. During a hearing, the practitioner may be represented by an attorney or another practitioner.

70. Jeff was an enrolled agent. He was recently disbarred from practice during his hearing with an administrative law judge. Jeff wants to appeal the judge's decision. Where should Jeff file his appeal after this initial hearing?

A. The Secretary of the Treasury.
B. The Office of Professional Responsibility.
C. The Internal Revenue Service Examination Division.
D. The U.S. Tax Court.

71. A "covered opinion" is which of the following?

A. Written advice given to an employer by a full-time employee.
B. The preparation of delinquent returns.
C. Written advice prepared for a taxpayer after the tax return has been prepared.
D. Written advice a practitioner gives a client regarding a tax shelter.

72. In which of the following cases does an IRS power of attorney expire or terminate?

A. When the client becomes incapacitated.
B. When the client leaves the country.
C. When the practitioner changes office locations.
D. When the client dies.

73. An ERO may originate the electronic submission of tax returns by:

A. Electronically sending the return to a Transmitter that transmits the return to the IRS.
B. Directly transmitting the return to the IRS.
C. Providing a return to an Intermediate Service Provider for processing prior to transmission to the IRS.
D. All of the above are allowable procedures for transmitting an electronic return.

74. In which of the following situations must the tax preparer obtain permission from the client to disclose sensitive tax return information?

A. The preparer receives a grand jury subpoena requesting client records.
B. A 10% general partner in a partnership requests copies of the partnership return.
C. An executor requests copies of a return for a deceased taxpayer's estate.
D. None of the above.

75. Robin is an enrolled agent. She has two clients who have recently divorced, and there is a clear conflict of interest between both parties. How should Robin proceed?

A. Robin may represent both of her clients so long as the conflict of interest is disclosed in writing to both parties and both parties agree.
B. Robin may represent both of her clients so long as the conflict of interest is disclosed to at least one party and he or she agrees.
C. Robin may not represent either client if a clear conflict of interest exists.
D. Robin may only represent one of the clients if a clear conflict of interest exists. The other client must be dismissed.

76. How often do enrolled agents renew their enrollment?

A. Every three years.
B. Every five years.
C. Every year.
D. None of the above.

77. For which of the following reasons would the Return Preparer Office not accept a waiver of continuing professional education?

A. Health issues.
B. Active deployment for military personnel.
C. Absence from the United States for employment or other reasons.
D. Because the tax practitioner did not receive his or her enrollment renewal.

78. Which of the following statements is false regarding an IRS power of attorney?

A. A newly filed power of attorney concerning the same matter will revoke a previously filed power of attorney.
B. The filing of Form 2848 will not revoke any Form 8821 (Document Information Authorization) that is in effect.
C. A signed Form 8821 is sufficient for a practitioner to represent a taxpayer before the IRS.
D. A power of attorney held by a student of a Low Income Tax Clinic is valid for only 130 days from the received date and will automatically be revoked.

79. What is the Taxpayer Advocate Service?

A. A private tax litigation firm.
B. A branch of the U.S. Tax Court that helps resolve taxpayer issues.
C. An independent organization within the IRS to help taxpayers resolve problems with the IRS.
D. A state agency designed to ensure federal and state compliance with current tax laws.

80. Alana owes $5,000 to the IRS, but she cannot pay in full. She applies for a payment plan by completing Form 9465, *Installment Agreement Request*. What is the maximum number of months that she can request to pay off her balance?

A. 12 months.
B. 24 months.
C. 60 months.
D. No maximum, so long as she continues to make her minimum payments on time.

81. The Freedom of Information Act (FOIA) does not require the IRS to release all documents that are subject to FOIA requests. The IRS may withhold information:

A. Due to budget cuts.
B. Due to the statute of limitation for FOIA requests.
C. If the requester fails to provide notarized identification along with the request.
D. For an IRS record that falls under one of the FOIA's nine statutory exemptions or by one of three exclusions under the Act.

82. Don is an enrolled agent. He sent out an advertisement announcing a flat rate of $100 for preparation of a single tax return. Don later changes his mind and wants to increase the price. Don is bound by this advertised rate for a minimum of _____ days after the last date on which the fee schedule was published:

A. 20 days.
B. 30 days.
C. 45 days.
D. 60 days.

83. Which of the following statement is false about the IRS and court cases?

A. The IRS must respect and follow the decisions of every court case.
B. The IRS may choose to appeal any court decision other than a decision by the Supreme Court.
C. The IRS publishes its acquiescence and non-acquiescence in the Internal Revenue Bulletin.
D. The IRS does not announce acquiescence or non-acquiescence in every case.

84. Which of the following facts regarding Revenue Rulings is false?

A. Revenue rulings *can* be used to avoid IRS penalties.
B. Revenue rulings *cannot* be used to avoid IRS penalties.
C. A Revenue ruling is an official interpretation by the IRS of the Internal Revenue Code.
D. A Revenue ruling can be challenged in court.

85. What is the mission of the Office of Professional Responsibility (OPR)?

A. The Office of Professional Responsibility is duty-bound to license enrolled practitioners.
B. The Office of Professional Responsibility is designed to support effective tax administration by ensuring all tax practitioners, tax preparers, and other third parties in the tax system adhere to professional standards and follow the law.
C. The Office of Professional Responsibility provides small businesses top quality service by educating and informing them of their tax obligations, developing educational products and services, and helping them understand and comply with applicable laws.
D. The Office of Professional Responsibility provides America's taxpayers with top quality service by helping them to understand their tax responsibilities and by enforcing the law with integrity and fairness to all.

86. Which of the following sanctions will the Office of Professional Responsibility not impose on a practitioner?

A. Permanent disbarment.
B. Sanctions.
C. Formal reprimand.
D. Criminal penalties.

87. Which of the following disputes may not be resolved by a proceeding in the U.S. Tax Court?

A. Gift tax.
B. Income tax.
C. Employment taxes.
D. Innocent spouse relief.

88. An IRS power of attorney must contain all of the following information except:

A. The type of tax involved.
B. The name and address of the representative.
C. The name and Social Security Number of the taxpayer.
D. The specific date the tax return was filed, if delinquent.

89. A paid preparer is required by law to _____.

A. Charge a fee for e-filing.
B. Sign the return and fill in the preparer areas of the form.
C. Include his Social Security Number on the tax return.
D. None of the above.

90. Webster is an enrolled agent, and he wants to apply to become an authorized e-file provider. Which of the following is not a requirement to become an IRS e-file provider?

A. To be a United States citizen or a legal U.S. alien lawfully admitted for permanent residence (a "green card" holder).
B. To be at least 21 years old as of the date of application.
C. To have a permanent business location *outside* his or her home, in order to ensure the safety of client confidentiality and client records.
D. To meet applicable state and local licensing or bonding requirements for the preparation and collection of tax returns.

91. The IRS must give a taxpayer reasonable notice before contacting third parties in connection with examinations or collecting tax liability. However, the IRS is not required to give notice in which of the following instances?

A. Any pending criminal matter.
B. When providing notice would jeopardize collection of any tax liability.
C. When providing notice may result in reprisal against any person.
D. When the taxpayer authorized the contact.
E. All of the above.

92. Enrolled agents are allowed a limited confidentiality privilege with their clients. Confidential communications do not extend to:

A. Noncriminal tax matters before the IRS.
B. Noncriminal tax proceedings brought in court.
C. Correspondence audits.
D. Tax shelter opinions.

93. Which of the following statements is false?

A. A taxpayer is prohibited from recording his meeting with an IRS auditor unless the taxpayer is represented by an enrolled agent, CPA, or tax attorney.
B. A taxpayer may record the examination interview with the IRS.
C. The request to record the examination meeting should be made in writing.
D. A taxpayer must notify the IRS ten days in advance in order to record an examination.

94. The IRS offers fast track mediation for all of the following issues except:

A. Examinations (audits).
B. Offers in compromise.
C. Trust fund recovery penalties.
D. Cases that are docketed in the district court.

95. Which of the following statements regarding the IRS Collection Appeals Program (CAP) is false?

A. A taxpayer cannot appeal a CAP hearing decision to the U.S. Tax Court.
B. The CAP process is generally quicker and is available for a broader range of collection actions.
C. A Low Income Tax Clinic may represent taxpayers who qualify.
D. A taxpayer may go to court if he disagrees with the CAP decision.

96. Penny has an installment agreement in place with the IRS. In March 2012, she gets into a bad car accident and misses a payment. The IRS sends her a notice 30 days later and terminates her installment agreement. Which of the following statements is false?

A. Penny has no appeal rights once the installment agreement is in default.
B. The IRS cannot levy until 30 days after the termination of an installment agreement.
C. If Penny appeals within a 30-day period after the termination, the IRS will be prohibited from levying until her appeal is completed.
D. Penny may call the telephone number shown on the notice and explain that she wants to appeal the termination.

97. Trent decided to represent himself in an IRS audit. When he arrived at the IRS office, he became agitated during the initial examination interview and requested to speak to a representative. Which of the following statements is correct?

A. The taxpayer may leave the examination and finish the audit through correspondence.
B. An IRS interview must be suspended when the taxpayer clearly requests the right to consult with a representative.
C. If the taxpayer chooses to suspend the interview, he must return in person with his representative.
D. The IRS is not required to cease an examination when the taxpayer requests a representative.

98. What is a CP-2000 notice?

A. A CP-2000 notice shows proposed changes to a taxpayer's income tax return.
B. A CP-2000 notice demands a payment from a taxpayer.
C. A CP-2000 notice shows proposed changes to a taxpayer's examination.
D. A CP-2000 notice alerts the taxpayer of an impending IRS examination.

99. If there is substantial unreported income (over 25%), the IRS may audit tax returns for up to _____ after the filing date.

A. Three years.
B. Five years.
C. Six years.
D. Indefinitely.

100. Juanita is an enrolled agent. Her client, Clive, had his return rejected. Clive will be given _____ from the date of a rejected return to resubmit the return, even if the submission is made after the due date of the return.

A. 24 hours.
B. 5 days.
C. 10 days.
D. 30 days.

Please review your answers with the answers in the back.

Test Answers

Individuals: Answers

Exam #1 Individuals: Answers

1. The answer is C. Since the trip was mainly for business, Pam can deduct the roundtrip airfare, parking, hotel costs, and the meals (subject to the 50% limit) connected with her professional continuing education. The meal costs incurred while sightseeing are not deductible. The answer is figured as follows:

Roundtrip airfare to New Orleans	$360	$360
Parking at the airport	$24	$24
Meals while at the conference	$220	$220 X 50% = **$110**
Meals while sightseeing	$72	**NO**
Hotel costs during the conference	$450	$450
Allowable costs before application of the 2%-of-AGI limit		**$944**

2. The answer is B. They are not required to file a return, because they are under the income threshold for their age and filing status. Randall is over 65, and Paula does not have any taxable income. Their gross income for the year is $19,500, and the inheritance is not reportable. Therefore, the table shows they do not have a filing requirement for 2012.

2012 Filing Requirements for Most Taxpayers		
Filing Status	**Age**	**Filing Requirement Threshold**
Single	under 65	$9,750
	65 or older	$11,200
Married Filing Jointly	under 65 (both spouses)	$19,500
	65 or older (one spouse)	$20,650
	65 or older (both spouses)	$21,800
Married Filing Separately	any age	$3,800
Head of Household	under 65	$12,500
	65 or older	$13,950
Qualifying Widow(er) With Dependent Child	under 65	$15,700
	65 or older	$16,850

This table does not apply to taxpayers who have self-employment income. A taxpayer is required to file a return if he or she has self-employment income of $400 or more. See IRS **Publication 17**, *Your Federal Income Tax.*

3. The answer is C. Income derived from a business carried on by an estate (or trust) generally is not included in determining the self-employment earnings of the estate. Even if a taxpayer was self-employed while he or she was alive and the business continues to generate revenues after the death, those revenues are not subject to self-employment tax. However, they will be subject to income tax.

4. The answer is C. For 2012 IRA contributions, a taxpayer may contribute at any time during 2012 and up until April 15, 2013. Filing an extension does not extend the IRA contribution deadline. However, if the taxpayer makes a contribution after January 1 but before the April 15th deadline, he will need to designate the contribution year.

5. The answer is A, figured as follows:

Wages #1 job	$5,000
Wages #2 job	$18,500
Gross wages	**$23,500**
Subtract *allowable* capital loss	($3,000)
Gross income	**$20,500**
Early withdrawal penalty	($130)
Adjusted gross income	**$20,370**

The wages must be added together. Then the allowable capital loss is subtracted, which provides the gross income. The early withdrawal penalty from a certificate of deposit is allowed as an adjustment to income.

6. The answer is D. Business casualty losses are not an AMT preference item. Business-related casualty losses are not subject to phase-outs and are deductible in full. AMT preference items are items that trigger the AMT because they are calculated differently (or are disallowed) for AMT purposes. The following items are some common AMT preference items.

- Medical and dental expenses
- Taxes on Schedule A
- Net operating loss deduction
- Home Mortgage Interest adjustment
- Miscellaneous itemized deductions on Schedule A
- Depletion
- Investment interest expense
- Qualified small business stock
- Disposition of property
- Other adjustments, including income-based related adjustments
- Married filing separately special adjustment

- Personal exemptions

The alternative minimum tax (AMT) attempts to ensure that higher income earners pay at least a minimum amount of tax. The AMT provides an alternative set of rules for calculating income tax.

7. The answer is D. Child care is not a medical expense. Taxpayers may deduct transportation related to medical care, as well as treatment for drug and alcohol addiction. The cost of smoking programs and prescription drugs are also deductible.

8. The answer is C. A taxpayer who files married filing separately does not qualify for the Earned Income Credit. See IRS **Publication 17** for more information.

9. The answer is D. Unlike divorce, an annulment legally invalidates a marriage, which is retroactive. A court decree of annulment deems that no valid marriage ever existed. Therefore, the taxpayer is considered unmarried even if he or she filed joint returns for earlier years. Taxpayers may choose to file jointly if they are:
- Married and living together as husband and wife.
- Living together in a common law marriage recognized by their state.
- Married and living apart but not legally separated under a decree of divorce or separate maintenance.
- Separated under an interlocutory (not final) decree of divorce.
- Married to a nonresident alien (the nonresident spouse must request an ITIN in order to file jointly). This is an election.

10. The answer is A. If a taxpayer's spouse dies during the year, the surviving spouse is considered married for the entire year and can choose either the married filing jointly or married filing separately as his or her filing status. See IRS **Publication 17** for more information.

11. The answer is B. Wayne may deduct up to $25,000 of his rental losses from his active income. The disallowed amount ($2,000) becomes a carryover to the next year. If a taxpayer actively participates in a passive rental real estate activity that produces a loss, the taxpayer can deduct the loss from non-passive income, up to $25,000. This special $25,000 allowance is only allowed for rental activities. However, there are income limitations. If modified adjusted gross income (MAGI) is $100,000 or less ($50,000 or less if MFS), the taxpayer can deduct losses up to $25,000. If MAGI **exceeds** $100,000 ($50,000 if MFS), the special allowance is limited to 50% of the difference between $150,000 ($75,000 if MFS) and MAGI. If MAGI is $150,000 or more ($75,000 or more if MFS), the losses are disallowed and must be carried forward. See **Publication 527**, *Residential Rental Property (Including Rental of Vacation Homes)*.

12. The answer is C. Their adjusted gross income is $165,000, so they are phased out for claiming the rental losses. The answer is figured as follows:

Wages for Ellie	$60,000
Wages for Timothy	$105,000
Income from a passive investment partnership	$4,000
ALLOWABLE rental losses from residential real estate	($4,000)
Adjusted gross income	**$165,000**

The $4,000 passive income from the investment partnership offsets $4,000 of the passive losses from the real estate activity. Since the taxpayers' joint MAGI exceeds $150,000, the rental losses are disallowed. However, the disallowed rental loss of $500 may be carried forward to the next year. See **Publication 527**, *Residential Rental Property (Including Rental of Vacation Homes).*

13. The answer is C. Ryan has a $370 ($1,320 sale price - $950 transferred basis) long-term capital gain. The basis of a gift generally remains the same for the receiver as it was for the donor. This is called a transferred basis. Therefore, Ryan's basis in the stock, for purposes of determining gain, is $950 (transferred basis). The holding period is also transferred, so the three years that Frank held the stock is tacked on to Ryan's holding period, which makes the disposition a long-term capital gain. See **Publication 551**, *Basis of Assets.*

14. The answer is B. Traditional IRA distributions are taxable to the receiver. In the case of a deceased IRA holder, the distribution to the beneficiary is subject to income tax, but not subject to the 10% early withdrawal penalty, regardless of the age of the beneficiary. See **Publication 525**, *Taxable and Nontaxable Income.*

15. The answer is A. The depreciable basis for the building is limited to the value of the building ($150,000). Land is never depreciated. Since residential rental property is depreciated over 27.5 years, $150,000 would generate depreciation of $5,455 per year ($150,000/27.5 years). Rental activity is reported on **Schedule E,** *Supplemental Income and Loss.* The depreciation of rentals is reported on **Form 4562,** *Depreciation and Amortization.* See **Publication 527**, *Residential Rental Property (Including Rental of Vacation Homes).*

16. The answer is C. Gary may claim the American Opportunity Credit for Devon and Brianna, but not for Keisha, because she is a graduate student. The credit is only allowed for students who are working on their undergraduate degrees. A taxpayer can claim the American Opportunity Credit for qualified education expenses paid for a dependent child, the taxpayer, or a spouse. If a taxpayer has multiple qualifying students, the taxpayer can claim multiple credits on the same return. In Gary's case, since he has two qualifying students, he can claim a maximum of $5,000 ($2,500 x 2) in American Opportunity Credits. Gary may be able to take the Lifetime Learning Credit for Keisha's education expenses, if she otherwise qualifies.

17. The answer is B. The Lifetime Learning Credit is limited to $2,000 *per return*. The credit is calculated as 20% of the first $10,000 of qualifying costs, regardless of the number of qualifying students, with a maximum credit of $2,000 ($10,000 X 20%). The Lifetime Learning Credit can be used for a student who is not eligible for the American Opportunity Credit. However, a taxpayer cannot claim both the American Opportunity Credit and the Lifetime Learning Credit for the same student on the same return.

18. The answer is D. Matthew's AGI is $20,000, which is multiplied by the AGI limit of 7.5% ($20,000 X 7.5% = $1,500). From $1,700 (his gross medical costs), Matthew must subtract $1,500. This leaves a deduction of $200 ($1,700 - $1,500). See **Publication 502**, *Medical and Dental Expenses*.

19. The answer is A. Life insurance proceeds payable to Amelia's beneficiaries would be included in the calculation of her gross estate. The gross estate includes the value of property that the taxpayer owns at the time of death. The gross estate also includes the following:
- The value of certain annuities payable to the estate or to the taxpayer's heirs
- The value of certain property transferred within three years before the taxpayer's death.

See **Publication 950,** *Introduction to Estate and Gift Taxes.*

20. The answer is A. The basis of the new property is $37,000 (the adjusted basis of the old property, $17,000, plus the amount she paid, $20,000). The basis of the property *received* is generally the same as the adjusted basis of the property *given up*. If a taxpayer trades property in a like-kind exchange and also pays money, the basis of the property received is the adjusted basis of the property given up *increased* by the money paid. Calculation: $17,000 old basis + $20,000 boot paid = $37,000 basis in new property. See IRS **Publication 544,** *Sales and Other Dispositions of Assets.*

21. The answer is C. Brandy must report $300 of the recovery in her taxable income. The only amount of the $900 reimbursement that must be included in her income for 2012 is $300—the amount that was actually deducted. A taxpayer must include a recovery in income in the year it is received, *but only up to the amount* by which the deduction reduced tax in the earlier year. For more information, see **Publication 525**, *Taxable and Nontaxable Income.*

22. The answer is D. All the gain is excludable from income. Aiden meets the ownership and use tests in order to exclude the gain, because during the five-year period ending on the date of sale, he owned and lived in the home for more than two years. The required two years of ownership and use do not have to be continuous nor do they have to occur at the same time. A taxpayer will meet the tests if he can show that he owned and lived in the property as a main home for either 24 full months or 730 days (365 × 2) during the five-year period ending on the date of sale. See **Publication 523,** *Selling Your Home.*

23. The answer is B. Municipal bond interest is exempt from federal tax, but must be reported on the taxpayer's return. *Excludable income*, which is not shown on a return, includes gifts, inheritances, life insurance proceeds, and employee reimbursements made under an accountable plan. *Exempt* income includes interest income from certain types of investments. There are some instances when exempt income is shown on a return but not included in the income tax computation, such as is the case with tax-exempt interest income (which includes municipal bond interest). For more information, see **Publication 525,** *Taxable and Nontaxable Income.*

24. The answer is D. The wages, interest, alimony, and unemployment compensation are taxable income and will be shown on Donna's tax return. Child support, inheritance, and workers' compensation are nontaxable income and will not be shown on Donna's tax return. Unlike unemployment compensation, workers' compensation is not taxable, because it is a form of insurance providing wage replacement and medical benefits to employees injured in the course of employment. Compensation for injuries (workplace or otherwise) is generally not taxable. For more information, see **Publication 525,** *Taxable and Nontaxable Income.*

25. The answer is C. A taxpayer cannot contribute to a traditional IRA unless the taxpayer has qualifying compensation. Alimony income is considered earned income for purposes of an IRA contribution. Earned income is typically any income received for work, such as wages or business income. Unearned income is any income produced by investments, such as interest on savings, dividends on stocks, or rental income. In order to contribute to a traditional IRA, the taxpayer must:
- Be under the age of 70½ at the end of the tax year.
- Have qualifying compensation, such as wages or income from self-employment. Taxable alimony and nontaxable combat pay are treated as qualifying compensation for IRA purposes, but child support is not.

26. The answer is C. Individuals who receive $20 or more per month in cash tips from one job must report their tip income to their employer. Tips are taxable as follows:

- Tips paid in cash of **$20 or more** per month are taxable as wages. These tips are subject to FICA, FUTA, and income tax.
- Tips of **less than** $20 a month are not subject to FICA or FUTA. However, the amounts are still subject to income tax.
- The fair market value of noncash tips (such as tickets or movie passes) is not subject to FICA or FUTA. However, the FMV of the noncash tips are still subject to income tax.

The employee is required to report the tip income on Form 1040. See **Publication 531,** *Reporting Tip Income*.

27. The answer is D. Allie has a loss on the sale of the rental property, calculated as follows:

($230,000 FMV on the date of conversion - $18,000 depreciation) = $212,000 tax basis
($212,000 tax basis -$205,000 sale price) = $7,000 loss

Losses from the sale of a primary residence are not deductible. However, if a primary residence is converted to a rental, a loss is generally deductible. In the case of a converted property, the loss is calculated on the tax basis of the rental property, which is the lesser of:

- The cost basis when the property is placed in service as a rental; or
- The fair market value when it is placed in service.

To figure the adjusted basis, add any improvements that were made while the property was a rental, and deduct any depreciation. See **Publication 551,** *Basis of Assets*.

28. The answer is A. Form 1098 reports expenses a taxpayer has **paid** (specifically, mortgage interest paid by a borrower), while Form 1099-MISC reports income a taxpayer has **received**.

29. The answer is A. Herb has a $1,000 short-term capital loss and a $7,000 ($5,000 + $2,000) long-term capital gain. The loss on the sale of the ABC Co. stock is short-term, because he owned the stock for less than a year. The gain on the sale of the empty lot is long-term gain, because inherited property is always treated as long-term property, regardless of how long the beneficiary holds the property. The gain on the sale of the XYZ Co. stock is also long-term gain, because Herb held the stock for over a year. See **Publication 550,** *Investment Income and Expenses*.

30. The answer is C. Natalie has $104,500 in gross income, but only her wages ($90,000) qualify for the foreign earned income exclusion. The interest and annuity payments are not qualifying income for purposes of the foreign earned income exclusion. Qualifying foreign earned income does not include the following:

- Pension or annuity payments, including Social Security benefits
- Pay received as a military or civilian employee of the U.S. government
- Pay for services conducted in international waters (not a foreign country)
- Unearned income, such as interest, dividends, and alimony

U.S. citizens and resident aliens who live abroad are taxed on their worldwide income. However, they may qualify to exclude a portion of their foreign earnings (up to $95,100 for 2012). In this case, only the wages qualify for exclusion. Only a **qualifying individual** with **qualifying income** may elect to exclude foreign earned income, and this exclusion applies only if a tax return is filed and the income is reported. See **Publication 54,** *Tax Guide for U.S. Citizens and Resident Aliens Abroad.*

31. The answer is B. Martina will report $30,850 on Form 1040, line 7. This is the total of her Forms W-2 income and her unreported tip income ($25,600 + $4,950 + $300). The unemployment compensation and the taxable state refund would be reported elsewhere on the return but not as wages.

32. The answer is C. Larry may choose to report the bond interest in one of two ways. He can:

- Report $250 of interest income only once when the bond matures (this is the difference between the $500 value at maturity and the amount he paid for the bond); or
- Report $7 of interest income at the end of the first year. This is the increase in value at the end of the year ($257 - $250 = $7). Larry would be required to report interest income each year until maturity.

See **Publication 550**, *Investment Income and Expenses.*

33. The answer is A. The alternate valuation date is **six months** from the date of death (not 180 days). If a taxpayer dies on March 31, the alternate valuation date is September 30. The alternate valuation date is an election made by the executor of an estate after an individual taxpayer has died. A taxpayer's gross estate will be valued either on the date of death or six months after the date of death, the alternate valuation date. See **Publication 950,** *Introduction to Estate and Gift Taxes.*

34. The answer is D. The cleaning deposits are refundable to the tenants, so they are not considered rental income. Karen would calculate her rental income as follows:

$11,700 ($1,300 x 9 months in 2012)
$1,800 ($600 x 3 months in 2012)
$600 (rent paid in advance)
$14,100 rental income for 2012

The advance rent must be included in Karen's 2012 rental income. This is because Karen had *constructive receipt* of the rent, and advance rent is always taxable when it is received, regardless of the taxpayer's accounting method. A taxpayer is deemed to have *constructive receipt* of income when the amount is made available to him or her *without restriction*. A taxpayer cannot hold checks or postpone taking possession of income from one tax year to another in order to avoid paying tax. The fact that Karen waited to cash the check is irrelevant, because she had rights to the funds. See **Publication 527**, *Residential Rental Property*.

35. The answer is D. Employee business expenses are a miscellaneous itemized deduction, not an adjustment to income. Some of the most common adjustments to income include:

- Individual Retirement Arrangements (IRAs)
- Alimony paid
- Bad debt deduction
- Moving expenses
- Student loan interest deduction
- Tuition and fees deduction
- Educator expense deduction
- Self-employed health insurance
- Jury duty pay given to the taxpayer's employer

See **Publication 17**, *Your Federal Income Tax*.

36. The answer is D. Because Greg does not meet the age test, Sandy's son is not her qualifying child. Because he does not meet the gross income test, Greg is not her qualifying relative. As a result, he is not Sandy's qualifying person for head of household purposes and she cannot claim her son as a dependent. However, if Greg was permanently disabled, he would be considered a qualifying child, regardless of his age. For more information, see **Publication 501,** *Exemptions, Standard Deduction, and Filing Information*.

37. The answer is A. IRA transfers due to divorce are tax free. If an interest in a traditional IRA is transferred from a spouse by a divorce decree, the interest in the IRA, starting from the date of the transfer, is treated as the receiving spouse's IRA. Transfers incident to a divorce are treated like a rollover, so the transfer is tax free. For more information, see **Publication 590,** *Individual Retirement Arrangements.*

38. The answer is B. Using an IRA as security for a loan is a prohibited transaction. A prohibited transaction is the improper use of a traditional IRA by a taxpayer, a beneficiary, or any other disqualified person (disqualified persons include a fiduciary and family members). Prohibited transactions include:

- Borrowing money from an IRA
- Selling property to an IRA
- Receiving unreasonable compensation for managing an IRA
- Using the IRA as security for a loan
- Buying property for personal use with IRA funds

If a prohibited transaction occurs, the IRA ceases to be an IRA, and the full amount of the account becomes taxable as of the first day of that year. The other actions listed in the question (early withdrawal of IRA funds, making excess contributions, and failing to take required minimum distributions) are not *prohibited transactions,* but they will result in additional taxes and penalties for the taxpayer. For more information, see **Publication 590,** *Individual Retirement Arrangements.*

39. The answer is B. Yes, Tina may contribute to a Roth, but her contribution is subject to a phase-out because of her AGI. Taxpayers can contribute to a Roth IRA if they have qualifying compensation and their modified AGI is less than:

- $183,000 (phase-out begins at $173,000) for married filing jointly or qualifying widower
- $125,000 (phase-out begins at $110,000) for single, head of household, or married filing separately and the taxpayer did not live with his or her spouse at any time during the year, or
- $10,000 (phase-out begins at $0) for married filing separately (living with spouse)

For more information, see **Publication 590,** *Individual Retirement Arrangements.*

40. The answer is C. In 2012, a taxpayer can convert a traditional IRA to a Roth IRA, and the conversion is treated as a rollover. Prior to 2010, taxpayers were not allowed to convert their traditional IRA accounts to Roth IRA accounts if their AGI exceeded $100,000. However, the rules were changed in 2010 to allow taxpayers to convert their traditional IRA accounts to Roth accounts, as long as the individual paid taxes on the conversion. This type of conversion results in taxation of any previously untaxed amounts in the traditional IRA, but is not subject to the early withdrawal penalty. The conversion is reported on **Form 8606**, *Nondeductible IRAs*. For more information, see **Publication 590,** *Individual Retirement Arrangements.*

41. The answer is D. The full amount is subject to SE tax and income tax. Theo must report the $2,500 cash payments as self-employment income along with the $12,400 on his Schedule C. It does not matter whether he receives a **1099-MISC** or not. All of the income is taxable as self-employment income. Therefore, it is subject to income tax, as well as to self-employment tax. See **Publication 334,** *Tax Guide for Small Business.*

42. The answer is A. The expenses paid for an unsuccessful adoption attempt may still be deductible. Qualified adoption expenses include court costs, attorney fees, traveling expenses (including meals and lodging while away from home), and other expenses directly related to the legal adoption of an eligible child. Expenses paid in an unsuccessful attempt to adopt an eligible child before finalizing the adoption of another child may still qualify for the credit. Qualified adoption expenses do not include expenses for adopting a spouse's child, expenses for a surrogate arrangement, or any expenses that were reimbursed by an employer or any other organization. Expenses connected with a foreign adoption (where the child was not a U.S. citizen or resident at the time the adoption process began) qualify only if the adoption is successful.

43. The answer is A. Capital gain distributions are taxable income that come from mutual funds and real estate investment trusts (REITs). These distributions are treated as long-term capital gains, regardless of how long the taxpayer holds the shares. The other types of distributions listed are not taxable. A return of capital reduces a taxpayer's stock basis. Stock dividends also reduce stock basis. Dividends paid to cash-value life insurance policyholders are also considered nontaxable distributions, but are not included in taxable income. ***Note:** Do not confuse *capital gains* with *capital gain distributions*. A capital gain occurs when a taxpayer sells stock, shares of a mutual fund, or other capital asset. A capital gain *distribution* occurs when the mutual fund sells assets for more than their cost and distributes the realized gain to the shareholders. See **Publication 550,** *Investment Income and Expenses.*

44. The answer is A. The American Opportunity Credit allows 40% of the credit to be refundable to taxpayers who meet certain requirements. The Lifetime Learning Credit and the Child Care and Dependent Care Credit are nonrefundable credits. The Adoption Credit was refundable in 2011, but is no longer refundable in 2012. See **Publication 970,** *Tax Benefits for Education.*

45. The answer is B. Lupe's dividends should be reported on **Form 1040.** Lupe meets the requirements for reporting the capital gain distribution directly on **Form 1040**. If the total amount of dividends received is over $1,500, **Schedule B** must also be filed with the tax return. Since Lupe's dividends did not exceed $1,500, **Schedule B** is not required. The capital gain from the sale of stock should be reported on **Schedule D**. See **Publication 550,** *Investment Income and Expenses.*

46. The answer is B. Danni may file as single, claiming her daughter as a dependent, and claim the Earned Income Credit. Jennifer is a qualifying child of both Danni and Fred, because she meets the relationship, age, residency, support, and joint return tests for both Fred and Danni. However, only one taxpayer can claim the child as a dependent. Since Danni did not pay the costs of keeping up the home, she does not qualify for head of household filing status.

47. The answer is B. Leslie does not need to pay estimated tax because she expects her income tax withholding ($10,250 in 2012) to be at least 90% of the tax to be shown on her 2013 return ($11,270 × 90% = $10,143). Therefore, Leslie qualifies for the safe harbor rule and is not required to make estimated tax payments. A taxpayer is not required to pay estimated tax for 2013 if:
- The taxpayer had no tax liability in the prior year
- The taxpayer was a U.S. citizen or resident alien
- The 2012 tax year covered a 12-month period.

The taxpayer also does not have to pay estimated tax if she pays enough through withholding so that the tax due on the return is less than $1,000. In most cases, a taxpayer must pay estimated tax if he or she expects withholding (plus any refundable credits) to be less than the *smaller* of:
- 90% of the tax to be shown on the 2012 tax return, or
- 100% of the tax shown on the 2013 tax return.

See IRS **Publication 505,** *Tax Withholding and Estimated Tax.*

48. The answer is B. Royalties from copyrights, patents, and oil, gas, and mineral properties are taxable as ordinary income. In most cases, royalties are reported as passive income on Schedule E. The amounts are generally subject to income tax, but not to self-employment tax. However, taxpayers who are in business as self-employed writers, inventors, artists, etc. must report this income on **Schedule C,** in which case the amounts would be subject to SE tax as well as to income tax.

49. The answer is D. A taxpayer has up to **seven years** to amend a return in order to take a loss from a worthless security. This is an exception to the regular three year rule. In general, if a refund is expected on an amended return (or a delinquent return that is being filed late), taxpayers must file the return within three years from the **due date** of the original return, or within two years after the date they paid the tax, whichever is later. There are a few other exceptions to the three-year limit rule, such as taxpayers having ten years to amend a return and claim the Foreign Tax Credit. See **Publication 550**, *Investment Income and Expenses*.

50. The answer is D. Only the amount that exceeds the value of the benefit received (the dinner) would be deductible as a charitable gift. Therefore, Pearl must deduct the value of the dinners ($20 X 6 tickets = $120) from the amount she paid. The answer is $160 ($280 - $120 = $160). See **Publication 526,** *Charitable Contributions*.

51. The answer is A. VA disability compensation is exempt from federal or state income tax. The veteran must have been terminated through separation or discharge under honorable conditions. The VA does not issue **Form W-2, Form 1099-R,** nor any other document for veterans' disability benefits. See **IRS Publication 3**, *Armed Forces Tax Guide.*

52. The answer is C. Stacy is entitled to claim five *dependency* exemptions. She may claim a dependency exemption for each of her children and one for Racine, her dependent parent. An exemption is a dollar amount that can be deducted from an individual's total income, thereby reducing the taxable income. Taxpayers may be able to claim two types of exemptions:
- Personal exemptions, which taxpayers can generally claim for themselves (and for a spouse)
- Dependency exemptions, which taxpayers claim for qualifying dependents

The **total** exemptions claimed on her return will be six (one personal exemption for Stacy and five dependency exemptions). See **Publication 501**, *Exemptions, Standard Deduction, and Filing Information.*

53. The answer is B. Angelo will not pay an underpayment penalty. Even though he will owe tax at the end of 2012, Angelo will not incur the underpayment penalty for 2012 because he had no tax liability in 2011. See **Publication 505**, *Tax Withholding and Estimated Tax.*

54. The answer is A. All the gain is excludable, because Cristina meets the ownership and use tests. Cristina meets the use test because she lived in the home for four years with Joe. She also meets the ownership test because if ownership of a home is transferred to a former spouse in a divorce, the transferee is considered to have owned it during any period of time when the other spouse owned it. In other words, since Joe was required to transfer the property due to their divorce settlement, any of the time that Joe owned the home is also considered time that Cristina owned the home. This is called the "tacking on" of the ownership period. Therefore, all Cristina's gain is excludable under section 121. See **Publication 17.**

55. The answer is C. Gabriel may claim the American Opportunity Credit for Marcus. He can take the Lifetime Learning Credit for Billy and Jason. The American Opportunity Credit is a better credit, but it applies only to undergraduate study (the first four years of college). Since Jason is a graduate student, his education expenses do not qualify for the AOC. Billy is ineligible for the AOC because he has a felony drug conviction on his record. Gabriel is still allowed to take a credit for a portion of Billy's education expenses using the Lifetime Learning Credit.

Note: A taxpayer can claim both the American Opportunity Credit and the Lifetime Learning Credit on the same return—but not for the same student. See **Publication 970,** *Tax Benefits for Education.*

56. The answer is A. Health insurance for a sole proprietor is deductible, but not on Schedule C. Instead, it is claimed as an adjustment to income on page one of Form 1040. For self-employed individuals filing a Schedule C or Schedule F, the insurance policy can be either in the name of the business or in the name of the individual. See **Publication 535,** *Business Expenses.*

57. The answer is C. The Lifetime Learning Credit is limited to $2,000 **per return**. The Lifetime Learning Credit is easy to calculate, because it is based on 20% credit for allowable expenses, calculated up to $10,000 in expenses ($10,000 X 20% = $2,000 maximum credit). Since Jim and Peggy have $11,700 ($4,800 + $6,900) in qualified education expenses, their maximum deduction is $2,000. Neither is eligible for the American Opportunity Credit because they are graduate students. The AOC only applies to the first four years of undergraduate study. See **Publication 970,** *Tax Benefits for Education.*

58. The answer is A. The answer is $8,200. The amount is figured as follows:

New computer system	$4,600
New multi-line phone system	$3,600
Total qualifying section 179 purchases	**$8,200**

Section 179 only applies to certain asset purchases. The telephone bills would be a regular business expense, not a section 179 item. The bathroom renovation is not a qualifying section 179 expense. The cost of improvements to a building must be capitalized and depreciated using MACRS. See **Publication 946,** *How To Depreciate Property.*

59. The answer is A. A tax preparer should advise Braden to amend his tax return using **Form 1040X,** removing his personal exemption from the return. Once the amended return is processed, Larissa may file her tax return normally, claiming her son as a dependent. Taxpayers should file amended returns (**Form 1040X**) when a return that has already been filed needs to be corrected. Taxpayers should file an amended return if they:

- Received another Form W-2, a corrected Form W-2, or another income statement that was not reported on the original return
- Received an additional Form 1099 that was not reported on the original return
- Claimed their own personal exemption on the return when someone else was entitled to claim it
- Claimed deductions or credits they should not have claimed
- Did not claim deductions or credits they could have claimed
- Should have used a different filing status

See **Publication 17,** *Your Federal Income Tax.*

60. The answer is B. If Rafael has his amended return postmarked on or before April 15, 2013, it will be within the three-year limit and the return will be accepted. But if the amended 2009 return is postmarked after that date, it will fall outside the three-year statute of limitations, and he will not receive the refund. See **Publication 17,** *Your Federal Income Tax.*

61. The answer is C. Failing to withdraw an RMD by the applicable deadline may result in the taxpayer owing the IRS an excise tax of 50% of the amount *not withdrawn.* A taxpayer cannot keep retirement funds in a traditional IRA forever. A taxpayer is required to start taking withdrawals from an IRA account when he or she reaches age 70½. However, unlike traditional IRAs, Roth IRAs do not require withdrawals until after the death of the owner. See **Publication 590,** *Individual Retirement Arrangements (IRAs).*

62. The answer is A. Unlike traditional IRAs, Roth IRAs do not require withdrawals until after the death of the owner. See **Publication 590,** *Individual Retirement Arrangements (IRAs).*

63. The answer is D. The standard deduction for MFJ in 2012 is $11,900. Since Robert is over 65 and blind, he is allowed an additional standard deduction amount for blindness and for being over 65 ($1,150 X 2). Therefore, their standard deduction is $14,200 ($11,900 + $1,150 + $1,150). See **Publication 501,** *Exemptions, Standard Deduction, and Filing Information.*

64. The answer is D. A statutory nonemployee is the most likely to be subject to estimated taxes. There are three categories of statutory nonemployees: direct sellers, licensed real estate agents, and certain companion sitters. These taxpayers are treated as self-employed for FICA purposes and are usually required to pay estimated taxes. Social Security and Medicare taxes of most wage earners are figured by their employers. A and C are incorrect, because household employees and statutory employees would both have their Medicare and Social Security taxes withheld by their employers. Answer B is also incorrect, because if a taxpayer is subject to back-up withholding, taxes are already being withheld from their earnings. Also, investment income is not subject to SE tax. See IRS **Publication 505**, *Tax Withholding and Estimated Tax.*

65. The answer is A. Married taxpayers who file separately and whose spouses itemize deductions must either claim "0" as their deduction or itemize their deductions. Since Rita does not have any deductions to itemize, she must claim "0" as her standard deduction amount. See **Publication 17,** *Your Federal Income Tax.*

66. The answer is A. The medical expenses are subject to a 7.5%-of-AGI limit. The unreimbursed work expenses are subject to a 2% of AGI limit. The gambling losses are limited by the gambling winnings ($3,000).

Medical expenses (gross amount)	$10,400	$7,910	Subject to 7.5% floor
Mortgage interest on main home	$6,700	$6,700	Allowable in full
Property tax on main home	$2,300	$2,300	Allowable in full
Misc. unreimbursed work expenses	$1,200	$536	Subject to 2% floor
Charitable donation to his church	$1,600	$1,600	Allowable in full
Gambling losses	$4,600	$3,000	Limited to gambling winnings
Allowable deduction on Schedule A		**$22,046**	

To figure the allowable amount of medical expenses:
    $33,200 AGI X 7.5% =$2,490
    $10,400 medical expenses - $2,490 =$7,910 allowable expense
To figure the allowable miscellaneous unreimbursed work expenses:
    $33,200 AGI X 2% =$664
    $1,200 employee expenses - $664 = $536 allowable expense
See **Publication 17**, *Your Federal Income Tax.*

67. The answer is B. Itemized deductions should be calculated after determining the taxpayer's adjusted gross income. The preparer needs to know the taxpayer's AGI in order to determine the deductible portion of some itemized expenses. See **Publication 17**, *Your Federal Income Tax.*

68. The answer is B. Qualified foreign income taxes may be deducted on Schedule A as an itemized deduction. Taxpayers have the option to choose a foreign tax credit or deduct their foreign income taxes as an itemized deduction. A taxpayer may also elect to take a deduction one year and a credit the following year.

69. The answer is B. The life insurance premiums and vitamins are not qualified medical expenses. The new total must then be adjusted by the 7.5%-of-AGI limit. The answer is figured as follows:

Copayments for prescription drugs:	$500
Dentist fees	$1,200
Medical insurance premiums	$300
Life insurance premiums	NO
Long-term care insurance premiums	$100
Vitamins	NO
Hospital bill	$3,000
Prescription eyeglasses	$350
Total qualified medical expenses	**$5,450**

To figure the AGI limit, multiply the AGI ($48,000) by 7.5%
($48,000 X 7.5%) = $3,600
$5,450 qualified expenses - $3,600 = **$1,850 allowable deduction on Schedule A.** See **Publication 502,** *Medical and Dental Expenses.*

70. The answer is D. In the case of personal-use property, (such as a personal home or vehicle) any casualty losses are subject to a $100 and 10%-of-AGI limit. This means that once the taxpayer has subtracted any insurance reimbursement, he or she must subtract $100 from each casualty. Then the taxpayer must further reduce the amount by 10% of adjusted gross income. The answer is figured as follows:

$58,000 casualty loss - $50,000 insurance reimbursement = $8,000 realized loss
$8,000 loss - $100 limitation= $7,900
$22,000 AGI X 10% =$2,200
$7,900 - $2,200 (10% of the taxpayer's AGI) = **$5,700 allowable casualty loss deduction**

*Note: Casualty losses of business property are not subject to the $100 and 10%-of-AGI limitations. Business casualty losses are deductible in full. See **Publication 547**, *Casualties, Disasters, and Thefts.*

71. The answer is C. Suzy needs to report the mortgage interest and taxes that she paid on two separate schedules. The mortgage interest and taxes for the rental property should be listed on **Schedule E**. Rental real estate income is calculated on **Schedule E,** and the income will be offset by various deductions, including the deduction for mortgage interest paid. The mortgage interest and the taxes for the primary residence should be listed on **Schedule A** as an itemized deduction. See **Publication 527**, *Residential Rental Property*.

72. The answer is B. Astrid may only deduct the job search expenses that are related to her occupation as a dental assistant. To qualify for a deduction, the expenses must be related to the taxpayer's current occupation. A taxpayer may not deduct expenses incurred while looking for a job in a new occupation. A taxpayer also cannot deduct job search expenses while looking for a job for the first time. Job search expenses are claimed as a miscellaneous itemized deduction on **Schedule A.** The deduction is subject to the 2%-of-AGI limit. For more information about job search expenses, see IRS **Publication 529**, *Miscellaneous Deductions*.

73. The answer is D. The alternative minimum tax will not increase a taxpayer's refund. In fact, it will do the opposite. The AMT attempts to ensure that higher income earners pay at least a minimum amount of tax. The AMT provides an alternative set of rules for calculating income tax.

74. The answer is B. Veronica is required to repay this credit. If a taxpayer claimed the First Time Homebuyer Credit on her income tax return for 2008, she must repay the credit. It is repaid as an additional tax on her tax return. Veronica is required to repay the credit in equal payments over 15 years. To repay the credit, she must attach a completed **Form 5405** to her tax return each year.

75. The answer is C. Caitlyn's disabled son is still considered a qualifying child for EITC purposes, regardless of his age. Certain work offered to individuals with physical or mental disabilities is considered *sheltered employment*. The qualified locations are:

- Sheltered workshops
- Hospitals and similar institutions
- Homebound programs
- Department of Veterans Affairs (VA) sponsored homes

If a qualifying child works for minimal pay under a special program for individuals with disabilities, the IRS will not consider it "substantial gainful activity" under EITC rules. See **Publication 4935**, *Guide to Everything Earned Income Tax Credit.*

76. The answer is A. Phil does not have a theft loss deduction because his loss after applying the $100 rule ($1,900) is less than 10% of his adjusted gross income ($2,050).

Loss after insurance	$2,000
Loss after $100 rule	$1,900
Subtract 10% X $20,500 =$2,050	$2,050
Theft loss deduction	$0

77. The answer is D, figured as follows:

Wages reported on Form W-2	$42,000
Gambling winnings	$2,000
Gambling losses	NO
Dependent care benefits (spent $3,200 on childcare)	NO
Capital loss carryover from prior year	($3,000)
Gross income shown on return	**$41,000**

The dependent care benefits are not taxable because the taxpayer's dependent care expenses exceeded the benefit payments. The gross gambling winnings must be included in income. The gambling losses are only deductible as an itemized deduction. If the taxpayer does not itemize, he cannot deduct gambling losses. The capital loss carryover is deductible, but only up to $3,000, which is the capital loss limit. See **Publication 547,** *Casualties, Disasters, and Thefts.*

78. The answer is D. Neither Harold nor Trish has taxable income from this exchange. Although canceled debt is usually included in income, since Trish files for bankruptcy, the canceled debt is excludable. See **Publication 4681,** *Canceled Debts, Foreclosures, Repossessions, and Abandonments.*

79. The answer is D. Jayden will not report any income until he completes five years of service. Since the stock is subject to restrictions, it is not considered taxable income until the restriction is lifted. In most cases, employees who are issued restricted stock are required to complete some type of employment contract or meet some type of employment or sales goals before the shares will be released. See **Publication 538,** *Accounting Periods and Methods.*

80. The answer is A. The distribution from the estate would be reported to Madison on **Schedule K-1 (Form 1041).** Nonpassive distributions would be reported on **Schedule E (Form 1040).** How a taxpayer reports distributions from an estate depends on the character of the income in the *hands of the estate.*

Each item of income retains the same character. For example, if the income distributed includes dividends, tax-exempt interest, or capital gains, it would retain the same character in the hands of the beneficiary. Business income and other nonpassive income that is distributed from an estate would be reported on Part III of the taxpayer's **Schedule E (Form 1040)**.

The estate's personal representative (executor) should provide a **Schedule K-1 (Form 1041)** to each beneficiary that receives a distribution from the estate. The personal representative handling the estate must furnish the **Schedule K-1** to each beneficiary by the date on which the **Form 1041** is filed. See **Publication 559,** *Survivors, Executors, and Administrators.*

81. The answer is B. Abigail must include $4,000 in her gross income. The distributable net income is less than the currently distributable income, so Abigail must include $4,000 in her gross income [($5,000 ÷ $7,500) × $6,000], and the daughter must include $2,000 in her gross income [($2,500 ÷ $7,500) × $6,000]. See **Publication 559,** *Survivors, Executors, and Administrators.*

82. The answer is B. If income from an estate is credited or must be distributed to a taxpayer, the income must be reported in the year that the distribution is credited, *even if the income has not been distributed.* The personal representative can elect to treat distributions paid within 65 days after the close of the estate's tax year as having been paid on the last day of that tax year. If this election is made, the beneficiary must report the distribution on his return for that year. See **Publication 559,** *Survivors, Executors, and Administrators.*

83. The answer is A. Each will be treated as having received $900 in rents ($1,800 X 50%) and $600 of taxable interest ($1,200 X 50%). An amount distributed to a beneficiary retains the **same character** for the beneficiary that it had for the estate. See **Publication 559,** *Survivors, Executors, and Administrators.*

84. The answer is B. In order to qualify for the Child Tax Credit, the dependent must be under the age of 17 and claimed on the taxpayer's return. The Child Tax Credit is worth as much as $1,000 per qualifying child.
- Qualifications: A qualifying child is someone who meets the qualifying criteria of six tests: age, relationship, support, dependent, citizenship, and residence.
- Age Test: To qualify, a child must have been **under age 17** – age 16 or younger – at the end of the year.
- Relationship Test: The child must be a son, daughter, stepchild, foster child, brother, sister, stepbrother, stepsister, or a descendant of any of these in-

dividuals. An adopted child includes a child lawfully placed with the taxpayer for legal adoption.

- Support Test: In order to claim a child for this credit, the child must not have provided more than half of his or her own support.
- Dependent Test: The taxpayer must claim the child as a dependent on his or her federal tax return.
- Citizenship Test: The child must be a U.S. citizen, U.S. national, or U.S. resident alien.
- Residence Test: The child must have lived with the taxpayer for more than half the year. Temporary absences (for school or hospitalization, etc.) are allowable.

The Additional Child Tax Credit is the refundable component of this credit. If the amount of the Child Tax Credit is greater than the amount of tax liability on the return, the taxpayer may qualify for the Additional Child Tax Credit. See IRS **Publication 972**, *Child Tax Credit*.

85. The answer is A. This is a wash sale, so Shane's losses are disallowed. A wash sale occurs when a taxpayer sells securities at a loss and within 30 days before or after the sale purchases identical securities. In this case, Shane's losses would be disallowed (not deductible) but the disallowed losses would increase the basis of his newly purchased stock ($3,100 purchased stock + $2,220 disallowed losses = $5,320 new basis). See **Publication 550,** *Investment Income and Expenses.*

86. The answer is C. A taxpayer may deduct the mortgage interest on two personal homes. A home can include a boat, RV, or anything with sleeping, cooking, and toilet facilities. Therefore, Sophia may claim the mortgage interest on the RV and her primary residence, since it gives her a larger deduction ($15,000 + $6,700 =$21,700) than if she deducted the interest on her residence and the second home. A taxpayer may not deduct mortgage interest for more than two homes. For more information regarding a qualified residence, see **Publication 936**, *Home Mortgage Interest Deduction.*

87. The answer is C, figured as follows: ($35,000 + $80,000 + $2,300 =$117,300). If a taxpayer buys property and assumes an existing mortgage on the property, the basis includes the amount of the assumed mortgage. The basis also includes the settlement fees and closing costs for buying a property. All the following items are settlement fees or closing costs that are includable in a property's basis.
- Abstract fees (abstract of title fees)
- Charges for installing utility services
- Legal fees and recording fees
- Transfer taxes

- Owner's title insurance
- Any amounts the seller owes that the buyer agrees to pay, such as delinquent property taxes or interest, recording or mortgage fees, charges for improvements or repairs, and sales commissions

This list is not exhaustive. See **Publication 551**, *Basis of Assets* for more information.

88. The answer is A. Charlene would report $1,200 in business income. Generally, the FMV of property exchanged for services is includable in income. However, if services are performed for a price agreed on beforehand, the price will be accepted as the FMV if there is no evidence to the contrary. See **Publication 551**, *Basis of Assets* for more information.

89. The answer is D. $14,960 ($14,000 + $960 sales tax). Generally, the FMV of property exchanged for services is includable in income. The basis of property is usually its cost. However, if services are performed for a price agreed on beforehand, the price will be accepted as the FMV if there is no evidence to the contrary. Since Scott charged $14,000 for his services and agreed to the transfer, $14,000 will be accepted as the FMV. The sales tax on purchase is always added to the basis of an asset, capitalized, and depreciated. The following charges are added to an asset's basis (rather than expensed). The basis of an asset also includes the following items:

- Sales tax
- Freight in (shipping costs)
- Installation and testing
- Excise taxes
- Legal and accounting fees (when they must be capitalized)
- Real estate taxes (if assumed for the seller)

See **Publication 551**, *Basis of Assets* for more information and a similar example.

90. The answer is D. Mason must report $12,000 in gambling winnings. He should also report the $1,300 withholding on his return. Mason can deduct his gambling losses as an itemized deduction on **Schedule A**, but the losses are limited to gambling winnings. Therefore, Mason cannot deduct more than $12,000 in gambling losses. If a taxpayer does not itemize, he is not allowed to deduct gambling losses. See **Publication 529**, *Miscellaneous Deductions*.

91. The answer is A. If Zoe had too much Social Security tax withheld, she may claim the excess as a credit against her income tax. Most employers must withhold Social Security tax from wages. Sometimes when an employee works for more than one employer, too much Social Security tax is withheld. In this case, the taxpayer may claim the excess as a credit against income tax. See **Publication 505**, *Tax Withholding and Estimated Tax*.

92. The answer is D. The "kiddie tax" only applies to investment income and other forms of unearned income, not to wages. Therefore, Colton's income will not be subject to the kiddie tax. Under the provisions of the kiddie tax, any *unearned income* that is more than $1,900 will be taxed at the parent's marginal rate. See **Publication 929,** *Tax Rules for Children and Dependents.*

93. The answer is B. The answer is figured as follows:

Cost of shipping her horse	$450
Gasoline costs during the move	$120
Cost of packing and shipping household goods	$6,400
Hotel costs while in transit	$310
Meals while in transit	NO
Cost of breaking her lease at her old apartment	NO
Lost deposit on her old apartment	NO
Cost of connecting a phone line at her new home	$120
Total deductible moving expenses	**$7,400**

Only certain expenses qualify for the moving expense deduction. Deductible moving expenses include:

- The cost of moving household goods, pets, and family members.
- Storage costs (only while in transit and up to 30 days after the day of the move).
- Travel expenses (including lodging but not meals) for one trip per person. However, family members are not required to travel together. The taxpayer may choose to deduct actual costs or mileage.
- Any costs of connecting or disconnecting utilities required because a taxpayer is moving his household goods, appliances, or personal effects.

Moving expenses that are not deductible for income tax purposes include:

- Pre-move househunting expenses, including travel to a new location to view apartments or houses before the actual move takes place.
- Temporary living expenses (hotel costs *while in transit* are allowable).
- Meals while traveling.
- Expenses of buying or selling a home, improvements to help sell a home, or loss on a home sale.
- Car tags, driver's license renewal fees.
- Storage charges (except those *paid in-transit* and for foreign moves).
- The cost of breaking a lease.

If a taxpayer chooses to drive himself to the new location, car expenses such as gas and oil are tax deductible if accurate records are kept, or he can use the standard mileage rate instead. Parking fees and tolls are also tax deductible, but general car repairs, maintenance, and car insurance are not. See **Publication 521**, *Moving Expenses.*

94. The answer is D. Regardless of an individual taxpayer's particular situation, the maximum taxable amount of a taxpayer's Social Security benefits subject to tax is 85%. Therefore, the maximum amount that is taxable on Mariah's net benefits is 85% or $10,540 = ($12,400 X 85%). See **Publication 915**, *Social Security and Equivalent Railroad Retirement Benefits.*

95. The answer is A. A nonrefundable credit can only reduce tax liability to zero but not below that. A refundable credit can reduce tax liability to zero, and the IRS will pay back (refund) any remaining credit to the taxpayer. See **Publication 17,** *Your Federal Income Tax.*

96. The answer is B. In 2012, the Adoption Credit is nonrefundable. Therefore, Vanessa will get a carryover of $1,500 that she can use in the following year. To take the credit, the taxpayer must complete **Form 8839** and attach it to his or her **Form 1040.**

97. The answer is A. Section 179 does not apply to rental activities, so none of Alton's expenses would qualify. The window repair is deductible as an ordinary expense ($350). The cost of the stoves and the roof must be capitalized and depreciated over their useful life using MACRS tables. See **Publication 527,** *Residential Rental Property.*

98. The answer is A. Since Kenneth's wages were only $4,500 for the year, Kenneth has made a $1,500 *excess contribution* to his IRA. He must correct the excess contribution, or he will have to pay an excise tax on any excess amounts that remain in the account at the end of the year. The excise tax on excess contributions is 6%. The unemployment compensation is not qualifying income for purposes of an IRA contribution. See **Publication 590**, *Individual Retirement Arrangements (IRAs)* and **Publication 560**, *Retirement Plans for Small Businesses.*

99. The answer is C. Chester has $1,100 in net long-term capital gain ($1,600 gain - $500 loss). The gain on the Harrington stock is short-term because the shares were not held for more than a year, and so they are not included in the equation.

Activity	Bought	Sold	Gain/Loss	Character
1400 shares for $3,000 (basis $1,400)	1/3/10	12/1/12	$1,600	LT gain
200 shares for $500 (basis: $1,000)	1/3/09	12/25/12	($500)	LT loss
50 shares for $1,700 (basis: $1,500)	2/1/12	9/12/12	$200	ST gain

See **Publication 550,** *Investment Income and Expenses.*

100. The answer is A. The points are deductible mortgage interest on **Schedule A.** Points are charges paid by a borrower to a lender in order to secure a loan or to secure a lower interest rate. They are also called:

- Loan origination fees (including VA and FHA fees)
- Maximum loan charges
- Premium charges
- Loan discount points
- Prepaid interest

Points are deductible as mortgage interest on **Schedule A**. Points paid to *refinance* a mortgage are generally not deductible in full the year the taxpayer paid them. Instead, points paid during a refinance must be amortized over the life of the loan.

Exam #2 Individuals: Answers

1. The answer is B. Jenni is allowed to take some of the rental losses, but her deduction is limited. The special allowance is limited to $12,500 for married individuals who file MFS, if they lived apart from their spouses during the tax year. For married taxpayers who **live together** and file separately, the rental losses are completely disallowed and must be carried forward. See **Publication 527**, *Residential Rental Property (Including Rental of Vacation Homes)*.

2. The answer is B. Passive income can only be generated by a passive activity. There are only two sources of passive income:
1. A rental activity, or
2. A business/activity in which the taxpayer does not materially participate.

Nonpassive activities are businesses in which the taxpayer works on a regular, continuous, and substantial basis. In addition, passive income does not include salaries, portfolio, or investment income. Income and losses from the following activities generally would be considered passive: equipment leasing, rental real estate, and operation of a farm or any other business in which the taxpayer does not actually participate. There are two exceptions to this passive activity loss limitation. First, when a taxpayer materially participates in a business, it is not generally considered a passive activity. Second, although rental income is generally considered passive income, there is an exception in the law for real estate professionals. Passive losses are generally deductible only to the extent of passive income. Regardless of whether income is deemed to be passive or nonpassive, it must be reported somewhere on the return, most typically on **Schedule E.**

3. The answer is A. The nanny is a household employee. Household employees include housekeepers, maids, babysitters, gardeners, and others who work in or around a taxpayer's private residence as employees. If an employer pays a household employee wages of $1,800 or less in 2012, the employer does not have to report and pay Social Security and Medicare taxes on that employee's wages. For more information, see Social Security and Medicare wages in **Publication 926**, *Household Employer's Tax Guide.*

4. The answer is C. Employees use **Form 2106** to deduct ordinary and necessary expenses related to their job. An employee can use Form 2106 to deduct expenses that were not reimbursed by his employer. Amounts included in box 1 of the employee's **Form W-2** are not considered reimbursements, because those amounts have been taxed as regular wages. See **Publication 529**, *Miscellaneous Deductions.*

5. The answer is D. A PTIN is a Preparer Tax Identification Number that is used by preparers only, not by taxpayers. There are only three types of Taxpayer Identification Numbers: the Social Security Number (SSN), the Adoption Taxpayer Identification Number (ATIN), and the Individual Tax Identification Number (ITIN). An Employer Identification Number (EIN) is used by entities, not by individuals.

6. The answer is C. Courtney is not required to file a tax return. She is blind and entitled to an increased exemption amount for blindness. She had only passive income. Therefore, she would not have to file a return unless her total *unearned* income exceeds $2,400. Whether a dependent has to file a return depends on the amount of his or her earned and unearned income and whether the dependent is married, is age 65 or older, or is blind. A dependent who has only unearned income must file a return if the income exceeds the amounts listed below:

Marital Status	Filing Threshold
Single	
Under 65 and not blind	$950
Either 65 or older, or blind	$2,400
65 or older and blind	$3,850
Married	
Under 65 and not blind	$950
Either 65 or older, or blind	$2,100
65 or older and blind	$3,250

For more information, see **Publication 929,** *Tax Rules for Children and Dependents.*

7. The answer is B. The rules for HSAs are similar to the rules for inherited IRA accounts. Since Chase is not a spousal beneficiary, the account ceases to be an HSA in the year of Patty's death. The fair market value of the HSA would also become taxable to the Chase in 2012. In the case of a spousal beneficiary, the spouse can elect to treat the HSA as his own account and roll over any inherited amounts into his own HSA. If an estate is the beneficiary of the account, the value of the HSA is included on the taxpayer's final income tax return. The amount taxable to a beneficiary (other than an estate) would be reduced by any medical expenses for the decedent that are paid by the beneficiary within one year after the date of death. See **Publication 969,** *Health Savings Accounts and Other Tax-Favored Health Plans.*

8. The answer is B. Gambling losses may be claimed as a miscellaneous itemized deduction, <u>not subject</u> to the 2% floor, on **Schedule A.** However, the amount of losses deducted *may not exceed* gambling winnings. A taxpayer can only deduct gambling losses if he itemizes deductions. For more information, see **Publication 529**, *Miscellaneous Deductions*.

9. The answer is C. The taxpayer is not required to request an EIN if he operates multiple businesses, as long as those businesses are all sole proprietorships without employees. The taxpayer will need an EIN if any of the following is true:

- He files bankruptcy under Chapter 7 (liquidation) or Chapter 11 (reorganization) of the Bankruptcy Code.
- He incorporates or takes in partners to operate as a partnership.
- He establishes a pension, profit sharing, or retirement plan.
- He files employment or excise tax returns.

He will not need a new EIN if any of the following is true:

- He changes the name of his business.
- He changes the location or adds locations (stores, plants, enterprises, or branches of the same entity).
- He operates multiple businesses (including stores, plants, enterprises, or branches of the same entity).

For more information, refer to **Publication 334**, *Tax Guide for Small Business*.

10. The answer is B, figured as follows:

Required textbooks	$450
Student health fees	NO
Required lab equipment	$1,260
Tuition ($6,800 - $4,750)	$2,050
Qualifying costs for the AOC	**$3,760**

The GI Bill is a benefit that is not taxable or reportable. However, to figure the amount of qualifying educational expenses for purposes of the AOC credit, Reggie must first subtract the $4,750 GI Bill payment from his qualified education expenses ($6,800 - $4,750). The books and lab equipment are allowable expenses, but the student health fees are specifically disallowed (even if they are mandatory). See **Publication 970**, *Tax Benefits for Education*.

11. The answer is C. Amounts contributed to an FSA are not subject to employment or federal income taxes. Health flexible spending arrangements (FSAs) allow employees to be reimbursed for medical expenses. FSAs are usually funded through voluntary salary reduction agreements with an employer. Employers may also contribute. Unlike HSAs or Archer MSAs which must be reported on Form 1040, there are no reporting requirements for FSAs on a taxpayer's individual return. See **Publication 969,** *Health Savings Accounts and Other Tax-Favored Health Plans.*

12. The answer is C. A taxpayer may be eligible to file as head of household if the dependent who qualifies the taxpayer for this filing status is born or dies during the year. Even if a child lives for a very short time, he or she may still be claimed as a dependent. The child must be born alive. Stillborn births do not qualify. There must be proof of a live birth shown by an official document such as a birth certificate. Under these unique circumstances, if the taxpayer does not have a Social Security Number for the child, the taxpayer instead may attach a copy of the child's birth certificate and death certificate and enter "DIED" on **Form 1040.** This is a very special exception that is outlined in **Publication 17.** The tax return cannot be e-filed and must be submitted on paper with a copy of the birth certificate and the death certificate.

13. The answer is B. His father must apply for an Individual Taxpayer Identification Number (ITIN), and then Rodrigo can claim his father as a dependent. If a dependent is a resident or nonresident alien who is not eligible for an SSN, he must apply for an ITIN by using **Form W-7,** *Application for IRS Individual Taxpayer Identification Number.* In order for a taxpayer to claim a dependency exemption for someone, a residency test must be met. To meet the "citizen, national, or resident test," an individual must be a citizen of the United States, a resident of the United States, or a citizen or resident of Canada or Mexico. For more information, see **Publication 501.**

14. The answer is A. In 2012, anyone can make a qualified rollover contribution to a Roth IRA regardless of the taxpayer's modified AGI. If a taxpayer wants to convert a traditional IRA to a Roth IRA, he is required to pay federal income taxes on any pretax contributions, as well as any growth in the investment's value. Once the funds are converted to a Roth, all of the investment grows tax-free, and funds can be withdrawn on a tax-free basis. Although there are still income limits to who can *participate* in a Roth IRA, beginning with tax year 2010, anyone may convert an existing traditional IRA to a Roth IRA. For more information, see **Publication 17.**

15. The answer is A. Adam does not have a deductible casualty loss. The loss deduction is figured as follows:

Loss after insurance	$2,000
Subtract $100	$100
Loss after $100 rule	$1,900
Subtract 10% × $29,500 AGI	$2,950
Theft loss deduction	**$–0–**

Adam does not have a casualty loss deduction because his loss after applying the $100 rule ($1,900) is less than 10% of his adjusted gross income ($2,950). Each personal casualty or theft loss is limited to the excess of the loss over $100. In addition, the 10%-of-AGI limit continues to apply to the net loss in most cases. For more information, see **Publication 17**.

16. The answer is D. Brittany is allowed to make a traditional IRA contribution in 2012, but she must designate the contribution as nondeductible. Because she was covered by a retirement plan at work and her modified AGI was over $68,000, she cannot deduct the contribution. Her traditional IRA contribution is subject to a phase-out. Although she is allowed to contribute, she will not get the benefit of a tax deduction for the IRA contribution. She must designate this contribution as a "nondeductible contribution" by reporting it on **Form 8606**. See **Publication 590,** *Individual Retirement Arrangements (IRAs)*.

17. The answer is B. Dianne can file as head of household because her husband did not live with her for the last six months of the year. There is a special exception that applies to married persons who live apart from their spouses for at least the last six months of the year. In this case, the taxpayer will be "considered unmarried" for head of household filing purposes.

18. The answer is B. A nonresident alien who is married to a U.S. citizen is not automatically treated as a resident for tax purposes. An election can be made by both spouses to treat a nonresident spouse as a U.S. resident for tax purposes. All of the other answers are taxpayers who would automatically be treated as U.S. residents for income tax purposes. Aliens are considered residents for tax purposes if they are lawful permanent residents of the United States (holders of green cards) at any time during the calendar year, regardless of their domicile. Individuals holding green cards have automatic U.S. resident status unless it is taken away from them or is administratively or judicially determined to be abandoned. See **Publication 54**, *Tax Guide for US Citizens and Resident Aliens Abroad*.

19. The answer is D. Daniel and Maria may take three exemptions on their tax return. Daniel can take a personal exemption for himself and, since he is married, one for his spouse. They can also take an exemption for Daniel's stepmother. If a taxpayer's qualifying person is a dependent parent, the taxpayer may still take a dependency exemption even if the parent does not live with the taxpayer.

20. The answer is D. Hailey must file MFS, and she will also be forced to itemize. On an MFS return, if one spouse itemizes deductions, the other spouse must also itemize and cannot claim the standard deduction. Hailey also cannot claim the dependency exemption for Sam, because she is not the custodial parent. If the parents separated during the year and the child lived with both parents before the separation, the custodial parent is the one with whom the child lived for the greater number of nights during the rest of the year. Neither spouse qualifies for head of household, because they did not separate until September 2012. For more information, see **Publication 501**, *Exemptions, Standard Deduction, and Filing Information*.

21. The answer is C. Chad provided more than half of his own support for the year. Therefore, he is not Amber's qualifying child or her qualifying relative. To meet the Support Test, the child cannot have provided more than half of his own support for the year. See **Publication 501**, *Exemptions, Standard Deduction, and Filing Information*.

22. The answer is C. Only Aaron qualifies for the Child Tax Credit. A qualifying child for this credit must be **under** age 17 and a U.S. citizen or national or a U.S. resident. For purposes of the Child Tax Credit, a child must:
- Be a son, daughter, stepchild, foster child, brother, sister, stepbrother, stepsister, or a descendant of any of them (for example, a grandchild, niece, or nephew);
- Be under age 17 at the end of 2012;
- Have not provided over half of his or her own support for 2012;
- Have lived with the taxpayer for more than half of 2012;
- And be a U.S. citizen, a U.S. national, or a U.S. resident alien.

For more information, see **Publication 972,** *Child Tax Credit.*

23. The answer is D. Gambling income does not qualify as earned income for purposes of the EIC. For purposes of the EIC, earned income includes wages and self-employment income. Taxable earned income also includes:
- Wages, salaries, and tips
- Union strike benefits
- Long-term disability benefits received prior to minimum retirement age
- Net earnings from self-employment
- Nontaxable combat pay

The taxpayer can elect to have nontaxable combat pay included in earned income for the Earned Income Credit. See **Publication 596**, *Earned Income Credit (EIC).*

24. The answer is C. The maximum amount of investment income he can have and still claim the Earned Income Credit is $3,200 for 2012. See **Publication 596**, *Earned Income Credit (EIC).*

25. The answer is A. Melanie turned 13 on May 1 and is no longer a qualifying person for purposes of this credit. For the Child and Dependent Care Credit, the child must be under the age of 13 (or be disabled, of any age). Rayna can use the $2,000 of expenses for Melanie's care January through April before she turned 13 to figure her credit because it is less than the $3,000 yearly limit for one qualifying child. If there is more than one qualifying child, the total amount of the credit is $5,000 in 2012. For more information, see **Publication 503**, *Child and Dependent Care Expenses.*

26. The answer is A. The other answers are incorrect. A foster child may be treated just like a biological child for purposes of the Earned Income Credit. A child is an eligible foster child if the child is placed with the taxpayer by an authorized placement agency or by judgment, decree, or other order of any court. See **Publication 596**, *Earned Income Credit (EIC).*

27. The answer is A. Francesca's filing status is single. Unlike divorce, an annulment is retroactive. If a taxpayer obtains a court decree of annulment, which holds that no valid marriage ever existed, the taxpayer is considered unmarried even if he or she filed joint returns for earlier years. The taxpayer must file amended tax returns claiming single or head of household status (if applicable) for each tax year affected by the annulment that is not closed by the statute of limitations for filing a tax return. The statute of limitations generally does not end until three years after the original return was filed. See **Publication 17,** *Your Federal Income Tax.*

28. The answer is C. Eligible educators can deduct up to $250 of qualified expenses as an adjustment to income. The deduction is claimed on either line 23 of Form 1040 or line 16 of **Form 1040A**. If the taxpayer and spouse are both educators, they can deduct up to $500, but neither can deduct more than their first $250. For courses in health and physical education, expenses are deductible if they are related to athletics. Teachers can deduct these expenses even if they do not itemize deductions. Only certain teachers qualify. An eligible educator must work at least 900 hours a school year in a school that provides elementary or secondary education (K-12). College instructors do not qualify. The term *educator* includes:

- Teacher
- Instructor
- Counselor
- Principal
- Teacher's aide

Any excess expenses may be treated as an itemized employment-related deduction on **Schedule A.** See **Publication 17,** *Your Federal Income Tax.*

29. The answer is D. Rebecca is a statutory nonemployee. Veranda properly issues Rebecca a **Form 1099-MISC** for commissions, and Rebecca files a **Schedule C** to report her income and expenses. There are generally two categories of statutory nonemployees: direct sellers and licensed real estate agents. They are treated as self-employed for all federal tax purposes, including income and employment taxes, if:

- Substantially all payments for their services as direct sellers or real estate agents are directly related to sales or other output, rather than to the number of hours worked, and
- Their services are performed under a written contract providing that they will not be treated as employees for federal tax purposes. (See **Publication 15-A**, *Employer's Supplemental Tax Guide*.)

30. The answer is D. The maximum amount of wages subject to Social Security tax for 2012 is $110,100. There is no limit on the amount of wages subject to Medicare tax. In most cases, employees in the United States must pay Social Security and Medicare taxes. The employee's payment of these taxes contributes to the individual's coverage under the U.S. Social Security and Medicare system. See **Publication 17,** *Your Federal Income Tax.*

31. The answer is B. Any amount that is reduced due to a contingency related to the child (such as the child dying, getting married, or going to school) is considered by the IRS to be child support, rather than alimony. Child support payments are neither deductible by the payer nor taxable to the payee. See **Publication 504**, *Divorced or Separated Individuals.*

32. The answer is C. The gift is not taxable, but it must be reported on Form 709. The gift limit in 2012 is $13,000. However, gift splitting between two spouses allows each spouse to gift *up to the annual limit.* Therefore, in 2012, gift splitting allows married couples to give up to $26,000 to a person without making a taxable gift. Gift splitting creates a filing requirement, and the donors must file a gift tax return (Form 709) even if half of the split gift is less than the annual exclusion. See **Publication 950**, *Introduction to Estate and Gift Taxes.*

33. The answer is A. Debt cancellation that occurs prior to the filing of bankruptcy does not qualify for the exclusion. However, canceled debts may be excluded from taxable income if the debts are forgiven as part of a Title 11 bankruptcy proceeding. The debt must be discharged through bankruptcy and not before the filing. For more examples of nontaxable debt cancellation, see **Publication 4681,** *Canceled Debts, Foreclosures, Repossessions, and Abandonments.*

34. The answer is B. All of the income is taxable except the inheritance. Amounts received in the form of gifts or inheritances are not included in taxable income. See **Publication 525,** *Taxable and Nontaxable Income.*

35. The answer is C. Tina, as the child's parent, will be the only one allowed to claim her son as a qualifying child for the Earned Income Credit. The IRS will disallow Tina's mother's claim to the dependency exemption. Tina cannot file as head of household, however, because she did not pay any of the costs of keeping up the home. The tiebreaker rules apply when two taxpayers cannot agree on who should claim the child as a qualifying child. Under the tiebreaker rule, the child is treated as a qualifying child in the following order:
- The parents, if they file a joint return
- The parent, if only one of the persons is the child's parent
- The parent with whom the child lived the longest during the tax year
- The parent with the highest adjusted gross income (AGI) if the child lived with each parent for the same amount of time during the year (if they do not file jointly)
- The person with the highest AGI, if no parent can claim the child as a qualifying child (for example, if the child did not live with either parent during the year)
- A person with the higher AGI than any parent who can claim the child as a qualifying child but does not

See **Publication 596**, *Earned Income Credit (EIC).*

36. The answer is B. Steve cannot claim the Earned Income Credit. As a noncustodial parent, he does not meet the residency test because the child did not live with him. Only a custodial parent can claim the Earned Income Credit based on a dependent child. If the noncustodial parent qualifies to claim the dependency exemption for a child, he *may* claim the Child Tax Credit if the other requirements for claiming the credit are met. The Child Tax Credit can only be claimed by the parent claiming the dependency exemption. See **Publication 596**, *Earned Income Credit.*

37. The answer is B. If a taxpayer earned over $1,500 in interest or dividend income, he is required to report the earnings on Schedule B and attach it to **Form 1040**. For more information, see **Publication 550,** *Investment Income and Expenses.*

38. The answer is C. Janice must file a **Schedule C** for the restaurant showing her net profit of $25,000, and Marty must file his own Schedule C for the carpentry business showing his net loss of $1,500. Janice's **Schedule SE** will show total earnings subject to SE tax of $25,000. Even if taxpayers file a joint return, they cannot file a joint **Schedule SE.** This is true whether one spouse or both spouses have earnings subject to self-employment tax. Married taxpayers cannot use losses from each other's businesses to offset self-employment tax. However, if an individual taxpayer operates multiple businesses, he must combine the net profit (or loss) from each to determine total earnings subject to SE tax. A loss from one business reduces the profit from another business. For example, if Janice had been running two businesses, the loss from the second business would have reduced her overall profit and also her self-employment tax. For more information, see **Publication 334,** *Tax Guide for Small Business.*

39. The answer is D. All of the charges are deductible as mortgage interest. Their mortgage interest deduction is $14,370 ($12,200 + $50 + $120 +$2,000). Taxpayers can deduct a late payment charge on a mortgage loan as mortgage interest. Sometimes, if a person pays off his home mortgage early, he must pay a penalty. The taxpayer can deduct a prepayment penalty as home mortgage interest provided the penalty is not for a specific service performed or cost incurred in connection with the mortgage loan. When taxpayers sell their home, they may deduct home mortgage interest paid up to, but not including, the date of the sale. For more information, see **Publication 936,** *Home Mortgage Interest Deduction.*

40. The answer is C. Victoria may claim $26,400 in alimony paid as an adjustment to income on her individual **Form 1040,** the total of the medical expenses and the regular alimony paid ($15,000 + $11,400). Alimony paid is an adjustment to income, and is claimed on page 1 of **Form 1040**. A taxpayer does not need to itemize deductions in order to claim an adjustment for alimony paid. The payer can deduct the full amount if it is **required** by the divorce agreement. Alimony is a payment to or for a spouse or former spouse under a divorce or separation agreement. Alimony does not include voluntary payments that are not made under a divorce or separation decree. Payments to a third party (such as the payment directly to the hospital) on behalf of an ex-spouse under the terms of a divorce or separation agreement can qualify as alimony. These include payments for an ex-spouse's medical expenses, housing costs (rent, utilities, etc.), taxes, and tuition. The payments are treated as received by the spouse and then paid to the third party. For more information, see **Publication 504,** *Divorced or Separated Individuals.*

41. The answer is B. Laverne can deduct $4,500, subject to the 2% limit, as a miscellaneous itemized deduction. Legal fees for a divorce are not a deductible expense. However, because a taxpayer must include alimony received in gross income, she can deduct legal fees related to the collection of alimony. In addition, a taxpayer may deduct fees paid to appraisers, actuaries, and accountants for tax advice or for services related to the determination of correct tax. An individual taxpayer can deduct these legal fees only if she itemizes deductions on **Schedule A (Form 1040)**. They are reported as a miscellaneous itemized deduction subject to the 2%-of-adjusted gross income limit. For more information, see **Publication 504**, *Divorced or Separated Individuals*.

42. The answer is A. Kayla meets the support test because she did not provide half of her own support. The support test determines the level of support by the child, not the person who wants to claim the child as a dependent. Children generally cannot have provided more than half of their own support during the tax year. A person's own funds are not counted as support unless they are *actually spent* for support. Since Kayla's income was deposited into a trust fund for college, it is not figured in the support calculation. Therefore, Kayla's parents may claim their daughter as a dependent on their return. See **Publication 501**, *Exemptions, Standard Deduction, and Filing Information*.

43. The answer is C. In order to qualify for the Earned Income Credit, a taxpayer cannot file **Form 2555** or **Form 2555-EZ** (which excludes foreign earned income). None of the other examples would exclude a taxpayer from claiming the EIC. Choice A is incorrect because resident aliens (green card holders) are generally taxed the same way as American citizens. Aliens are considered residents for tax purposes if they are lawful permanent residents of the United States (green card holders) at any time during the calendar year. Choice B is incorrect because head of household filing status does not disqualify a taxpayer from claiming the EIC. Choice D is incorrect because taxpayers are allowed to file a joint return with a deceased spouse in the year of death. See **Publication 596**, *Earned Income Credit (EIC)*.

44. The answer is D. The amounts for loss of wages and emotional distress are taxable as ordinary income ($4,000 + $10,000 = $14,000). The damages awarded for physical injury are not taxable. Damages for emotional distress are usually taxable, except for any amounts that were paid for medical care related to the emotional distress (such as a person who is treated for depression after an incident). See **Publication 525**, *Taxable and Nontaxable Income*.

45. The answer is C. For an involuntary conversion in a federally declared disaster area, the taxpayer has up to four years to replace his or her principal residence or to pay tax on any gain. See **Publication 544**, *Sales and Other Dispositions of Assets*.

46. The answer is B. The Adoption Credit is not refundable in 2012. Gabrielle may claim the Adoption Credit only for the amount of her tax liability of $3,500.

47. The answer is C. An employee can generally exclude $5,000 from an employer-financed flexible spending account. However, if a taxpayer is filing MFS, the maximum she can exclude is $2,500. Benefits that are in excess of those limits ($5,000/$2,500 for MFS) are included in gross income. Terry cannot take the Child and Dependent Care Credit for any of the remaining amounts because in order to claim this credit, the taxpayer's filing status must be single, head of household, qualifying W\widow(er), or married filing jointly. For more information, see **Publication 503**, *Child and Dependent Care Expenses.*

48. The answer is A. These expenses are deductible on **Schedule A** as a miscellaneous itemized deduction, subject to the 2% floor. They are deductible because they relate to Matt's investment activity. The tax code allows for a deduction for the production or collection of income, such as the management of investments. Since investing is not a self-employment activity (unless a person is a bona fide securities dealer), the costs related to this activity, such as the safe deposit box and the subscriptions to the investing magazines, would not go on **Schedule C**. For more information, see **Publication 550,** *Investment Income and Expenses.*

49. The answer is C. Tom may choose to take a lump sum distribution or start taking minimum distributions from the retirement plan. The distribution will be subject to income tax, but it will not be subject to the 10% early withdrawal penalty. He cannot roll over the inherited retirement plan into his own plan. The IRS generally imposes a 10% early withdrawal penalty on early distributions (distributions before age 59½). However, there are many exceptions to this rule, and one is when the original owner of the plan dies. Since Tom was Leigh's son, he cannot choose to roll over the amounts into his own plan (only surviving spouses have the option to do this). Current tax law allows a beneficiary of an inherited IRA to choose between taking a full distribution immediately, which is taxable, or continue tax-deferred growth and take minimum annual distributions over his lifetime. See **Publication 590,** *Individual Retirement Arrangements,* for additional information.

50. The answer is D. The Smiths must report the amount that was credited to their mutual fund account, regardless of the amount that was actually distributed to them. The amounts from a mutual fund are always reported as a long-term capital gain regardless of how long someone has held the shares. Investors may have to pay taxes on any capital gains distribution they receive — even if the fund performed poorly after they bought shares. That is because the law requires mutual funds to distribute capital gains to shareholders if they sell securities for a profit

231

that cannot be offset by a loss. For more information, see **Publication 564,** *Mutual Fund Distributions.*

51. The answer is D. Ellen's at-risk amount for this activity includes all her costs, investment, and the debt that she personally absorbs for the business. Since Ellen used her own credit cards for the purchase of business materials, this is also considered an investment in her business. If any of the debt had been nonrecourse, then an individual is not considered at-risk for amounts that are protected from loss through nonrecourse financing. See **Publication 334,** *Tax Guide for Small Business.*

52. The answer is B. Generally, the expenses of renting a property, such as maintenance, insurance, taxes, and interest, can be deducted from the rental income. If a taxpayer owns a partial interest in rental property, he can deduct expenses paid according to the percentage of ownership. The cost is a repair, not an improvement, because the window was broken. If all the windows had been replaced with energy-efficient windows, it would have been considered an improvement and would have been added to the property's basis. For more information, see **Publication 527,** *Residential Rental Property.*

53. The answer is D. The full amount of $5,000 is taxable to Clark because the IRS stipulates that if a student is not a degree candidate, all scholarships are subject to federal income tax, even if it is spent on educational expenses. The student must also attend an eligible educational institution. For more information, see **Publication 970,** *Tax Benefits for Education.*

54. The answer is A. The American Opportunity Credit is a maximum credit of up to $2,500 for the cost of qualified tuition and related expenses paid during the taxable year for each eligible student. Taxpayers receive a tax credit based on 100% of the first $2,000 of tuition, fees, and course materials paid, plus 25% of the next $2,000 of qualified expenses paid. This is a per-student limit. The expenses for Lynette do not qualify, because the American Opportunity Credit can only be claimed for expenses for the first four years of post-secondary education. The American Opportunity Credit is partially refundable in 2012. For Lynette's expenses, Ursula may be able to take the Lifetime Learning Credit instead.

55. The answer is B. Because David's new job location is 57 miles farther from his former home than the distance from his former home was to his old job location, he meets the distance test. A move will meet the distance test if the new main job location is *at least 50 miles* farther from the former home than the old job location was from the former home. For example, if the old job location was three miles from the former home, the new main job location must be at least 53 miles from that former home. Deductible moving expenses include moving household goods and personal effects (including in-transit or foreign-move storage expenses), and traveling (including lodging but not meals) to a new home. A taxpayer can include the cost of storage and insuring household goods within any period of 30 consecutive days before or after the moving day. For more information, see **Publication 521**, *Moving Expenses*.

56. The answer is B. Individuals who have been physically present for at least 183 days over a three-year period, including the current year, meet the requirements of the substantial presence test. This includes 183 days over a three-year period comprising the current year (must be at least 31 days); one-third of the days in the first year before the current year; and one-sixth of the days in the second year before the current year. The rules define residency for tax purposes in a way that is very different from immigration laws. Although the immigration laws of the United States refer to aliens as immigrants, non-immigrants, and undocumented (illegal) aliens, the **tax** laws of the United States refer only to *resident* and *nonresident aliens*. In general, the controlling principle is that resident aliens are taxed in the same manner as U.S. citizens on their worldwide income, and nonresident aliens are taxed according to special rules contained in certain parts of the Internal Revenue Code. A major distinguishing feature of this special tax treatment concerns the source of income: a nonresident alien is subject to federal income tax only on income that is derived from sources within the United States and/or income that is effectively connected with a U.S. trade or business. On the other hand, a taxpayer that meets residency tests for the U.S. will be taxed on worldwide income. For more information, see **Publication 519**, *U.S. Tax Guide for Aliens*.

57. The answer is B. Ramon can claim head of household status since his spouse is a nonresident alien who will not file a joint return with him, and he meets all the other qualifications for head of household. There is a special exception in the tax code that allows U.S. citizens and resident alien spouses who live with their nonresident alien spouses to file as head of household. All of the following requirements must be met:

- The taxpayer is a U.S. citizen or resident alien for the entire year and meets all the rules for head of household except for living with the nonresident alien spouse.
- The nonresident alien spouse does not meet the substantial presence test.
- The nonresident alien spouse does not choose to file a joint return.

For more information, see **Publication 54**, *Tax Guide for US Citizens and Resident Aliens Abroad*.

58. The answer is B. Since their combined gross income is $16,000 (which is under $21,300), Carol and Joaquin are not required to file a return. They do not qualify for the Earned Income Credit because they are both over 65 years old. (This age test only applies to taxpayers without any qualifying children.) See **Publication 17,** *Your Federal Income Tax.*

59. The answer is C. Self-employed individuals generally are required to file an annual return and pay estimated tax quarterly. A taxpayer is required to file an income tax return if net earnings from self-employment are $400 or more. See **Publication 17,** *Your Federal Income Tax.*

60. The answer is D. If a taxpayer must file a U.S. tax return, or is listed on a tax return as a spouse or dependent and does not have and cannot obtain a valid SSN, he must apply for an ITIN.

61. The answer is B. Taxpayers should keep the supporting documentation for their tax returns for at least three years from the date the return was filed, or two years from the date the tax was paid, whichever is later. This also includes applicable worksheets, receipts, and other forms. For more information see **Publication 552,** *Recordkeeping for Individuals.*

62. The answer is B. Alice's original basis per share was $11 ([[$1,050 + $50 broker's commission= $1,100] ÷ 100). After the stock dividend, her $1,100 basis must be spread over 110 shares (100 original shares plus the additional 10 shares). Therefore, if Alice's basis in the stock was $1,100 for 100 shares, the ten additional shares mean Alice's basis per share decreased to $10 per share ($1,100 ÷ 110). For additional information, see **Publication 551,** *Basis of Assets.*

63. The answer is C. Both taxpayers must file. Taxpayers who are under 65, use the married filing separately status, and earn at least $3,800 are required to file a return.

64. The answer is A. Although Lenny owned the ten shares he received as a nontaxable stock dividend for only three months, all the stock has a long-term holding period. Stock acquired as a stock dividend has the same holding period as the original stock owned. Because he bought the stock for $1,500 three years ago, his holding period is long-term. Lenny has a long-term capital gain of $530 on the sale of the 510 shares.

65. The answer is B. Nora does not need to itemize in order to claim the adjustment for the penalty on early withdrawal of savings. The deduction can be claimed on **Form 1040** or **Form 1040A**. She cannot use Form **1040EZ**. See **Publication 17,** *Your Federal Income Tax.*

66. The answer is C. If a child of divorced or separated parents is claimed as a dependent on either parent's return, each parent may deduct the medical expenses they individually paid for the child. This is a special exception for divorced and separated individuals. For more information, see **Publication 502,** *Medical and Dental Expenses.*

67. The answer is A. Harvey is over the age limit for a traditional IRA contribution. If Harvey was under the age of 70½ and married filing separately, he could contribute no more than his $2,000 compensation. There is no age limit for Roth IRA contributions. For more information, see **Publication 590,** *Individual Retirement Arrangements.*

68. The answer is D. All her expenses are qualifying medical expenses, including the amounts paid for her son. If a child of divorced or separated parents is claimed as a dependent on *either* parent's return, each parent may deduct the medical expenses he or she individually paid for the child. Taxpayers can deduct only the amount of unreimbursed medical expenses that exceeds 7.5% of their adjusted gross income (AGI). The answer is figured as follows:

- $6,600 + $2,000 = $8,600 qualified medical expenses
- $38,000 X 7.5% = $2,850 AGI limit
- $8,600 - $2,850 = $5,750 allowable deduction on Schedule A.

See **Publication 502,** *Medical and Dental Expenses.*

69. The answer is A. The term points is used to describe certain interest charges paid by a borrower to obtain a home mortgage. Points may also be called loan origination fees, maximum loan charges, loan discount points, or discount points. A taxpayer generally cannot deduct the full amount of points in the year paid. Taxpayers must calculate and amortize points on a monthly basis, calculated over the life of the loan. In this case, the taxpayer had a 30 year loan which began on November 1, 2012. The answer is figured as follows:

- $1,800 ÷ 30 years = $60 in deductible interest per year
- $60 ÷ 12 months = $5 of interest per month
- $5 X two months (November and December) = $10 of deductible interest in 2012

This means that Whitney may claim a deduction of $10 in 2012. See **Publication 936**, *Home Mortgage Interest Deduction.*

70. The answer is C. Olga's total itemized deduction for taxes is $4,000 ($2,000 + $1,900 +$100 = $4,000). The $250 homeowners' association fee is not deductible. All the other costs are deductible as taxes. For more information, see **Publication 600**, *State and Local General Sales Taxes* and **Publication 17,** *Your Federal Income Tax.*

71. The answer Is B. Hana's distribution was not made after the five-year period beginning with the first taxable year she made a contribution to her Roth IRA. Therefore, only the return of her regular contributions is not included in her gross income. Any earnings would be taxable. She would also have to report the withdrawal on **Form 8606**, *Nondeductible IRAs*, even though portions of the withdrawal might not be taxable. Distributions from a Roth IRA are tax-free and may be excluded from income if the following requirements are met:

- The distribution is made after the five-year period beginning with the first taxable year for which a contribution was made to a Roth IRA, **and** the distribution is:
  - Made on or after age 59½, or
  - Made because the taxpayer was disabled, or
  - Made to a beneficiary or to an estate, or
  - To pay certain qualified first-time homebuyer amounts (up to a $10,000 lifetime limit)

72. The answer is A. Keith and Tiffany can deduct the interest on their loans because the total of these loans throughout 2012 ($72,000) does not exceed $100,000, and the total amount of the home equity loan ($72,000) is not more than the home's fair market value minus any outstanding acquisition debt ($230,000 - $30,000 = $200,000). For more information, see **Publication 936,** *Home Mortgage Interest Deduction.*

73. The answer is C. In the case of charity volunteers, transportation expenses, including bus fare, parking fees, tolls, and either the cost of gas and oil or a standard mileage deduction of 14 cents per mile, can be deductible as an itemized deduction on Schedule A. Raffle tickets (or any type of gambling expense) are never deductible as a charitable contribution, even if the event directly benefits a charity. Blood donations are not deductible, but the cost of travel to make a blood donation is a deductible expense. A taxpayer cannot deduct a donation that is made directly to a needy individual.

74. The answer is B. Travel for medical reasons is deductible as a medical expense. However, there are certain restrictions. The cost of meals is not deductible. Lodging costs are limited to $50 a night. However, a taxpayer can also include the cost of lodging for an additional person, so a parent traveling with a child can deduct up to $100 per night (2 X $50 limit). The cost of plane fare, mileage, or other transportation expenses is fully deductible. The answer is figured as follows:

Hotel costs for seven days (limited to $100 per night)	$700
Meals while traveling	NO
Cost of train tickets	$220
Qualified medical expenses	**$920**

See **Publication 502**, *Medical and Dental Expenses*.

75. The answer is B. The $30,000 in debt cancellation is treated as a reduction in basis in the property and should be reported on **Form 982**. The debt cancellation is covered by the qualified principal residence indebtedness exclusion and is not counted as taxable income on the return. **Form 8949** and **Schedule D** are not required because Paloma did not dispose of the home.

76. The answer is B. Mai Lin may only deduct $15,000 ($25,000 - [50% x $20,000]) of the rental losses in the current year. Taxpayers who actively participate in a rental real estate activity can deduct up to $25,000 of loss from the activity from non-passive income. But the $25,000 allowance is phased out if modified adjusted gross income (MAGI) is between $100,000 and $150,000. The $25,000 limit gets phased out by $1 for every $2 that the taxpayer earns over $100,000. If the taxpayer's MAGI is $150,000 or more ($75,000 or more if married filing separately), there is no special allowance. This special allowance is an exception to the general rule disallowing losses in excess of income from passive activities. For more information, see **Publication 527**, *Residential Rental Property*.

77. The answer is A. All tips are taxable. The value of noncash tips, such as tickets, passes, or other items of value, are only subject to income tax (not to FICA or FUTA). Noncash tips should not be reported to the employer. The employee is not required to pay Social Security and Medicare taxes on these tips. See **Publication 531,** *Reporting Tip Income*.

78. The answer is C. Raymond is allowed to roll over his traditional IRA into a government deferred-compensation plan (section 457 plan).Taxpayers are allowed to roll over their traditional IRA to any of the following plans without incurring tax or penalty:

- A rollover into another traditional IRA
- A qualified plan
- A tax-sheltered annuity plan (section 403(b) plan)
- A government deferred-compensation plan (section 457 plan)

IRAs cannot be held jointly, so spouses are not allowed to roll over funds into each other's retirement plans. However, a taxpayer is allowed to roll over an IRA from a *deceased* spouse. After death, the surviving spouse may elect to treat the IRA as his own, and roll it over into another traditional IRA.

79. The answer is B. The sales price was $4,400, which was $1,900 more than the original basis of $2,500 ($2,400 cost + $100 commission) of the shares. The broker's commission would be deducted when figuring the amount of gain. The gain is the difference between the sales price and the adjusted basis.

80. The answer is B. The adjusted basis of the house at the time of the change in its use was $182,000. The basis for depreciation on the house is the fair market value on the date of the change ($147,000), because it is less than Carlos's adjusted basis ($182,000). When a primary residence is changed to rental use, the basis for depreciation will be the lesser of fair market value or adjusted basis on the date of conversion. Land is not subject to depreciation. For more information, see **Publication 527**, *Residential Rental Property*.

81. The answer is B. On Kyle's tax return, he can deduct $3,000 of the capital loss. The unused part of the loss, $4,000 ($7,000 – $3,000), can be carried over to the following year. Kyle's adjusted gross income is $29,000 ($32,000 – $3,000 capital loss). Capital losses can be deducted on a taxpayer's return and used to reduce other income, such as wages, up to an annual limit of $3,000 (or $1,500 if married filing separately).

82. The answer is A. In general, the deadlines for performing certain actions applicable to his taxes are extended for the period of Kevin's service in the combat zone, plus 180 days after his last day in the combat zone. This extension applies to the filing and paying of his income taxes that would have been due April 15. During his extension period, assessment and collection deadlines will be extended, and he will not be charged interest or penalties attributable to the extension period.

83. The answer is B. The donor is generally responsible for paying the gift tax. A gift is not taxable to the recipient but may need to be reported on Form 709. The annual exclusion for gifts made to a donee during 2012 is $13,000, unchanged from

2011. The general rule is that any gift over $13,000 is a taxable gift. However, there are many exceptions to this rule. Generally, the following gifts are not taxable gifts:

- Gifts that are not more than the annual exclusion ($13,000 in 2012).
- Tuition or medical expenses paid for someone directly to a college or a medical provider (the educational and medical exclusions).
- Gifts to a spouse who is a U.S. citizen.
- Gifts to a political organization for its own use.

84. The answer is B. Josh and Heather may each make a maximum contribution of $5,000 to a traditional IRA. This is because Josh, who has no compensation, can add Heather's compensation, reduced by the amount of her IRA contribution ($50,000 − $5,000 = $45,000) to his own compensation ($0) to figure his maximum contribution to a traditional IRA. For more information, see **Publication 590,** *Individual Retirement Arrangements.*

85. The answer is C. If a taxpayer claims a deduction for a charitable contribution of noncash property worth more than $5,000, the taxpayer is required to obtain a qualified appraisal and must fill out Form 8283. See **Publication 526,** *Charitable Contributions.*

86. The answer is B. The maximum amount taxpayers may claim for the nonrefundable Child Tax Credit is $1,000 for each qualifying child. The amount actually claimed on Form 1040 depends on the taxpayer's tax liability, modified adjusted gross income (MAGI), and filing status. This credit is phased out once MAGI reaches the following income levels:

- Married filing jointly - $110,000
- Single, head of household, or qualifying widow(er) - $75,000
- Married filing separately - $55,000

87. The answer is B. Chelsea has a taxable gain of $30,000. Her basis in the new home is $80,000. The part of her gain that is taxable is $30,000 ($130,000 − $100,000), the unspent part of the payment from the insurance company. The rest of the gain ($20,000) is not taxable, because it was reinvested into the replacement home. This follows the rules for involuntary conversions (IRC section 1033). The basis of the new home is figured as follows:

Cost of replacement home	$100,000
Minus: Gain not recognized	($20,000)
Basis of the replacement home	$80,000

For more information, see **Publication 523**, *Selling Your Home.*

88. The answer is C. Chuck can exclude up to $250,000 of gain on a separate or joint return for 2012. The $500,000 maximum exclusion for joint returns does not apply because Jayme does not meet the use test. For more information, see **Publication 523**, *Selling Your Home.*

89. The answer is A. There is a special rule known as the *15-Day Rule* for homes that are rented for fewer than 15 days a year. In this case, the rental income is not reported. The mortgage interest on a second home or a vacation home is deductible on Schedule A. For more information, see **Publication 527,** *Residential Rental Property (Including the Rental of Vacation Homes).*

90. The answer is C. Wilson's office is 20% (240 ÷ 1,200) of the total area of his home. Therefore, his business percentage is 20%. His expenses for the year were $12,000 ($1,000 per month x 12 months) and $600 ($50 x 12 months). The answer is figured as follows:

$12,000 total rent
$600 total utilities
$12,600 total expenses for the year X 20% (business use percentage) = $2,520.

For more information, see **Publication 587,** *Business Use of Your Home.*

91. The answer is C. Angel's deductible expense would be calculated as follows: $300 + $245 + $150 + $30 ($60 X 50%) = $725. All of the expenses are qualifying work-related educational expenses, but the meal expense must be reduced by 50%. Employees can deduct work-related educational expenses as a miscellaneous itemized deduction on Form 1040, Schedule A; the expense is subject to the 2% of adjusted gross income limit. For more information on educational expenses, refer to **Publication 970,** *Tax Benefits for Education.*

92. The answer is D. Taxpayers can deduct the cost and upkeep of uniforms, if the uniforms are not suitable for everyday use. (Taxpayers cannot deduct the cost of regular clothing used for work.) The clothing must be specifically required by the employer. Scott can only claim the amount of expenses that exceeds 2% of his adjusted gross income. The expense is deductible on Schedule A (Form 1040) as a miscellaneous itemized deduction, subject to the 2% floor. For more information on work-related expenses and miscellaneous deductions, see **Publication 529,** *Miscellaneous Deductions.*

93. The answer is A. The value of the free use of a taxpayer's property is not a charitable deduction. Qualified contributions must be made in cash or property. For more information, see **Publication 526**, *Charitable Contributions.*

94. The answer is A. The casualty loss is figured as follows:

Basis of property	$4,000
Minus (*the $100 Rule)	(100)
Allowable loss	$3,900
Less 10% of $24,000 AGI (*the 10% Rule)	(2,400)
Audrey's loss deduction	$1,500

Individuals are required to claim their casualty losses as an itemized deduction on Form 1040, Schedule A. For property held for personal use (not business-use property), the taxpayer must subtract $100 from each casualty that occurred during the year. Those amounts are then added before 10% of adjusted gross income is subtracted from the total to calculate the allowable casualty and theft losses for the year. For more information, see **Publication 547**, *Casualties, Disasters, and Thefts.*

95. The answer is A. The credit amount limit for energy-efficient windows in 2012 is 10%, up to $200. The 2012 credit for windows is limited to a combined limit for all tax years after 2005 of $200. For certain other energy-efficient improvements, a taxpayer can deduct a maximum of $500 for all tax years after 2005. The Residential Energy Efficient Property Credit increases the energy tax credit for homeowners who make energy efficient improvements to their existing homes. This credit applies to improvements such as adding insulation, energy-efficient exterior windows, and energy-efficient heating and air conditioning systems.

96. The answer is A. Unlike a traditional IRA, Roth IRAs do not require minimum distributions at age 70½. For more information, refer to **Publication 590**, *Individual Retirement Arrangements (IRAs).*

97. The answer is D. Gregory has a wash sale, and he cannot take the capital loss. In general, a wash sale occurs when a taxpayer sells stock or other securities at a loss and, within 30 days before or after the sale or disposition, the taxpayer buys or acquires substantially identical stock or securities. The wash sale rules also apply if a taxpayer sells stock and then the taxpayer's spouse immediately buys identical stock. Since Gregory's wife purchased identical securities within 30 days after Gregory sold his stock, he has a wash sale. The wash sale rules apply regardless of whether a husband and wife file separate tax returns. Gregory's $4,000 loss is instead added to the cost basis of the new stock. The result is an increased basis in the new stock. This adjustment postpones the loss deduction until the disposition of the new stock or securities. The holding period for the new stock includes the holding period of the stock or securities sold.

98. The answer is D. For income tax purposes, Pastor Green excludes $31,000 from gross income ($24,000 fair rental value of the parsonage plus $7,000 from the allowance for utility costs). He will report $60,000 as regular income ($59,500 salary plus $500 of unused utility allowance). His income for SE tax purposes, however, is $91,000 ($67,000 salary + $24,000 fair rental value of the parsonage). Services that a duly ordained, commissioned, or licensed minister performs in the exercise of his ministry are generally covered under the Self-Employment Contributions Act. That means the minister is exempt from Social Security and Medicare withholding, but he is then responsible for paying self-employment tax on his net earnings from self-employment. The fair rental value of a minister's parsonage is excludable from income only for income tax purposes. No exclusion applies for self-employment tax purposes. For more information, refer to **Publication 517**, *Social Security and Other Information for Members of the Clergy and Religious Workers.*

99. The answer is A. A taxpayer can include in medical expenses the costs of buying, training, and maintaining a guide dog or other service animal to assist a visually-impaired or disabled person. For more information, see **Publication 502**, *Medical and Dental Expenses.*

100. The answer is B. Brock's gross profit percentage is 12.5% ($15,000 ÷ $120,000). Brock would report 12.5% of each payment, (12.5% x $30,000) = $3,750), as installment sale income from the sale for the tax year he receives the payment (after subtracting interest, if any). The balance of each payment is the tax-free return of his adjusted basis. For more information, refer to **Publication 537,** *Installment Sales.*

Businesses: Answers

Exam #1 Businesses: Answers

1. The answer is A. Since Daley Company is on the accrual basis, it reports income when it is *earned*, not when it is received. Daley must include the entire payment of $22,000 in 2012 income because that is when it was earned.

2. The answer is C. Derrick must include $10,000 in partnership income on his tax return. The answer is figured as follows:

1. $55,000 - $5,000 guaranteed payment = $50,000 in ordinary income
2. $50,000 X 10% = $5,000 Derrick's share of the partnership's ordinary income
3. ($5,000 guaranteed payment + $5,000 ($50,000 × 10%) distributive share) = $10,000

Guaranteed payments are determined without regard to the partnership's income. They are deducted as a business expense when figuring the partnership's ordinary income. The individual partner who receives the guaranteed payments reports the payments on **Schedule E (Form 1040)** as ordinary income, along with his or her distributive share of the partnership's other ordinary income. See **Publication 541,** *Partnerships.*

3. The answer is D. Codex should first carry back the $8,000 excess capital losses to a prior year, and carry forward any remaining amounts. The treatment of capital losses for C corporations is very different than the treatment for individuals. There is no favorable treatment for long-term capital gains for corporations. Also, unlike individuals, there is no $3,000 allowance for capital losses. A corporation can only offset capital losses with capital gains. If there are any unused losses, the corporation carries its capital losses backward up to three years, and forward up to five years. Any capital losses that are not used within the three year and five year period is forfeited. A corporation also cannot choose which year to carry back the losses. The losses must be used in the earliest year they can be used.

4. The answer is B. Form 1099-DIV is used to report the distribution of dividends to shareholders.

5. The answer is C. By definition, an S corporation is not a personal service corporation. A C corporation is classified as a personal service corporation if its shareholders are also employee-owners that perform the personal services within the corporation (more than 20% of the corporation's compensation costs). If a corporation is classified as a PSC, there are three major drawbacks:

- Personal service corporations pay a flat corporate rate of 35%. The graduated corporate tax rates that apply to other C corporations do not apply to PSCs.
- A personal service corporation cannot elect to have a fiscal year without prior IRS approval.
- Unlike other C corporations, the at-risk rules and passive loss rules apply to personal service corporations.

6. The answer is D. The capital loss carryforward is $17,000. The net capital losses for 2012 are $50,000 ($100,000 - $50,000). Corporate capital losses are carried back three years and carried forward five years. The net capital losses cannot be carried back to 2009 because there were no capital gains that year, so the $24,000 in gains from 2010 must be offset first. This leaves $26,000 in capital losses. The $9,000 in capital gains from 2011 may also be offset, which leaves a carryforward of $17,000. This amount may be applied to any gains that are earned in the subsequent five tax years. *Note: Do not confuse capital loss carryback rules with the net operating loss (NOL) carryback rules, which are different.

7. The answer is D. The transfer is not a qualified 351 exchange because Runway Corporation is an investment company. In a qualified section 351 exchange, no gain or loss is recognized provided:
- The transferor receives only stock in exchange for property (or money), and
- The transferor is in control of the corporation immediately after the exchange. This means at least 80% of the voting stock and at least 80% of all other classes of stock of the corporation.

However, section 351 does not apply when:
- The corporation is an investment company.
- The transferor transfers property during a bankruptcy in exchange for stock used to pay creditors.
- The stock received in exchange for the corporation's debt (other than a security) or for interest on the corporation's debt (including a security) that accrued while the transferor held the debt.

In these cases, the nonrecognition treatment that is afforded by section 351 would be disallowed.

8. The answer is C. Payments made to an employee under an accountable plan would not be included on the employee's Form W-2. These are amounts that are not taxable to the employee and not reportable as wages. An accountable plan is a formal or written arrangement whereby an employer reimburses an employee for business expenses. The employee provides proof of the expense, and the employer is allowed to deduct the expenses as normal business expenses. The employee does not have to recognize the reimbursements as income.

9. The answer is D. A closely held corporation generally has a small number of shareholders (usually family) and no public market for its corporate stock. The corporate ownership and management often overlap. A corporation is considered to be closely held if all of the following apply:

- It is not a personal service corporation.
- At any time during the last half of the tax year, more than 50% of the value of its outstanding stock is, directly or indirectly, owned by or for five or fewer individuals. An individual in this case includes certain trusts and private foundations.

Closely held corporations are exempt from certain at-risk and passive activity limits, which can provide substantial tax benefits.

10. The answer is B. Most real property is considered like-kind"\ property. For example, real property that is improved may be exchanged with vacant land. One exception for real estate is that property within the United States cannot be exchanged with property outside of the United States. In order for the exchange to be valid, both properties must be used in a business, or held for investment. Property used primarily for personal use, such as a primary residence or vacation home, does not qualify for like-kind exchange treatment. The other answers are all prohibited under the section 1031 rules. Like-kind property does not include the exchange of property from inside the United States with property from outside the United States, or the exchange of property for personal use with property used for business or trade (personal-use property is excluded altogether.) Section 1031 also specifically excludes the following:

- Inventory
- Stocks, bonds, or notes
- Other securities or debt
- Partnership interests

Taxpayers must report a section 1031 exchange on Form 8824, *Like-Kind Exchanges*. See **Publication 544,** *Sales and Other Dispositions of Assets*.

11. The answer is A. A corporate distribution is taxable to a shareholder as a dividend, but only to the extent of earnings and profits (including current and accumulated profits). Any distribution in excess of earnings is treated as a return of capital and would reduce the shareholder's basis in his stock. In this case, there are two equal shareholders, April and Charles; the gross distribution is $100,000; and the corporation only had $90,000 in E&P. The answer is figured as follows:

- Distribution to Charles: $50,000 = ($100,000 X 50%)
- Amount treated as a dividend: $45,000 = (90,000 X 50%)
- Amount treated as a reduction in shareholder stock basis: $5,000 ($50,000 - $45,000)

12. The answer is C. With regards to corporations, "book income" and tax income are reported differently. Differences in accounting rules for financial (book) and tax reporting purposes can lead to differences in the amount of income reported to shareholders and tax authorities. A tax professional must understand how to reconcile "book" and tax differences. The answer is figured as follows:

Net book income	$90,000
Capital losses	$8,000
Capital gains	$4,000
Tax exempt interest	$12,000
Accrued federal income tax	$22,000

Starting book income	$90,000
Add back:	
Federal income tax	$22,000
Net capital losses ($8,000 -$4,000)	$4,000
Subtotal	$116,000

Subtract	$116,000
Tax exempt interest income	-$12,000
Taxable income	**$104,000**

The differences in "book income" and taxable income are reconciled for tax reporting purposes on Schedule M-1 (or on Schedule M-3 for large corporations) of Form 1120. Some examples of items that would be included in the reconciliation on Schedule M-1 or Schedule M-3, if applicable, are:

- Charitable contribution carryover (the amount of charitable contributions that are disallowed for tax purposes and must be carried over to the next taxable year.)
- Travel and entertainment in excess of the allowable 50% limit.
- Income subject to tax that is not included in the books.
- Federal income taxes paid or accrued, which are deductible for accounting purposes but not for tax purposes.
- Advance rental income.

13. The answer is D. Contributions to the capital of a corporation, whether or not by shareholders, are paid-in capital. These contributions are not taxable to the corporation. The basis of property contributed to capital by a person other than a shareholder is zero. See **Publication 542**, *Corporations*.

14. The answer is B. The corporation's basis in the land is $650,000. To figure this problem, begin with the contributing shareholder's basis in the building (Logan's basis is $450,000), then add any gain that is recognized by Logan. Logan's recognized gain is the **lesser of:** his realized gain or the boot received in the transaction. Logan's realized gain is $250,000 ($700,000 FMV - $450,000 basis). The boot he received was $200,000. Therefore, the gain recognized is $200,000, and the corporation's basis in the land is $650,000 ($450,000 basis + $200,000 boot).

15. The answer is D. Section 1245 applies to most depreciable personal property, but generally not to real property (buildings, homes, etc.). Section 1245 property does not include most *permanent* buildings and structural components. The term "building" also includes a house, barn, warehouse, or garage.

16. The answer is C. Assessments for local improvements are items that tend to increase the value of property, such as streets and sidewalks, and are added to the basis of a taxpayer's property. These items cannot be deducted as taxes. However, a business can deduct assessments for local benefits if they are for the maintenance, repairs, or interest charges related to the improvements.

17. The answer is B. Lori's basis in the stock after a tax-free exchange under section 351 is $3,700 ($6,200 basis of the machinery - $2,500 relief of liabilities that was assumed by the corporation). Generally, when liabilities are assumed in an exchange, the party that is relieved of debt is treated as having a gain (boot). However, in a section 351 transaction, the liability relief is not treated as boot for recognition purposes. Instead, the basis of the transferor's stock is reduced by the liability assumed by the corporation. See **Publication 542,** *Corporations*.

18. The answer is C. Golden Touch Partnership is required to use April 30 as its tax year-end. A partnership generally must conform its tax year to its partners' tax years. If multiple partners having the same tax year own an interest in partnership profits and capital of more than 50% (a majority interest), the partnership must use the tax year of those partners. In this case, since Daisy Corporation and Aster Corporation both share the same tax year and their combined partnership interest exceeds 50%, then Golden Touch Partnership is required to use April 30 as it tax year-end.

19. The answer is B. A distribution that gives cash or other property to some shareholders and an increase in the percentage interest in the corporation's assets or earnings and profits to other shareholders would cause a stock dividend to be a taxable event. Generally, stock dividends and stock rights are not taxable. However, in the following cases, a stock dividend would be taxable:

- The distribution gives cash or other property to some shareholders and an increase in the percentage interest in the corporation's assets or earnings and profits to other shareholders.
- Some shareholders are permitted to choose cash or other property instead of stock or stock rights.
- The distribution is in convertible preferred stock, or some shareholders are allowed to receive preferred stock and others receive common stock.

If a stock dividend is deemed taxable, it would be included in the shareholder's income at its FMV at the time of distribution. See **Publication 542,** *Corporations.*

20. The answer is A. If a corporation pays an employee who is also a shareholder a salary that is unreasonably high considering the services actually performed, the excessive part of the salary may be treated as a constructive distribution of earnings to the employee-shareholder. For more information on corporate distributions to shareholders, see **Publication 542,** *Corporations.*

21. The answer is A. Christopher must recognize dividend income of $150,000 and a taxable gain of $20,000. He must also reduce his stock basis to zero. In this case, the shareholder received dividend income of $150,000 (which was the amount of the corporation's accumulated earnings and profits). Christopher's stock basis was $30,000, so, after reducing his stock basis to zero, he must recognize a taxable gain of $20,000, which is the excess of the distribution over the amount of his stock basis. The answer is figured as follows:

($200,000 distribution - $150,000 accumulated E&P) = $50,000
($50,000 remaining distribution - $30,000 stock basis [reduced to zero]) = $20,000
$20,000 is treated as a gain from the sale or exchange of stock.

See **Publication 542,** *Corporations*.

22. The answer is A. Jerry recognizes a taxable gain of $175,000 on the transaction. In order for the transfer to be nontaxable, Jerry would have to have at least 80% of the total stock. Since he only received 75% of the stock, the exchange does not qualify for section 351 nonrecognition treatment. See **Publication 542,** *Corporations.*

23. The answer is B. Susan's basis in the factory machinery is $12,000. Her partnership basis is reduced to zero. In a nonliquidating distribution, Susan's basis in the partnership must first be reduced by the cash distribution ($6,000). Her basis in the machinery then would be the lesser of: her remaining basis or the partnership's adjusted basis in the machinery. The answer is figured as follows:

Susan's starting partnership basis	$18,000
Reduced by cash distribution	($6,000)
Lesser of: $12,000 remaining basis or the partnership's basis in the property	$12,000

24. The answer is B. The domestic production activities deduction cannot exceed 50% of W-2 wages paid. The domestic production activities deduction, authorized by IRC section 199, is designed to stimulate domestic manufacturing and farming. In 2012, the DPAD is equal to 9% of the *lesser* of:

- The business's qualified production activities income, or
- Taxable income determined without regard to the DPAD.

The deduction is limited to 50% of wages paid on Form W-2 by the company for the year. Therefore, if a company does not have any employees, it is not eligible for this deduction.

25. The answer is A. A *de minimis* fringe benefit is deductible by the employer but not taxable to the employee. The IRS defines a de minimis benefit in this way: a benefit for which, considering its value and the frequency with which it is provided, is so small as to make accounting for it unreasonable or impractical. De minimis fringe benefits include occasional snacks, coffee, or doughnuts provided in a company's break room, and limited employee use of a business copy machine for personal purposes. The following are common examples of fringe benefits that do **not** qualify as *de minimis*:

- Cash (except for rare and infrequent meal money to allow overtime work)
- Cash equivalents (i.e., savings bond, gift certificate for general merchandise at a department store)
- Certain transportation passes or costs
- Use of employer's apartment, vacation home, or boat
- Commuting use of employer's vehicle more than once a month.
- Membership in a country club or athletic facility

These exceptions are outlined in **IRS Publication 15-B,** *Taxable Fringe Benefit Guide.*

26. The answer is A. An S corporation may have a shareholder that is an estate. S corporations cannot be owned by C corporations, partnerships, or nonresident aliens. Some exempt entities (notably 501(c)3 charities) may own stock in an S corporation. Answer "C" is incorrect because an S corporation that was previously a C corporation cannot have passive investment income that exceeds 25% of its gross receipts for three consecutive tax years. If this occurs, the S election will be terminated and the corporation will revert back to C corporate status. Answer "D" is incorrect because an S corporation cannot have *more than* 100 shareholders.

27. The answer is B. This is a section 1033 involuntary conversion. Travis has until December 31, 2014 to reinvest the insurance proceeds in a new tractor. The replacement period begins on the date of the casualty. The replacement period generally ends two years after the close of the first tax year in which the taxpayer realizes gain from the involuntary conversion. Travis is not required to report the insurance proceeds on his tax return unless he fails to reinvest the proceeds in qualifying replacement property.

28. The answer is C. Guaranteed payments are paid in accordance with the partnership agreement, and they are treated as salary payments. Guaranteed payments are deductible from the partnership's ordinary income. See **Publication 541,** *Partnerships.*

29. The answer is C. Kerry's basis in her partnership interest is calculated by adding the cash contributed ($10,000) to the basis of the property contributed ($18,000). Her partnership interest is $28,000 ($10,000 + $18,000). See **Publication 541,** *Partnerships.*

30. The answer is A. Unlike limited partners, general partners have joint and several liability in a partnership's debt obligations. Limited partners are only liable up to the amount of their investment. See **Publication 541,** *Partnerships.*

31. The answer is A. An individual partner's basis is increased by his share of taxable and nontaxable income. Since Christian is a 50% partner, the income items must be allocated based on his partnership percentage. The answer is figured as follows:

Starting partnership basis		$1,000
Ordinary income X 50%	$40,000	$20,000
Tax exempt income X 50%	$20,000	$10,000
Rental income X 50%	$4,000	$2,000
Christian's year-end basis		**$33,000**

See **Publication 541,** *Partnerships.*

32. The answer is A. A partnership terminates when one of the following events takes place:

- All its operations are discontinued.
- At least 50% of the total interest in partnership capital and profits is sold or exchanged within a 12-month period, including a sale or exchange to another partner.

Answer "B" is incorrect, because a corporation can legally own an interest in a partnership. Answer "C" is incorrect because the death of a partner will not necessarily dissolve a partnership if the partners have expressly agreed to continue the partnership. Answer "D" is incorrect because there must be a change of 50% in *both* capital and profits for the partnership to terminate. Therefore, a sale of a 40% interest in capital and a 60% interest in profits will not automatically terminate the partnership. ***Exception:** Unlike other partnerships, an "electing large partnership" does not terminate on the sale or exchange of 50% or more of the partnership interests within a 12-month period. An electing large partnership is a partnership with at least 100 partners or more. A partnership chooses electing large partnership (ELP) status by filing **Form 1065-B** instead of **Form 1065**. This election cannot be revoked without IRS permission.

33. The answer is A. An individual partner's basis is increased by her share of partnership debt and decreased by the amount of debt relief. Since Holly was a 30% partner, the basis items must be allocated based on her partnership percentage. The answer is figured as follows:

Beginning basis (her adjusted basis in the building)	$60,000
Mortgage debt assumed by partnership	($30,000)
Holly's share of the debt ($30,000 X 30%)	$10,000
Holly's basis in the partnership interest	**$40,000**

See **Publication 541**, *Partnerships*.

34. The answer is C. An S corporation's accumulated adjustment account includes all items of income and expenses with the exception of tax-exempt income (and expenses related to tax-exempt income).

35. The answer is C. The dividends received deduction is 70% when the receiving corporation owns less than 20% of the stock.

36. The answer is A. Passive loss limits do not apply to C corporations. Partnerships, estates, and individuals are all subject to the passive loss rules. However, there are special rules for closely-held corporations and personal service corporations. A closely held corporation can offset net active income with its passive activity loss. It also can offset the tax attributable to its net active income with its passive activity credits. However, a closely held corporation cannot offset its portfolio income with its passive activity losses. A personal service corporation cannot offset passive losses against either active income or portfolio income.

37. The answer is C. Corporations generally are allowed to choose a fiscal year-end unless:

- The corporation is a personal service corporation
- The corporation is an S corporation

Personal service corporations and S corporations are generally required to use a calendar year-end.

38. The answer is D. The answer is figured as follows:

Start with book income	$380,000
Subtract: Municipal bond interest income	($60,000)
Add back: Federal income tax	$120,000
Add back: Municipal bond interest expense	$4,300
Taxable income on Schedule M-1	**$444,300**

See **Publication 542,** *Corporations*.

39. The answer is D. A controlled group is a group of corporations that are related through common ownership, typically as either parent-subsidiary or brother-sister. A parent-subsidiary controlled group involves a parent corporation that owns at least 80% or more of the voting power of at least one other corporation (with possible additional corporations that are at least 80% owned by either the common parent or one of the subsidiary entities). A brother-sister controlled group involves situations in which five or fewer individuals, estates, or trusts own 80% or more of the combined voting power for multiple corporations, and have identical common ownership within the individual corporations of at least 50%. Members of controlled groups are subject to rules regarding related party transactions that may require deferral of recognition for losses or expenses incurred by one party. See **Publication 542,** *Corporations*.

40. The answer is C. Misty must report a taxable dividend of $160,000 ($260,000 FMV - $100,000 liability assumed). Her basis in the property is $260,000. When a corporation distributes property to a shareholder (rather than stock or cash), the amount distributed is based on the FMV of the property on the date of distribution. The amount distributed is reduced by any liabilities assumed by the shareholder.

254

The basis of the property in the hands of the shareholder would be the FMV on the date of distribution. See **Publication 542,** *Corporations.*

41. The answer is A. Hudson River Corporation would report a $110,000 gain ($200,000 FMV - $90,000 basis). Samuel would report a $200,000 dividend (the fair market value of the property). All distributions of appreciated property would trigger gain recognition for the corporation. The distribution to the shareholder is treated as a sale, and gain is reported on the transaction. However, a corporation would not recognize a loss on the distribution of property. See **Publication 542,** *Corporations.*

42. The answer is A. The distribution reduces Fitzmorris-Jones's E&P to zero. Leah must report a dividend of $210,000 and a capital gain of $10,000. The answer is figured as follows:

Accumulated E&P	$120,000
Current year E&P	$90,000
Current and accumulated E&P	**$210,000**

A distribution cannot create a deficit in a corporation's earnings and profits. Thus, the distribution to Leah reduces E&P to zero.

Gross distribution	$220,000
Current and accumulated E&P	-$210,000
Capital gain to Leah	$10,000

Leah must recognize a dividend of $210,000 (the amount of the distribution from current and accumulated E&P), and the remaining $10,000 would either reduce her stock basis or produce a capital gain for her. Since the problem stated that Leah's stock basis was already zero, the $10,000 would be reported as a capital gain. See **Publication 542,** *Corporations.*

43. The answer is D. The *extended* due date for all calendar-year partnerships is September 15. In the case of a fiscal year partnership, the return is due on the fifteenth day of the fourth month after the close of their tax year. September 15 is also the due date for corporate returns (Forms 1120, 1120A, 1120S) and trusts (Form 1041) if an extension was requested. See **Publication 541,** *Partnerships.*

44. The answer is C. Even though no distributions were made during the year, Tara is required to report her share of the partnership's income. The income is allocated based on her partnership interest, so the answer is figured as follows:
(30% X $40,000 partnership income) = $12,000 in ordinary income to Tara

Since no distributions were made, the income that was attributable to Tara increases her partnership basis: ($30,000 starting basis + $12,000 undistributed income) = $42,000 Tara's year-end basis. See **Publication 541**, *Partnerships*.

45. The answer is A. The final deadline for self-employed persons or small employers to establish a SIMPLE IRA for the year 2012 is October 1, 2013. A SIMPLE IRA plan can be set up effective on any date between January 1 and October 1, provided the plan sponsor did not previously maintain another SIMPLE IRA plan. If a SIMPLE IRA plan was previously established, a SIMPLE IRA plan may be set up effective only on January 1.

46. The answer is B. May 15 is the deadline for calendar-year nonprofit organizations to file their information returns (Form 990). The organization may also request an extension by using Form 8868. Even though a charity is organized as a corporation, it must still file Form 990, not Form 1120. An exempt entity on a fiscal year is required to file by the fifteenth of the fifth month after the end of its taxable year.

47. The answer is B. Section 1245 property excludes permanently-fixed buildings and structural components. However, there is an exception for single purpose agricultural or horticultural structures. A barn that houses different animals and is used to store supplies would not be section 1245 property because it is not a "single purpose" facility. Part or all of the gain of the sale of section 1245 property is treated as ordinary income under the rules of depreciation recapture.

48. The answer is A. Victor would report $35,000 in partnership losses and have a $6,000 loss carryforward. A partner may deduct partnership losses only to the extent of his adjusted basis in the partnership. Since Victor's distributive share of the loss exceeds his partnership basis, his basis is first reduced to zero, and the remaining loss is carried forward. The answer is figured as follows:

(Loss $82,000 X 50% Victor's owner's percentage) = $41,000 Victor's distributive share of losses. ($41,000 Victor's share of loss - $35,000 Victor's basis) = $6,000 loss carried forward

Victor's partnership basis is reduced to zero, and the excess loss is carried over to the next year. Partnership losses are never carried back. See **Publication 541**, *Partnerships*.

49. The answer is B. Both partners share income and loss equally, and they are required to report their share of partnership income, whether or not it is actually distributed. Therefore, each partner will report $55,000 ($110,000 X 50%) in taxable income from the partnership. An individual partner must report his allocable share of partnership income on his own tax return, regardless of whether the partnership made an actual distribution of the money earned by the partnership. Thus, for example, it would be possible for a partner to include $1,000 of partnership income on his own tax return in year one, but not receive a $1,000 distribution of cash until year two. See **Publication 541,** *Partnerships.*

50. The answer is A. Separately stated items of an S corporation are reported on Schedule K-1, Form 1120S.

51. The answer is B. Suspended passive activity losses would become deductible in the year of disposal of the entire interest of the passive activity. For example, if a partnership has suspended passive losses from an investment asset and then sells the investment (either at a loss or a gain), the suspended losses would be recognized upon the disposition of the asset. This is similar to the treatment of suspended losses for rental activities for individuals—if an individual taxpayer has suspended rental losses and then later decides to sell the rental, the suspended losses would become deductible in the year of disposition. Answer "A" is incorrect, because a partnership cannot use passive losses to offset ordinary income. Answer "C" is incorrect because in a like-kind exchange suspended losses are only deductible if there are gains recognized in the transfer. See **Publication 541,** *Partnerships.*

52. The answer is B. The S-election can be made anytime during 2012 or by March 15, 2013, and it will be valid retroactively for the 2012 tax year. Any election request made **after** March 15, 2013 will be applicable to the following year. A qualifying S-election requires unanimous consent from all the shareholders. However, a revocation of S status only requires the assent of a shareholder majority (over 50%). See **Publication 542,** *Corporations.*

53. The answer is C. An exempt entity on a fiscal year is required to file by the **fifteenth** of the **fifth month** after the end of their taxable year. The Reading Exchange's fiscal year ends June 30. Five months after that date is November 15. See **Publication 557,** *Tax-Exempt Status for Your Organization.*

54. The answer is B. A general partnership and a sole proprietorship do not require any type of formal agreement or state filing in order to create the entity. Corporations and LLCs require formal filing at the state level in order for the entity to be created.

55. The answer is A. Telecast has a $4,000 gain from the conversion. The adjusted basis of the property was $20,000, and Telecast received an insurance reimbursement of $45,000. Since Telecast only used $41,000 of the insurance reimbursement on qualifying replacement property, the company would recognize a gain of $4,000 ($45,000 - $41,000), the amount that was not reinvested. See **Publication 544**, *Sales and Other Dispositions of Assets.*

56. The answer is B. The distribution is treated as a sale. Helvetica Corporation would recognize income of $138,000 on the distribution ($200,000 - $62,000 basis). A corporation will recognize gain only when it makes a liquidating distribution to its shareholders. See **Publication 542,** *Corporations.*

57. The answer is D. The amount of current earnings and profits that is allocated to Valerie is $32,000 ($64,000 earnings X 50% stock ownership). Valerie must report dividend income of $32,000. The remaining amount of the distribution ($40,000 - $32,000 = $8,000) is treated as a return of capital and reduced Valerie's stock basis to $42,000 ($50,000 - $8,000). Corporate distributions will be treated as dividends to the extent of the shareholder's share of corporate earnings and profits. In the above example, Valerie's share of earnings is 50% of the earnings. The excess distribution then reduces her stock basis. See **Publication 542,** *Corporations.*

58. The answer is D. The built-in gains tax is imposed at the highest rate of tax that is applicable to corporations (currently, the tax rate is 35%).

59. The answer is B. Gains are recognized for distributions of appreciated property, but losses are not. The amount of gain is calculated as though the S corporation had sold the property to the shareholder at its fair market value. Even though the S corporation is a pass-through entity, this is one instance in which an S corporation differs greatly from a partnership. In the case of a partnership, gains from appreciated property that is distributed to a shareholder are generally deferred. With an S corporation, however, the gains must be recognized upon distribution.

60. The answer is D. A shareholder's basis in an S corporation will increase with:
- Additional contributions to capital, and
- The shareholder's share of corporate and exempt income.

Answer "A" is incorrect because the shareholder's share of nondeductible expenses will decrease basis, not increase it.

61. The answer is C. The DRD deduction for a corporation that owns less 20% of the stock is 70% of the dividends-received ($140,000 X 70% = $98,000). The DRD is limited to taxable income unless the deduction gives rise to an NOL (or adds to an existing NOL). In that case, the DRD would not be limited by income. See **Publication 542,** *Corporations*.

62. The answer is A. Partnerships and C corporations cannot own stock in an S corporation. Estates, trusts, individuals, and some exempt entities are permitted to own stock in an S corporation. An S corporation can have up to 100 shareholders.

63. The answer is C. The corporate charitable deduction for C corporations is limited to 10% of taxable income before figuring the dividends-received deduction. Therefore, the allowable charitable deduction is $12,500 = ($125,000 X 10%). The unused charitable contribution becomes a carryover to the following year and may be carried forward up to five years. After five years, any unused charitable deduction is lost. See **Publication 542,** *Corporations*.

64. The answer is C. A corporation whose S-election was revoked or terminated must wait five years before making an S-election again. There are exceptions for entities that are granted S-election earlier than the mandatory five year waiting period, but only with IRS consent. An S corporation may always choose to revoke its S status voluntarily, as long as a majority of the shareholders agree (over 50%).

65. The answer is A. The answer is calculated as follows:

Starting basis	**$95,000**
Ordinary losses	($15,000)
Long-term capital gain	$4,000
Short-term capital loss	($9,000)
Municipal bond interest income	$2,000
Year-end basis	**$77,000**

In computing stock basis, a shareholder starts with his initial capital contribution to the S corporation (the same as a C corporation). Basis is then increased and/or decreased based on the flow-through amounts from the S corporation. An income item will **increase** stock basis while a loss, deduction, or distribution will **decrease** stock basis. In an S corporation, a shareholder's tax basis is increased or decreased by the following:

INCREASES to basis
1. Ordinary income
2. Separately stated income items
3. Tax exempt income
4. Excess depletion

DECREASES to basis
1. Ordinary losses
2. Separately stated loss items
3. Nondeductible expenses
4. Nondividend distributions
5. Depletion for oil and gas

Stock basis is adjusted annually, on the last day of the S corporation year, in the following order:

- Increased for income items and excess depletion
- Decreased for distributions
- Decreased for nondeductible, noncapital expenses, and depletion, and
- Decreased for items of loss and deduction

When determining the taxability of a nondividend distribution, the shareholder looks solely to his/her stock basis (debt basis is not considered). A shareholder's stock basis cannot be decreased below zero. If a nondividend distribution is made in excess of stock basis, the distribution is taxed as a capital gain on the shareholder's personal return.

66. The answer is C. A fisherman or farmer who elects income averaging uses Schedule J, *Income Averaging for Farmers and Fishermen,* to figure his 2012 income tax. Certain farmers and fishermen may average all or some of their current year's farm income by allocating it to the three prior years. This may lower a farmer's current year tax if the current year is high and his taxable income from one or more of the three prior years was low. Income averaging is only available to farming businesses that are sole proprietorships or partnerships.

67. The answer is A. Brett must report a capital gain of $6,000 on his personal return ($30,000 - $24,000 = $6,000). A shareholder's stock basis cannot go below zero. Therefore, if a nondividend distribution is made in excess of stock basis, the distribution is taxed as a capital gain on the shareholder's personal return. See **Publication 542,** *Corporations.*

68. The answer is D. The answer is figured as follows:

Roger's starting basis	**$16,000**
Ordinary income (X 50%)	$40,000
Exempt income (X 50%)	$3,000
Year-end basis (before distribution)	**$59,000**
Subtract distribution	($50,000)
Year-end basis (after distribution)	**$9,000**

Roger is a 50% shareholder, so the ordinary income and exempt income is allocated according to his stock ownership percentage. The distribution is subtracted from the year-end basis.

69. The answer is A. A partnership's basis in its assets is known as *inside basis.* This is in contrast to a partner's basis in his partnership interest, which may be referred to as *outside basis.* The initial basis of a partnership interest is generally equal to the cash plus the adjusted basis of any property the partner contributed. The adjusted basis of a partner's partnership interest is ordinarily determined at the end of the partnership's tax year. However, if there is a sale or exchange of all or part of a partner's interest or a liquidation of his entire interest in a partnership, the adjusted basis must also be determined on the date of liquidation. See **Publication 541,** *Partnerships.*

70. The answer is C. In general, a partner's basis in distributed property will be the same as the partnership's basis in the property immediately before the distribution. However, in this case, the distributed property had a basis that exceeded Justine's remaining partnership interest. Therefore, her partnership basis is reduced to zero, and the basis of the property is $29,000.

Starting basis	$60,000
Cash distribution	$31,000
Remaining basis after cash distribution	$29,000

The remaining basis ($29,000) after the cash distribution is less than the adjusted basis of the property ($46,000). Therefore, Justine's basis in the property is $29,000. A partner's basis in distributed property may not exceed her basis in the partnership. See **Publication 541,** *Partnerships.*

71. The answer is D. There is no such thing as a casualty loss limitation. There are three shareholder loss limitations:
- Stock and debt basis limitations
- At risk limitations
- Passive activity loss limitations

If a shareholder is allocated an item of S corporation loss or deduction, the shareholder must first have adequate stock and/or debt basis to claim the loss. Even when a shareholder has adequate stock and/or debt basis to claim an S corporation loss, he must also consider the at-risk and passive activity loss limitations and therefore still may not be able to claim the loss. The fact that a shareholder receives a Schedule K-1 reflecting a loss does not mean that the shareholder is automatically entitled to claim it.

72. The answer is B. Before applying for tax exemption, the organization must be created using an *organizing document*. This document must limit the organization's purposes to those set forth in section 501(c)(3) and must specify that the entity's assets will be permanently dedicated to an exempt purpose. The organizing document should also contain a provision for distributing funds if it dissolves. In order to qualify for tax exemption section 501(c)(3, an organization must generally request exemption from the IRS by the end of the fifteenth month after it was created, with a 12-month extension available. See **Publication 557,** *Tax-Exempt Status for Your Organization.*

73. The answer is D. The answer is figured as follows: guaranteed payment $10,000 + $21,000 ($42,000 X 50%). Nicholas must report the guaranteed payment as income. He is a 50% partner, so he must also report 50% of the partnership's income. See **Publication 541,** *Partnerships.*

74. The answer is B. A partnership deducts guaranteed payments as a business expense. They are also listed on Schedules K and K-1 of the partnership return. The individual partner reports guaranteed payments on **Schedule E (Form 1040)** as ordinary income, along with his or her distributive share of the partnership's other ordinary income. See **Publication 541,** *Partnerships.*

75. The answer is B. Section 280F places limits on the amount of depreciation that can be taken on passenger cars used in business. Although section 280F's caption refers to "luxury automobiles," the restrictions apply to most new passenger cars. There are also special limits placed on the depreciation of sports utility vehicles. Each year, the IRS releases guidance regarding MACRS' limitations for automobiles set at specified amounts, adjusted for inflation, for various makes and models of vehicles.

76. The answer is B. Under the accrual method of accounting, income is realized when it is earned, regardless of when the income is actually collected. The purpose of an accrual method of accounting is to match income and expenses in the correct year.

77. The answer is D. Freelance authors, photographers, and artists are exempt from the uniform capitalization rules. Under UNICAP, a business must capitalize the direct costs and part of the indirect costs for production or resale activities. Businesses that create, purchase, and resell property or inventory are subject to UNICAP.

Smaller businesses that are exempt from the uniform capitalization rules are the following:

- Resellers of personal property with average annual gross receipts of $10 million or less for the three prior tax years
- Businesses that produce inventory but have average annual gross receipts of $1 million or less

78. The answer is A. Randy must report $10,000 in partnership income in 2012. After the distribution, his remaining partnership basis would be $500. Randy must report his share of partnership income in the year it is earned, whether or not the amounts are actually distributed. Since Randy had $10,000 in ordinary income from the partnership in 2012, he is required to report that amount in 2012, even if he did not receive it. The answer is figured as follows:

Randy's starting partnership basis	$0
Ordinary income	$10,000
Tax exempt income	$1,500
Basis at the end of 2012	**$11,500**
Cash distribution in 2013	$11,000
Basis after cash distribution	**$500**

The municipal bond interest is nontaxable interest, so it retains its character as nontaxable when it is distributed to Randy. However, the exempt income does increase Randy's basis in his partnership interest, so after the distribution he still has $500 in basis left. The basis of a partner' partnership interest is **increased** by his distributable share of:

1. Taxable income
2. Tax exempt income
3. Excess of the deductions for depletion over the basis of the property subject to depletion

See **Publication 541**, *Partnerships*.

79. The answer is B. A greenhouse is generally classified as section 1245 property, not section 1250, because it is a single purpose horticultural or agricultural structure. Section 1250 property generally consists of buildings (including their structural components), other inherently permanent structures, and land improvements of general use and purpose. Examples of section 1250 property include residential rental property, factory buildings, and office buildings. Since buildings are generally depreciated using the straight-line method, taxpayers usually get more favorable treatment of depreciation recapture for section 1250 property.

A

80. The answer is B. The sale of a partner's interest in a partnership usually results in capital gain or loss. The gain or loss is the difference between the amount realized and the adjusted basis of the partner's interest in the partnership. Therefore, Carl has an $8,000 capital gain upon the disposition of his partnership interest ($20,000 - $12,000 = $8,000). See **Publication 541,** *Partnerships*.

81. The answer is C. A disregarded entity is a single-member limited liability company that is disregarded for federal tax purposes. A domestic LLC with one member will be treated as a sole proprietorship for tax purposes, thus "disregarded" as separate from its owner for income tax purposes (but as a separate entity for purposes of employment tax and certain excise taxes). An individual owner of a single-member LLC is subject to the tax on net earnings from self-employment in the same manner as a sole proprietorship.

82. The answer is D. An LLC with at least two members can choose to be taxed as a partnership or a corporation (either a C corporation or an S corporation).

83. The answer is C. A private foundation is required to file an annual information return every year, regardless of income. Private foundations file Form 990-PF. See **Publication 557,** *Tax-Exempt Status for Your Organization*.

84. The answer is A. Cheryl has a $20,000 taxable dividend and a $10,000 capital gain. The amounts distributed would come first from earnings and profits ($20,000). This would be classified as a dividend. The remaining amount ($30,000 -$20,000) would be classified as a capital gain, because it exceeds Cheryl's stock basis, which is zero. A distribution will be treated as a dividend if there are earnings and profits. See **Publication 542,** *Corporations*.

85. The answer is B. The expenses incurred during a complete liquidation of a corporation can be deducted on the final corporate return.

86. The answer is C. A C corporation is taxed as a separate entity and does not have the characteristics of a flow-through entity. Income that is passed through to the shareholders does not retain its character, and it is taxed twice: at the corporate level and at the shareholder level. In contrast, partnerships, S corporations, and sole proprietorships are all flow-through entities. For example, a partnership is not a taxpaying entity. Each partner reports his or her distributive share of the partnership's income, gain, loss, deductions, and credits on his or her own individual tax returns.

87. The answer is D. Generally, the partnership's basis in contributed property is identical to the adjusted basis of the property in the hands of the contributing partner. Therefore, the partnership's tax basis in the contributed land is $10,000. The partnership's tax basis in the contributed equipment is $75,000. In addition, the partnership's holding period for the assets is the same as Kathryn's holding period, so if either asset is later sold, the holding period is "tacked on" for the partnership's recognition of long-term or short-term gains. See **Publication 541,** *Partnerships*.

88. The answer is A. Mark's partnership basis is increased to $71,000 ($46,000 + $25,000 [25% X $100,000]). The partnership has four partners, so each would increase the basis of his partnership interest by his share of the debt (25% X $100,000). IRC section 752(a) treats the $100,000 borrowing as if each partner had contributed $25,000 to the partnership. Mark's basis in his partnership interest is now $71,000 (starting basis of $46,000 plus $25,000 of debt share). See **Publication 541**, *Partnerships*.

89. The answer is B. Because the cash received does not exceed the basis of her partnership interest, Sydney does not recognize any gain on the distribution. Any gain on the land will be recognized when she later sells or disposes of it. The distribution decreases the adjusted basis of Sydney's partnership interest to $57,000 [$165,000 – ($80,000 + $28,000)]. See **Publication 541,** *Partnerships*.

90. The answer is A. The Quicker Relay Corporation would recognize a gain of $430,000 = ($620,000 liability - $190,000 basis). During a liquidation, a corporation will recognize gain or loss on distributions. In general, the gain or loss on a liquidating distribution is calculated by subtracting the basis of the property from the fair market value on the date of the distribution (FMV - basis = gain/loss). However, if the property is encumbered by a liability, the fair market value of the property cannot be used if the liability exceeds the FMV. See **Publication 542,** *Corporations*.

91. The answer is D. In the case of S corporations, any suspended losses in excess of stock basis (or debt basis) are carried forward indefinitely. Suspended losses due to basis limitations retain their character in subsequent years.

92. The answer is B. If a shareholder receives a nondividend distribution from an S corporation, the distribution is tax-free to the extent it does not exceed the shareholder's stock basis. Debt basis is not considered when determining the taxability of a distribution.

93. The answer is B. Partners can modify their partnership agreement after the close of the tax year but no later than the due date for filing the partnership return. This deadline does not include any extensions. See **Publication 541,** *Partnerships.*

94. The answer is C. The corporation's final return is due by October 15, 2012. It will cover the short period from January 1, 2012 through July 12, 2012. October 15 is the fifteenth day of the third month following the close of the corporation's tax year, which was a short year because the corporation dissolved. See **Publication 538,** *Accounting Periods.*

95. The answer is C. An S corporation cannot deduct charitable contributions. Only a C corporation can take a business deduction for charitable contributions of up to 10% of income. The two main reasons for electing S corporation status are:
- Avoiding double taxation on distributions
- Allowing corporate losses to flow through to shareholders

In addition, S corporations share the same liability protection benefits of C corporations.

96. The answer is D. For the sale of livestock due to drought, flood, or other weather-related conditions in an area eligible for federal assistance, the replacement period ends four years after the close of the first tax year in which the taxpayer realizes any part of his gain from the sale or exchange of livestock. The IRS may extend the replacement period on a regional basis if the weather-related conditions continue for longer than three years. See **Publication 544,** *Sales and Other Dispositions of Assets.*

97. The answer is A. A partnership does not pay income tax. However, a partnership can still be liable for other taxes, such as employment taxes (FUTA, Social Security, Medicare taxes) and excise taxes. See **Publication 541,** *Partnerships.*

98. The answer is D. The differences in book and taxable income are reconciled on Schedule M-1 of Form 1120 by small corporations with less than $10 million in assets. Larger corporations with over $10 million in assets use Schedule M-3. Schedule M-3 provides additional information and contains three main sections:
- Financial statement reconciliation
- Detail of income/loss items
- Detail of expenses/deductions

99. The answer is A. A corporation must carry an NOL back two years. If the NOL is not used in the prior two years, the remaining NOL can be carried forward for up to twenty years.

100. The answer is C. The corporation has an $80,000 DRD and a $10,000 NOL. Its taxable income is $70,000 ($100,000 dividends earned - $30,000 business losses) **before** figuring the dividends-received deduction. If APX Corporation claims the full dividends-received deduction of $80,000 ($100,000 × 80%) and combines it with its business loss of $30,000, it will have an NOL of ($10,000). Therefore, the 80% of taxable income limit does not apply. The corporation can deduct the full $80,000. See **Publication 542,** *Corporations*.

Exam #2 Businesses: Answers

1. The answer is A. In general, a partner's basis in distributed property is the same as the partnership's basis in the property immediately before the distribution. However, in this case, the distributed property had a basis that exceeded Tony's remaining partnership interest. Therefore, his partnership basis is reduced to zero, and the basis of the property is $50,000.

Starting basis	$65,000
Cash distribution	$15,000
Remaining basis after cash distribution	$50,000

A partner's basis in distributed property may not exceed his basis in the partnership.

2. The answer is B. The accumulated earnings tax is assessed on the accumulated earnings and profits of a C corporation. If a corporation allows earnings to accumulate beyond the reasonable needs of the business, it may be subject to an accumulated earnings tax of 15%. The IRS imposes this tax upon corporations with retained earnings deemed to be "unreasonable" and in excess of what is considered ordinary. The accumulated earnings tax does not apply to partnerships, sole proprietorships, or S corporations, because these businesses are pass-through entities and do not accumulate earnings from year to year, as a C corporation does. For more information, see **Publication 542**, *Corporations*.

3. The answer is B. The IRS only allows an employer to provide $50,000 of term life insurance coverage tax-free to an employee. There are no tax consequences if the total amount of the life insurance policy does not exceed $50,000. The value of any coverage over this amount must be included in wages and reported on Form W-2. The employer must calculate the taxable portion of the premiums for coverage that exceeds $50,000. For more information, see **Publication 15-B**, *Employer's Tax Guide to Fringe Benefits*.

4. The answer is C. The first corporate tax return is due March 15 of the following year. This short period return covers May 15, 2012 through December 31, 2012. Corporate tax returns are due on the fifteenth day two-and-a-half months after the end of the corporation's taxable year. Since the corporation elected the calendar year, the corporate return is due two-and-a-half months after the end of December. For more information, see **Publication 542**, *Corporations*.

5. The answer is D. A nonprofit entity (exempt organization) must file **Form 990**, not **Form 1120**. In order for an entity to qualify as exempt, it must be organized as a community chest, corporation, trust, fund, or foundation. A nonprofit entity may still be classified as a corporation, but its income is nontaxable (exempt), and it is required to file a nonprofit tax return, which is IRS **Form 990**.

6. The answer is B. If liabilities assumed by the corporation exceed the basis of the assets transferred, the relief from liabilities in excess of basis is treated as boot. In the case of a section 351 exchange, a taxpayer will not recognize any gain or loss in the transfer, so long as the following conditions are met:

- The taxpayer receives only stock in exchange for the property, and
- The taxpayer has a controlling interest in the corporation immediately after the exchange. In order to qualify, the taxpayer must have at least 80% ownership in corporate stock.

7. The answer is A. A family farming corporation may use the cash method of accounting if its average annual gross receipts are $25 million or less. A tax shelter must always use the accrual method, regardless of its gross receipts. A corporation with long-term contracts must always use the accrual method. A C corporation with gross receipts exceeding $5 million must use the accrual method of accounting.

8. The answer is B. A domestic LLC that has at least two members and does not file a **Form 8832** will automatically be classified by the IRS as a partnership for tax purposes.

9. The answer is C. The maximum section 179 deduction the company can claim for 2012 is $355,000 ($100,000 for the equipment + $5,000 computer + $250,000 for the qualifying leasehold improvements). In 2012 there is a special rule that allows taxpayers to elect to deduct a maximum of $250,000 of qualified real property (QRP) under section 179. This special provision only applies to certain industries and includes the following real property:

- Qualified leasehold improvement property
- Qualified restaurant property (such as a major renovation of a restaurant building)
- Qualified retail improvement property (such as a major interior upgrade of a retail clothing store)

The QRP portion of section 179 expenses is limited to $250,000. A business is still eligible to deduct an additional $250,000 of other qualifying property to reach the $500,000 section 179 limit for 2012.

10. The answer is C. If a business does not have a payee's Social Security Number or Taxpayer Identification Number, it must withhold federal income taxes at a 28% rate for U.S. citizens and resident aliens. This is called backup withholding. Most types of U.S. source income received by a foreign person are subject to a backup withholding rate of 30%, unless a reduced rate applies due to a tax treaty the United States has with a given country. See **Publication 505**, *Tax Withholding and Estimated Tax*, and **Publication 515**, *Tax Withholding of Tax on Nonresident Aliens and Resident Aliens.*

11. The answer is D. The partnership must include the fair market value (FMV) of the items it received in exchange for services. This is bartering income, and it is treated as though the partnership had received money. Therefore, the answer is $8,000 + $3,000 = $11,000.

12. The answer is A. Its final return is due by October 15, 2012 and will cover the short period from January 1, 2012 through July 22, 2012. The return is due on the fifteenth day of the third month after the close of its taxable year. In this case, the taxable year ended on the date the entity was dissolved. This is called a short year tax return. Even if a taxable entity was not in existence for the entire year, a tax return is required for the time it was in existence. Requirements for filing a short year return and figuring the tax are generally the same as the requirements for a return for a full tax year (12 months) ending on the last day of the short tax year.

13. The answer is B. Because they used the car 70% for business, they can deduct 70% of the expenses as a business expense. The answer is figured as follows:

$$[(\$235 + \$20 + \$25) = \$280] \times 70\% = \$196$$
$$\underline{(\$5,500 \times 70\%) = \$3,850}$$
Allowable expense: $4,046

See **Publication 334**, *Tax Guide for Small Businesses.*

14. The answer is A. The filing of a bankruptcy petition creates a bankruptcy estate, which consists of all the assets of the person (or entity) filing the bankruptcy petition. A separate entity is created if the bankruptcy petition is filed under chapter 7 or chapter 11 of the Bankruptcy Code. For additional information, refer to **Publication 908**, *Bankruptcy Tax Guide.*

15. The answer is C. A sole proprietorship with 100 employees is not required to file electronically. The IRS requires partnerships with more than 100 partners (Schedules K-1) to electronically file their return. A small tax-exempt organization that wishes to file **Form 990-N** must file electronically, as there is no paper version of this form available. Corporations that have assets of $10 million or more and file at least 250 returns annually are required to electronically file **Forms 1120** and **Form 1120S** (this applies to S corporations and C corporations).

16. The answer is D. The IRS has ruled that there must be substantial "noncompensatory" reasons for use of a phone which relate to the employer's business. Legitimate reasons include the employer's need to contact the employee at all times for work-related emergencies and the employee's need to be available to speak with clients away from the office. However, a cell phone provided simply to promote an employee's morale or to attract a prospective employee is considered a form of compensation. In those cases, the value of a cell phone would no longer be a de minimis benefit and must be added to an employee's wages. If an employer provides an employee with a cell phone primarily for noncompensatory business purposes, personal use of the phone also is excludable from an employee's income as a *de minimis* fringe benefit.

17. The answer is B. For businesses using the cash method of accounting, the general rule is that an expense paid in advance is deductible only in the year to which it applies. The expense for the business insurance must be prorated because the payment does not qualify for the 12-month rule. Therefore, only $500 (6/36 × $3,000) is deductible in 2012, $1,000 (12/36 × $3,000) is deductible in 2013, $1,000 (12/36 × $3,000) is deductible in 2014, and the remaining $500 is deductible in 2015. Under the 12-month rule, the cash-basis taxpayer is *not* required to capitalize amounts paid that do not extend beyond the earlier of the following:
- 12 months after the benefit begins, or
- The end of the tax year after the tax year in which payment is made.

See IRS **Publication 538,** *Accounting Periods and Methods.*

18. The answer is D. When Dwight died in 2012, his estate qualified for the full basic exclusion amount of $5,120,000. As a result of having reported the DSUE when Form 706 was filed for his estate, the amount of the DSUE is available in addition to Monica's basic exclusion amount of $5,120,000. Therefore, the amount of her taxable estate would have to exceed $10,240,000 in order to be subject to estate tax.

19. The answer is A. It is expected to be *more difficult* for a business to deduct certain costs that are now classified as repairs but are likely to be redefined as improvements under the new rules. The new IRS improvement standards apply to the building structure and to each of the building's major component systems separately. The guidelines divide a building into nine different structural components called "building systems," such as those for plumbing, heating and air conditioning, and electrical. The effects of a repair on a specific building system, rather than the building as a whole, must be evaluated under the new, narrower definition of an improvement. The final regulations are still being revised, and full implementation is being delayed until 2014. For tax year 2012, taxpayers have the choice to use the current rules or adopt the new ones.

20. The answer is B. Participant loans are not permitted. Participants are always 100% vested in all of the funds in their IRAs. Withdrawals are permitted anytime, but they are subject to income taxes (except for certain distributions from non-deductible IRAs and Roth IRAs). If the employee is under age 59½, there may also be a 10% penalty tax. With an IRA, an employee controls where his money is invested, and he also bears the investment risk. The financial institution holding the IRA manages the funds. An employee may also move IRA assets from one IRA provider to another. See **Publication 4587**, *Payroll Deduction IRAS for Small Businesses.*

21. The answer is C. The entire meal amount is a qualified expense, but subject to the 50% meal and entertainment limitation. Janelle can deduct the full amount of the travel in the taxi cab. Therefore, the deductible portion of the expense is figured as follows: ($250 X 50%) + $10 =$135.

22. The answer is B. The corporation does not recognize any income or loss from this exchange. However, Manny (now the majority shareholder) must recognize ordinary income of $13,000 as payment for services he rendered to the corporation. If a taxpayer transfers property (or money) to a corporation in exchange for stock and immediately gains control of the corporation, the exchange is usually not taxable. This nonrecognition treatment does not apply when a person exchanges *services* for stock. In order to be "in control" of a corporation, the taxpayer who transfers the property must own, immediately after the exchange, at least 80% of the stock. See **Publication 542**, *Corporations.*

23. The answer is B. Cassandra may not deduct the taxes as a current expense, since they are delinquent real estate taxes and the person who is legally liable for the debt is Alex. However, the taxes should be added to the property's basis and depreciated as part of the purchase price, since Cassandra intends to use the property as a rental. If a taxpayer agrees to pay the delinquent real estate taxes that the seller owes on real property, the buyer must treat those taxes as part of the asset's basis. The buyer cannot deduct them as taxes. See **Publication 551**, *Basis of Assets.*

24. The answer is A. Harrington's basis in the new plane is $70,000 (the $30,000 basis of the old plane plus the $40,000 paid). The FMV of the new plane has no bearing on the basis in a section 1031 exchange. If a business trades property in a qualified like-kind exchange and also pays money, the basis of the property received is the basis of the property given up, increased by the additional money paid. See **Publication 551**, *Basis of Assets.*

25. The answer is C. A new corporation establishes its tax year when it files its first tax return. Businesses must file **Form 1128** to adopt, change, or retain a tax year. The IRS will grant automatic approval to any C corporation so long as the entity has not changed its accounting period in the previous 48 months. If the business does not qualify for *automatic* approval, a ruling must be requested, and a user fee must be paid. See **Publication 538,** *Accounting Periods and Methods.*

26. The answer is D. The cost of shipping finished products to customers are not product costs and not part of the cost of goods sold (COGS) calculation. However, freight-in costs are part of the cost of goods calculation. There are several factors that go into determining COGS, including inventory at the beginning of the year; raw material purchases; direct labor costs (generally applies to manufacturing and mining operations); materials and supplies; other costs; and inventory at the end of the year. Starting inventory, net purchases, cost of labor, materials and supplies, and other costs are added together. Inventory at the end of the year is subtracted from this total to determine COGS. See **Publication 334**, *Tax Guide for Small Business.*

27. The answer is B. U.S. tax law requires businesses to submit a Form 1099 for every contractor paid at least $600 for services during a year. This requirement does not apply to corporations receiving payments.

28. The answer is A. Mario's basis is the cash he contributed, and Juan's basis is his adjusted basis in the property. The FMV does not affect the basis of the partner's interest. The basis of a partnership interest is the money (cash investment) plus the adjusted basis of any property the partner contributed. See **Publication 541,** *Partnerships.*

29. The answer is B. A nonresident alien cannot hold shares in an S corporation. All of the other entities would be permitted to be shareholders in an S corporation. Shareholders in an S corporation must be U.S. citizens or residents. Corporate shareholders and partnerships are excluded. However, certain trusts, estates, and tax-exempt corporations, most notably 501(c)(3) corporations, are permitted to be shareholders.

30. The answer is C. A guaranteed payment must actually be paid to a partner in order to be classified as a guaranteed payment. Guaranteed payments are those made by a partnership to a partner which are determined without regard to the partnership's income. In other words, the payments will be made even if the partnership loses money. In this respect, these payments are treated as though they are being made to someone outside of the partnership.

31. The answer is B. The basis of Doreen's partnership interest is $480,000, figured as follows:

Adjusted basis of contributed property	$800,000
Minus: Part of mortgage assumed by other partners (80% × $400,000)	$320,000
Basis of Doreen's partnership interest	$480,000

If contributed property is encumbered by a liability or if a partner's liabilities are assumed by the partnership, the basis of the contributing partner's interest is reduced (but not below zero) by the liability assumed by the other partners. This partner must reduce her basis because the assumption of the liability is treated as a distribution of money to that partner. The other partners' assumption of the liability is treated as a contribution by them of money to the partnership. See **Publication 541,** *Partnerships.*

32. The answer is D. The corporation's charitable contribution is limited to $40,000 and is figured as follows: ($600,000 - $200,000) X 10% = $40,000. A C corporation can claim a limited deduction for charitable contributions. The deduction is limited to 10% of taxable income, calculated *before* the charitable contribution, dividends-received deduction, and net operating loss or capital loss *carrybacks*. See **Publication 542**, *Corporations.*

33. The answer is B. If a taxpayer trades property and also pays money, the basis of the property received is the basis of the property given up, increased by any additional money paid. In a nontaxable property exchange, the additional money is called boot. The answer is figured as follows:

Cost of old equipment	$50,000
subtract depreciation on old equipment	$26,000
Adjusted basis old equipment	$24,000
Add cash paid (boot) for new equipment	$12,000
Adjusted basis new equipment	$36,000

34. The answer is C. A "prohibited transaction" is a transaction between a retirement plan and a disqualified person that is prohibited by law. Disqualified persons may include fiduciaries of the plan or employers who are administering the plan, among others.

An initial 15% tax is applied on the amount involved in a prohibited transaction for each year in a taxable period. If the transaction is not corrected within the taxable period, an additional tax of 100% of the amount involved is imposed. These taxes are payable by any disqualified person who takes part in a prohibited transaction. If more than one person takes part, each can be jointly and severally liable for the entire amount of tax. Prohibited transactions include the following:

- A transfer of plan income or assets to, or use for the benefit of, a disqualified person
- Any act of a fiduciary by which plan income or assets are used for his own benefit
- The receipt of money or property by a fiduciary for his own account from any party dealing with the plan in a transaction that involves plan income or assets
- The sale, exchange, or lease of property between a plan and a disqualified person
- Lending money between a plan and a disqualified person
- Furnishing goods or services between a plan and a disqualified person

35. The answer is B. Corporations generally must make estimated tax payments if they expect to owe tax (income tax less credits) of $500 or more. Sole proprietors, partners, S corporation shareholders, and self-employed individuals generally have to make estimated tax payments if they expect to owe tax of $1,000 or more when they file their return. See **Instructions for Form 1120.**

36. The answer is A. Because ABC Corporation has over 80% ownership of S&V Corporation, the dividends are not taxable. ABC Corporation may claim the dividends-received deduction for the dividends received from S&V Corporation.

37. The answer is D. None of these vehicles is categorized as listed property. Vehicles are excluded if they are used in the business of transporting persons (such as a tour bus or ambulance), or used in a property for hire (such as a taxi cab). Trucks or vans that are qualified non-personal use vehicles (such as a van used only for furniture delivery at a business location) are also not categorized as listed property. See **Publication 946,** *How to Depreciate Property.*

38. The answer is D. Livestock is eligible for the section 179 deduction. The other assets listed do not qualify for any type of accelerated depreciation. See **Publication 946,** *How to Depreciate Property.*

39. The answer is D. A stock distribution is generally not a taxable event. In a stock distribution, a corporation is not actually distributing money (which would then be taxable); instead, it distributes shares of its own stock. Distributions by a corporation of its own stock are also commonly known as stock dividends or stock rights. Stock rights are distributions by a corporation of rights to acquire the corporation's stock. Generally, stock dividends and stock rights are not taxable to shareholders and not deductible by the corporation.

40. The answer is B. The ordinary income is figured as follows ($50,000 - $20,000 in expenses). The tax-exempt interest and rental income is separately stated income, and the charitable contribution is also a separately stated item but is not used to figure an S corporation's income. The charitable contributions deduction is taken by the individual shareholder on her individual return (Schedule A, Form 1040). In this respect, the S Corporation is similar to a partnership in its tax treatment of charitable contributions. ***Note:** Do not confuse this treatment with charitable contributions of a C corporation. A C corporation is allowed to deduct a limited amount of charitable contributions directly from its taxable income.

41. The answer is B. Contributions to a partner's retirement account are treated as a distribution to the partner. The amount is a separately stated item on **Form 1065.** See **Publication 541,** *Partnerships.*

42. The answer is C. A C corporation is not a pass-through entity. There are many benefits to incorporation. However, one of the main drawbacks of a C corporation is the tax ramifications of this entity type. Unlike a partnership, a sole proprietorship, or an S corporation, the earnings of a C corporation are taxed twice. Corporate income is taxed when it is earned and then taxed again when it is distributed to shareholders as dividends. A corporation does not receive a tax deduction for the distribution of dividends to its shareholders.

43. The answer is A. If a corporation cancels a shareholder's debt without repayment by the shareholder, the amount canceled is treated as a distribution to the shareholder. A corporate distribution to a shareholder is generally treated as a distribution of earnings and profits.

44. The answer is A. Gracie Development must recognize a taxable gain of $60,000. This transaction is treated as a sale. It is as if Gracie Development sold the building for $250,000 and used the profits from the sale to pay the debt. Gracie Development must realize a taxable gain as if the property had been sold at its fair market value and the proceeds were used to pay off the creditor.

45. The answer is D. A personal service corporation pays corporate tax at a flat rate of 35%. The answer is figured as follows: ($68,000 - $22,000 NOL) X 35% = $16,100.

46. The answer is A. In this case, Gabe is considered to have 100% of constructive ownership in the partnership, because the rules for "constructive ownership" include the ownership of his family. For this rule, family includes only brothers, sisters, spouses, ancestors, and lineal descendants. Therefore, the ownership is figured as follows:

Gabe	20%
Gabe's son	20%
Gabe's brother	60%
Ownership	**100%**

See **Publication 550**, *Investment Income and Expenses*.

47. The answer is B. A corporation's treatment of distributions is different during a complete liquidation. In a liquidation, a corporation recognizes gain on appreciated assets and losses on depreciated property. Shareholders also recognize gain or loss on a corporation's distribution of assets during a liquidation. In this case, Gordon's gain would be figured as follows:

$10,000 + $12,000 = $22,000 distribution

$22,000 - $17,000 stock basis = $5,000 gain

Corporate liquidations of property generally are treated as a sale or exchange. Gain or loss generally is recognized by the corporation on a liquidating **sale** of its assets. Gain or loss generally is *also* recognized on a liquidating **distribution** of assets as if the corporation sold the assets to the distributee at fair market value. See **Publication 544,** *Sales and Other Dispositions of Assets*.

48. The answer is A. The IRS may reclassify the excess $1,500 per month in rental payments as a constructive dividend, and the corporation would lose that amount as a deduction. If a corporation rents property from a shareholder and the rent is unreasonably more than the shareholder would charge a stranger to rent the same property, the excessive part of the rent may be treated as a distribution to the shareholder. See **Publication 542**, *Corporations*.

49. The answer is B. If a corporation issues bonds and then later repurchases the bonds at a higher price than the original issue price, the corporation has a deduction for interest expense in the year of the repurchase. Therefore, the corporation should report interest expense of $30,000 ($580,000 - $550,000).

50. The answer is A. An unincorporated business jointly owned by a married couple is generally classified as a partnership for Federal tax purposes. However, a married couple who jointly operate a business may choose to file as a "qualified joint venture," filing on Schedule C. Unless a business meets the requirements of a qualified joint venture, a sole proprietorship must be solely owned by one spouse and the other spouse may work in the business as an employee. See **Publication 334,** *Tax Guide for Small Business.*

51. The answer is A. C corporations report income and loss on **Form 1120,** *U.S. Corporation Income Tax Return.*

52. The answer is C. A gain of $70,000 = ($160,000 – $90,000) must be recognized, because only $80,000 was reinvested. If property is condemned (or disposed of under the threat of condemnation), gain or loss is figured by comparing the adjusted basis of the condemned property with the net condemnation award. See **Publication 544,** *Sales and Other Dispositions of Assets.*

53. The answer is C. Wages of a child under age 18 who works for his parent in a business are not subject to Social Security and Medicare taxes if the trade or business is a sole proprietorship or a partnership in which each partner is a parent of the child (Note: this rule does not apply to corporations). Earned income, including wages that are paid to the taxpayer's own children, are not subject to the "kiddie tax," regardless of the child's age. Payments for the services of a child of any age who works for his parent are generally not subject to backup withholding. See **Publication 15,** *(Circular E), Employer's Tax Guide.*

54. The answer is D. Since XYZ is an accrual-basis corporation, the wages are deductible as they are accrued. The full amount of the bonus and other wages to the other employees is deductible in 2012.

55. The answer is D. Tips are considered taxable income and are subject to federal income taxes. Tips that an employee receives from customers are generally subject to withholding. Employees must report tips they receive to their employer by the tenth of the month after the month that the tips are received. Employers are required to collect income tax, employee Social Security tax, and employee Medicare tax on the employee's tips. See **Publication 15,** *(Circular E), Employer's Tax Guide.*

56. The answer is B. An LLC can file Form 8832 to elect its business entity classification. A business with at least two members can choose to be classified as a corporation or a partnership, and a business entity with a single member can choose to be classified as either a corporation or disregarded as an entity separate from its owner (a "disregarded entity").

57. The answer is B. An interest in a partnership or joint venture is treated as a capital asset when it is sold. However, any gain or loss from unrealized receivables or inventory items will be treated as ordinary gain or loss. See **Publication 541,** *Partnerships.*

58. The answer is B. If a partnership's debt is canceled because of bankruptcy or insolvency, the rules for the exclusion of the canceled amount from gross income and for tax attribute reduction are applied at the **individual partner level**. Thus, each partner's share of debt cancellation income must be reported on the partner's individual tax return. The allocation of debt cancellation income to a partner results in that partner's basis in the partnership being *increased* by that amount. At the same time, the reduction in the partner's share of partnership liabilities caused by the debt cancellation results in a deemed distribution, in turn resulting in a reduction of the partner's basis in the partnership. See **Publication 908**, *Bankruptcy Tax Guide.*

59. The answer is C. The corporation's *unextended* due date is September 15, 2012, so the six-month corporate extension to file makes the new due date March 15, 2013.

60. The answer is C. The answer is figured as follows:

($190,000 - $35,000) =	$155,000
($155,000 X 39%) =	$60,450

The capital loss can only offset capital gain. Therefore, the capital loss cannot be currently deducted and must be carried over to a future year.

61. The answer is C. Ned must reduce the basis of his stock. A nondividend distribution is a distribution that is not paid out of the earnings and profits of a corporation. A nondividend distribution reduces the basis of the shareholder's stock. It is not taxed until the basis in the stock is fully recovered. When the basis of the stock has been reduced to zero, any additional nondividend distribution that is received must be reported as a capital gain.

62. The answer is C. Form 990-T is currently used by tax-exempt organizations to report and pay the tax on unrelated business income. Any domestic or foreign tax-exempt organization must file **Form 990-T,** *Exempt Organization Business Income Tax Return,* if it has gross income from an unrelated trade or business of $1,000 or more.

63. The answer is A. Renee must reduce her basis in the partnership interest to zero. She will have a $32,000 basis in the land. A partner cannot have a negative partnership basis. She does not recognize any income in this transaction and will defer any gain on the land until she sells it. If Renee had received cash instead of property, she would have been forced to recognize the gain.

64. The answer is A. State incorporation fees are considered qualifying organizational costs. However, the following items are capital expenses that cannot be amortized:

- Costs for issuing and selling stock or securities, such as commissions, professional fees, and printing costs.
- Costs associated with the transfer of assets to the corporation.

See **Publication 535,** *Business Expenses.*

65. The answer is B. The video recorder, laptop, and digital camera are all considered listed property. The Small Business Jobs and Credit Act of 2010 removed cellular telephones from the category of listed property.

Video recorder	$195
Laptop	$450
Digital camera	$123
Total	**$768**

Special rules apply to listed property, which includes cars and other vehicles used for transportation; property used for entertainment, recreation, or amusement such as photographic or video-recording equipment; and certain computers. If an item is used for both business and personal purposes, deductions for depreciation and section 179 are based on the percentage of business use. Further, if business use is not more than 50%, section 179 deductions and bonus depreciation allowances are not allowed, and depreciation must be calculated using the straight-line method. See IRS **Publication 946,** *How to Depreciate Property.*

66. The answer is D. In general, a business can deduct only 50% of business-related meal and entertainment expenses. However, there are some examples where meals are not subject to this limit. The following meals are not subject to the 50% limit:

- Meals that are included in employees' wages as taxable compensation
- Meals that qualify as a *de minimis* fringe benefit, such as occasional coffee and doughnuts
- Meals furnished to employees when the employer operates a restaurant or catering service

- Meals furnished to employees as part of a teambuilding activity, such as a company picnic
- Meals that are required by federal law to be furnished to crew members of certain commercial vessels
- Meals furnished on an oil or gas platform or drilling rig located offshore or in Alaska

These meals are 100% deductible by the employer. See **Publication 463**, *Travel, Entertainment, Gift, and Car Expenses.*

67. The answer is A. Since Jacob received a $10,000 cash distribution when his basis was only $7,000, he must recognize gain of $3,000 and reduce his partnership basis to zero. Therefore, his basis on the distributed property is also zero. A partner cannot have a negative basis. Gain is not recognized in a partnership distribution unless the distribution exceeds the partner's basis in his partnership interest. A partnership also generally does not recognize any gain or loss because of distributions made to its partners. A partner generally recognizes gain on a partnership distribution only to the extent any money distributed exceeds the adjusted basis of the partner's interest. Any gain recognized is treated as capital gain. If partnership property (in this case, Jacob got a car) is distributed to a partner, he does not recognize any gain until the sale of the property.

68. The answer is B. When a partnership ceases all operations, it is called a partnership liquidation. When a partnership liquidates, all the following events are deemed to occur at the same time:
- All partnership liabilities become payable in full.
- All of the partnership's assets have a value of zero (except for property contributed to secure a liability).
- All property is disposed of by the partnership in a fully taxable transaction for no consideration except relief from liabilities for which the creditor's right to reimbursement is limited solely to one or more assets of the partnership.
- All items of income, gain, loss, or deduction are allocated to the partners.
- The partnership then liquidates.

69. The answer is D. All of the costs must be added to the basis of the land. The original basis of an asset includes:
- The purchase price, including any borrowed money to pay for the property
- Expenses of making the purchase, such as legal fees or realtor fees
- Any existing liabilities that the seller assumes (such as delinquent property taxes)

Any demolition costs are added to the basis of the land. Costs incurred to demolish a building are added to the basis of the land on which the demolished building was located. The costs cannot be claimed as a current deduction. See **Publication 551,** *Basis of Assets.*

70. The answer is C. Lynden Corporation must include the $12,000 on each employee's **Form W-2** because it is taxable as wages. The amounts are subject to withholding, as well as to Social Security and Medicare tax. The car allowance is treated as part of a nonaccountable plan. See **Publication 463,** *Travel, Entertainment, Gift, and Car Expenses.*

71. The answer is A. The death of a partner closes the partnership's tax year for that partner. Generally, it does not close the partnership's tax year for the remaining partners. The decedent's distributive share of partnership items must be figured as if the partnership's tax year ended on the date the partner died.

72. The answer is B. Software development in the United States qualifies for the domestic production activities deduction, which is authorized by section 199 and applies to activities related to installing, developing, improving, or creating goods that are "manufactured, produced, or grown within the United States." This deduction also applies to the construction of real property in the United States, domestic software development, and any qualified domestic film production (except for pornographic films.) The following types of business are specifically excluded from claiming the DPAD:
- Construction services that are cosmetic in nature, such as drywall and painting
- Leasing or licensing items to a related party
- Selling food or beverages prepared at restaurants or dining establishments
- The transmission or distribution of electricity, natural gas, or water
- Any advertising, product placement, customer service businesses, and other telecommunications services
- Most service type businesses

In 2012 the DPAD is equal to 9% of the lesser of the business's qualified production activities income or taxable income determined without regard to the DPAD.

73. The answer is A. *Depletion* is the using up of natural resources by mining, quarrying, drilling, or felling. The depletion deduction allows an owner to account for the reduction of a product's reserves. The industries that qualify for the depletion deduction are:
- Mining
- Timber
- Oil and gas

- Geothermal energy producers
- Other similar industries

A patent does not qualify for a depletion deduction because it is not a resource that gets used up. Instead, a patent would be amortized over its useful life.

74. The answer is D. The production of inventory is subject to the uniform capitalization rules (UNICAP). Under UNICAP, businesses must capitalize the direct costs for production of goods. In most cases, UNICAP also applies to businesses that purchase merchandise for resale to others. In essence, the rules affect most businesses that carry or produce inventory. The uniform capitalization rules do not apply to the following:

- Resellers of personal property with average annual gross receipts of $10 million or less for the three prior tax years
- Nonbusiness property (such as a hobby that is not operated for profit, but produces occasional income)
- Research and experimental expenditures
- Intangible drilling and development costs of oil and gas or geothermal wells
- Property produced under a long-term contract
- Timber raised, harvested, or grown, and the underlying land
- Qualified creative expenses incurred as freelance writers, photographers, or artists that are otherwise deductible on their tax returns
- Loan originations

75. The answer is B. An estate tax return is filed on **Form 706**, *United States Estate (and Generation-Skipping Transfer) Tax Return.*

76. The answer is A. Chris realizes $25,000 from the sale of his partnership interest ($10,000 cash payment + $15,000 liability relief). He reports $4,000 ($25,000 realized − $21,000 basis) as a capital gain. The sale of a partner's interest in a partnership usually results in capital gain or loss. Gain (or loss) is the difference between the amount realized and the adjusted basis of the partner's interest in the partnership. If the selling partner is relieved of any partnership liabilities, that partner must include the liability relief as part of the amount realized. See IRS **Publication 541, **
Partnerships.

77. The answer is A. Diamondback's taxable income is $80,000 ($100,000 dividends - $20,000 NOL). The tentative dividends-received deduction will not cause a net operating loss, so the Dividends-received deduction is limited to 70% of Diamondback's taxable income. The problem is figured as follows:

($100,000 dividends - $20,000 NOL) = $80,000 income (before the DRD)

$80,000 X 70% = $56,000

78. The answer is A. The cost of defending or perfecting a title *increases* an asset's basis. The following table shows common increases and decreases to basis:

Increases to Basis	Decreases to Basis
Putting an addition on a home	Nontaxable corporate distributions
Replacing an entire roof	Casualty or theft loss deductions and subsequent insurance reimbursements
Installing central air conditioning	Credit for qualified electric vehicles
Rewiring a rental property	Section 179 deduction
Assessments for local improvements	Deduction for clean-fuel vehicles and clean-fuel vehicle refueling property
Water connections, sidewalks, roads	Depreciation
Casualty losses (and subsequent repairs without insurance reimbursement)	Depletion
Restoring damaged property	Amortization
Legal fees	Rebates from a manufacturer

See **Publication 551**, *Basis of Assets*.

79. The answer is A. A trust must file IRS **Form 1041** in order to report income, loss, and distributions. The fiduciary fee is deductible in arriving at taxable income, and the fiduciary fee must be allocated between taxable and nontaxable income. The answer is figured as follows: ($4,000 - $500 fiduciary fee) = $3,500 in taxable income to be distributed.

80. The answer is C. Religious organizations (churches, mosques, etc.) are generally not required to file an information return to report their income and loss. This is the exception to the rule. Most exempt organizations are required to file **Form 990**. Churches are also exempted by law from payment of federal income tax and therefore they are not required to file an application for exemption with the IRS, but many churches still do seek formal exemption. Federal law imposes several reporting requirements on charitable organizations, but the main reporting requirements for churches have to do with employment taxes (when they pay employees) and unrelated business income tax, or UBIT. An exempt organization that has $1,000 or more of gross income from an unrelated business must file **Form 990–T**. Since Trinity does not have $1,000 of unrelated business income, it is not required to file **Form 990-T**, but it is still required to file employment tax returns (the **Form 941** series), because it pays employee wages. See IRS **Publication 557**, *Tax Exempt Status for Your Organization.*

81. The answer is B. In order to apply for recognition of exempt status by the IRS under section 501(c)(3) of the IRC, entities use Form 1023, *Application for Recognition of Exemption*. Tax-exempt organizations are organized primarily for religious, charitable, scientific, educational, or literary purposes. Organizations created to prevent cruelty to animals or children also qualify. There are two forms used by nonprofit organizations to request exemption. Organizations that *do not qualify* for exemption under section 501(c)(3) may still qualify for tax-exempt status under another code section. They can file Form 1024, *Application for Recognition of Exemption Under 501(a)*. See IRS **Publication 557**, *Tax Exempt Status for Your Organization.*

82. The answer is B. The exchange of partnership interests is not a qualifying 1031 exchange. Certain property does not qualify for section 1031 exchange treatment. Section 1031 does not apply to exchanges of:
- Inventory
- Stocks, bonds, notes, or other securities
- Livestock of different sexes
- Real property in the United States and real property outside the United States
- Shares of corporate stock in different companies
- Partnership interests in different partnerships

A 1031 exchange applies to business property or investment property only. Section 1031 says that owners may defer gain on the disposal of business property if they exchange it for another item of business property of a similar type (i.e., residential rental for an apartment building). The tax liability is not eliminated; it is simply *deferred* until the eventual sale or disposal of the newly acquired item. To qualify for a nontaxable 1031 exchange:
- The property must be business or investment property.
- The property must not be property held for sale (such as inventory, acquired specifically for resale).
- There must be an actual exchange of property.
- Tangible personal property can be either like-kind or like-class.
- Intangible personal property must be like-kind.

285

- The transferor must identify the property to be received within 45 days after the date the original property is given up in the exchange.
- The exchange must be completed within 180 days.
- A qualified intermediary must be used to facilitate the tax-deferred transaction.

83. The answer is A. Section 1245 property generally does not include buildings and their structural components, with the exception of certain single-purpose agricultural or horticultural structures (such as a greenhouse or a grain silo). For section 1245 property, any gain attributable to a previously deducted depreciation allowance is taxed as ordinary income.

84. The answer is C. Leisure Crafts Corporation will recognize neither gain nor loss on the sale of the asset. There is no loss recognized in this transaction because this is a sale to a related party. A loss on the sale of an asset to a related party is not allowed unless the distribution is done in a complete liquidation. In this case, "related parties" include members of a family, including brothers and sisters, spouse, ancestors (e.g., parents, grandparents), and lineal descendants (children, grandchildren). This list is not exhaustive, and related parties can also be entities. IRC section 267 not only applies to family members, but also includes related businesses, trusts, fiduciaries, and a host of other transactions.

85. The answer is D. An accrual-based C corporation is allowed to deduct charitable contributions authorized during the taxable year by the board of directors and paid by the 15th day of the third month following the close of the taxable year.

86. The answer is B. In general, a taxpayer has two years after the close of the year that the involuntary conversion occurred to replace the property and make the reinvestment. However, there are special rules for certain types of property. For real estate, the replacement period is generally three years after the close of the year in which the gain is realized. If the involuntary conversion property is not replaced within the allowed time period, an amended tax return would have to be filed, claiming the income as taxable.

87. The answer is A. Kristy will be forced to recognize $2,800 in imputed interest as dividend income. When a corporation makes an interest-free loan or a below-market loan to a shareholder, the imputed interest is deemed to be a taxable dividend. The corporation is not allowed to take a deduction for the imputed dividends that were paid. However, if the loan is made to an employee, the treatment of the imputed interest is different. When an employer makes an interest-free loan or a below-market loan to an employee, then the imputed interest is considered taxable compensation to the employee and is deductible by the employer. See **Publication 542**, *Corporations.*

88. The answer is B. A business may deduct up to $5,000 for start-up expenditures. If expenses exceed $50,000, there is a dollar-for-dollar reduction until the deduction is eliminated. The deduction for organizational costs is also $5,000 with a phase-out range of $50,000. Any remaining costs must be amortized over 180 months (15 years).

89. The answer is D. Prepayment penalties on a mortgage are deductible as interest expense. The other items listed cannot be taken as business expenses. Any type of political contribution, kickbacks, or any cost that is incurred to try to influence legislation is not deductible as a business expense. Repairs to equipment that add value to the asset or increase its useful life are considered improvements and must be capitalized and depreciated.

90. The answer is C. The original basis, which is $140,000 ($30,000 + $110,000), must be reduced by the depreciation. Therefore, Sam's adjusted basis in the building before the sale is $118,000 ($140,000 - $22,000). The gain is then figured as follows: ($205,000 - $118,000 basis) = $87,000 gain. The gain is allocated as follows: $22,000 of the $87,000 gain will be recognized as ordinary income (depreciation recapture) and the remaining $65,000 is taxed as a capital gain. See **Publication 544**, *Sales and Other Dispositions of Assets.*

91. The answer is D. An exempt entity may file a request for exemption within 15 months of initial organization. Retroactive exemption is still available within that time period.

92. The answer is B. The answer is figured as follows:

Gross receipts	$42,000
Supplies expense	($3,500)
Wages for part-time employee	($5,000)
Utility expenses	($800)
Income	**$32,700**

The amounts for the section 1231 gain and the charitable contributions are not reported on **Schedule C**. Section 1231 gains and losses are netted against each other in the same manner as capital gains and losses (for example, the gains and losses from a stock sale), except that a section 1231 gain is considered a capital gain, while a section 1231 loss is treated as an ordinary loss for tax purposes. See **Publication 544**, *Sales and Other Dispositions of Assets.*

93. The answer is C. Angie must include $27,000 = (30% X $90,000) in her gross income for the year. A partner pays tax on income that is earned, even if it is not distributed. In spite of having received only a $23,000 distribution, Angie must include $27,000 = (30% X $90,000) in her gross income for the year. Partnership income earned by a general partner is considered income from self-employment and is subject to self-employment tax.

94. The answer is C. Since Davenport Corporation operates on the accrual basis, it must meet the "all events test" and "economic performance" must have occurred before deducting and/or accruing the expense. Davenport is not required to pay the expense first. Under the accrual method of accounting, transactions are reported (and accrued) as they occur, regardless of when the actual cash (or other method of payment) is actually received or paid.

95. The answer is D. Guaranteed payments are only applicable to partnerships. Guaranteed payments are made to a partner without regard to the partnership's income. Corporations make distributions (not payments) to their shareholders.

96. The answer is B. The answer is figured as follows:

$120,000 X 80% = $96,000 dividends-received deduction

A corporation can deduct a percentage of certain dividends-received during its tax year. The dividends-received deduction is a tax deduction received by a corporation on the dividends paid to it by other corporations in which it has an ownership stake. If the corporation receiving the dividend owns 20% of the other corporation, the deduction is 80%.

97. The answer is A. Since Temple Corporation is on a fiscal tax year ending June 30, its payments are due October 15, December 15, March 15, and June 15. Installment payments for estimated tax are due by the fifteenth day of the fourth, sixth, ninth, and twelfth months of the corporation's tax year. If a corporation is on a calendar year, its tax year ends December 31. Installment payments are due April 15, June 15, September 15, and December 15. If any due date falls on a Saturday, Sunday, or legal holiday, the installment is due the next business day.

98. The answer is C. The section 179 deduction limit was unchanged at $500,000 in 2012. The total amount of qualifying property that can be purchased is $2 million, before the deduction is subject to a phase-out. Section 179 includes most new and used equipment. Businesses generally may not deduct the costs of real property under section 179. However, a special provision presently allows businesses to use up to $250,000 of the $500,000 limit for costs of qualified real property (QRP). This provision only applies to qualified leasehold improvement property, qualified restaurant property, and qualified retain improvement property.

99. The answer is C. An S-election may be revoked if shareholders holding more than 50% of the stock agree to the termination. Since Charlotte and Thomas own more than 50% of the outstanding stock, they can elect to revoke the S-election.

100. The answer is C. The corporation treats this $6,000 as a short-term loss that must be **carried back for three years** and **carried forward for up to five years**. When a corporation carries a net capital loss to another tax year, it is treated as a short-term loss. It does not retain its original identity as long-term or short-term. A corporation can deduct capital losses only up to the amount of its capital gains. In other words, if a corporation has an excess capital loss, it cannot deduct the loss in the current tax year. A capital loss is carried to other years in the following order:

- Three years prior to the loss year
- Two years prior to the loss year
- One year prior to the loss year

Any loss remaining is carried forward for five years. Capital losses incurred by a C corporation can only be used to offset capital gains, not ordinary income.

Representation: Answers

Exam #1 Representation: Answers

1. The answer is C. A tax practitioner may represent two clients when there is a clear conflict of interest, as long as both clients agree and sign a disclosure agreement. Tax practitioners may not notarize documents for the clients that they represent before the IRS. If the practitioner is a notary public and is employed as counsel, attorney, or agent in a matter before the IRS or has a material interest in the matter, he must not engage in any notary activities relative to that matter (Circular 230). Tax practitioners are allowed to charge contingent fees in some cases, but never on an original return. A tax preparer cannot endorse a client's refund check, even if permission is granted by the taxpayer.

2. The answer is D. A Third Party Authorization is not sufficient to designate a preparer to receive a tax refund check. A signed Form 2848, *Power of Attorney and Declaration of Representative*, must be used. Form 2848 is also used to authorize an individual to represent a taxpayer or an entity before the IRS. A Third Party Authorization will automatically end no later than the due date (without extensions) for filing the next year's return.

3. The answer is B. Preparers should review prior year returns in order to identify significant changes. The prior year return should always be checked for errors and to identify any carryover amounts from one year to the next.

4. The answer is B. Per IRC §6695(f) a $500 penalty may be imposed on a return preparer who endorses or negotiates a refund check issued to a taxpayer. This penalty is imposed on preparers who negotiate refund checks for returns they themselves prepared.

5. The answer is B. For Forms 941, *Employer's Quarterly Federal Tax Return* (and Forms 720, *Quarterly Federal Excise Tax Return*), the tax period is the first, second, third, or fourth quarter of the calendar year.

Form 941 is due on the last day of the month that follows the end of the quarter.		
Quarter Includes:	Quarter Ends	Form 941 Due
1. January, February, March	31-Mar	30-Apr
2. April, May, June	30-Jun	31-Jul
3. July, August, September	30-Sep	31-Oct
4. October, November, December	31-Dec	31-Jan

6. The answer is C. As of January 1, 2012, any tax preparer who files 11 or more Forms 1040, 1040A, 1040EZ and 1041 during a calendar year must use IRS e-file. However, clients may choose not to e-file their returns. Tax preparers should attach Form 8948, *Preparer Explanation for Not Filing Electronically*, to their client's paper return If a client is filing a joint return, only one spouse's signature is necessary on the choice statement.

7. The answer is A. Communications relating to tax advice between an enrolled agent and a taxpayer are confidential to the same extent that the communications would be privileged if it were between a taxpayer and an attorney, and the advice relates to:

- Noncriminal tax matters before the IRS, or
- Noncriminal tax proceedings brought in federal court by or against the United States.

This confidentiality privilege does not extend to:

- Communications regarding tax shelters
- Communications in furtherance of a crime or fraud
- Any criminal matter before the IRS
- The preparation of tax returns (IRC §7525)

8. The answer is A. A practitioner must, at the request of a client, promptly return any and all records belonging to him that he needs to comply with his federal tax obligations. This requirement does not include any forms or schedules that the practitioner prepared if the practitioner is withholding these documents pending the client's payment. The practitioner may retain copies of the records returned to a client.

9. The answer is B. In filing jointly, both taxpayers are *jointly and severally liable* for the tax and penalties on the joint return even if they later divorce. *Joint and several liability* means that each taxpayer is legally responsible for the entire liability. Thus, both spouses are generally held responsible for all the tax due even if one spouse earned all the income or claimed improper deductions or credits. This is also true even if a divorce decree states that a former spouse will be responsible for any amounts due on previously filed joint returns.

10. The answer is D. The practice of enrolled actuaries is limited to certain Internal Revenue Code sections that relate to their area of expertise, principally those sections governing employee retirement plans. See Publication 947, *Practice Before the IRS and Power of Attorney*.

11. The answer is A. Enrolled agents, like attorneys and certified public accountants (CPAs), have unlimited practice rights before the IRS. This means they are unrestricted as to which taxpayers they can represent, what types of tax matters they can handle, and which IRS offices they can represent clients before.

12. The answer is C. The Office of Professional Responsibility has the primary responsibility for matters relating to practitioner conduct, and exclusive responsibility for discipline, including disciplinary proceedings and sanctions. See Publication 947, *Practice Before the IRS and Power of Attorney*.

13. The answer is B. The Return Preparer Office is responsible for matters related to the authority to practice, including acting on applications for enrollment and administering competency testing and continuing education. See Publication 947, *Practice Before the IRS and Power of Attorney*.

14. The answer is C. An enrolled agent's practice rights do not extend to representation before the courts.

15. The answer is B. If an individual loses eligibility to practice, the IRS will not recognize a power of attorney that names the individual as a representative. Individuals who have been disbarred as a result of certain actions cannot practice before the IRS. See Publication 947, *Practice Before the IRS and Power of Attorney*.

16. The answer is D. If a disbarred practitioner seeks reinstatement, he or she may not practice before the IRS until the Office of Professional Responsibility authorizes reinstatement. Practitioners who are disbarred in a disciplinary proceeding are not allowed to practice before the IRS.

17. The answer is B. A disbarred practitioner can seek reinstatement from the Office of Professional Responsibility five years after disbarment.

18. The answer is A. Revenue rulings are written determinations released by the IRS that interpret the tax laws as applied to specific factual situations. A private letter ruling only applies to the individual taxpayer who requests the ruling. Technical advice memoranda provide nonbinding written advice in response to questions that arise from examinations. Information letters are issued in response to requests for general information by taxpayers. They are advisory only and have no binding effect on the IRS.

19. The answer is D. It is not required for a taxpayer to have filed for divorce when innocent spouse relief is requested. A taxpayer must meet all of the following conditions to qualify for "innocent spouse relief":

- The taxpayer filed a joint return that has an understatement of tax (deficiency) that is solely attributable to a spouse's erroneous item. An "erroneous item" includes income received by the other spouse, but which was omitted from the joint return. Deductions, credits, and property basis are also erroneous items if they are incorrectly reported on the return.
- When the taxpayer signed the joint return he or she did not know, and had no reason to know, that there was an understatement of tax on the return.
- Taking into account all the facts and circumstances, it would be unfair to hold the taxpayer liable for the understatement of tax.

Note: Previously, a taxpayer was required to request innocent spouse relief no later than two years after an IRS assessment. However, the two-year time limit no longer applies for innocent spouse requests for "equitable relief." Rather, the IRS will consider a request for equitable relief if the collection statute of limitations for the tax years involved has not expired, or, if the taxpayer is seeking a refund, if the refund statute of limitations has not expired. Many taxpayers that were previously denied because of the two-year limit may now reapply for relief if they qualify.

20. The answer is B. A formal complaint against a practitioner may be served in the following ways: Certified mail, First Class mail if returned undelivered by Certified mail; private delivery service; in person; or by leaving the complaint at the office of the practitioner. Electronic delivery, such as e-mail, is not a valid means of serving a complaint.

21. The answer is C. Best practices, according to Circular 230, include:

- Clearly communicating with clients and the IRS
- Establishing relevant facts, evaluating reasonableness of assumptions or representations, applying relevant legal authorities in arriving at a conclusion supported by the law and the facts (not the client's information)
- Advising the client regarding any potential penalties
- Acting fairly and with integrity in dealings with the IRS

22. The answer is D. The IRS does not recommend that all client information be stored electronically. The IRS requires tax preparers and other businesses to take appropriate steps to safeguard taxpayers' private information. The IRS makes the following specific recommendations:

- Take responsibility or assign an individual or individuals to be responsible for safeguards

- Assess the risks to taxpayer information in the office, including operations, physical environment, computer systems, and employees
- Make a list of all the locations taxpayer information is kept (computers, filing cabinets, bags, and boxes, etc.)
- Make a written plan on how the business will safeguard taxpayer information
- Put appropriate safeguards in place
- Use only service providers who have policies in place to also maintain an adequate level of information protection
- Monitor, evaluate, and adjust the security program as the tax preparer's business or circumstances change

See IRS Publication 4557, *Safeguarding Taxpayer Data.*

23. The answer is D. A "tax return preparer" includes a *non-signing* preparer who prepares all or a substantial portion of a return or claim for refund. A tax return preparer is any person who prepares returns for compensation, or who employs one or more persons to prepare for compensation, all (or a substantial portion) of any tax return. A signing tax return preparer is usually the tax preparer who has the primary responsibility for the overall accuracy of the return. Answer "A" and "C" are incorrect because VITA and TCE are volunteer programs where returns are not prepared for compensation. They offer free tax help for taxpayers who qualify (usually lower income individuals and individuals with simpler returns).

24. The answer is B. There is a six year statute of limitation period for the criminal offense of willfully attempting to evade or defeat any tax. See IRC § 6531 (periods of limitation on criminal prosecutions).

25. The answer is C. Failure to timely file tax returns or to pay taxes *may* be grounds for denying an application for enrollment. The Return Preparer Office will review all of the facts and circumstances to determine whether a denial of enrollment is warranted. Answer "A" is incorrect, because an enrolled agent is not required to have a Social Security number. Answer "B" is incorrect because U.S. citizenship is not required to practice before the IRS, and, in fact, many EAs, CPAs and attorneys work abroad helping expatriate taxpayers with their U.S. tax returns while they are living overseas.

26. The answer is A. A request for a collection due process (CDP) hearing will temporarily suspend the 10-year collection period and will also prohibit levy action in most cases. The amount of time the suspension is in effect will be added to the time remaining in the 10-year period. For example, if the 10-year period is suspended for six months, the time left in the period the IRS has to collect taxes will be extended by six months. See IRS Form 12153, *Request for a Collection Due Process or Equivalent Hearing*.

27. The answer is C. A lien is a legal claim to the property of the taxpayer as security for a tax debt. Generally, a federal tax lien will continue until the liability is satisfied, becomes unenforceable by lapse of time (the collection statute expires), or a bond is accepted in the amount of the liability.

28. The answer is B. The EIC will be disallowed, and the taxpayer will have a balance due, including penalties and interest. In addition, the taxpayer may be disallowed from claiming the EIC in future years.

29. The answer is B. Direct deposit of a taxpayer's refund should only be designated to an account in the taxpayer's name. It would be both illegal and unethical for a paid preparer to put his own bank account as the designated account to receive a taxpayer's refund.

30. The answer is D. Disbarred individuals are prohibited from practice before the IRS. However, a disbarred individual is still allowed to perform duties in certain capacities before the IRS. A suspended or disbarred individual may:

- Represent himself with respect to any matter (authorized under section 10.7(a)).
- Appear before the IRS as a trustee, receiver, guardian, administrator, executor, or other fiduciary if duly qualified/authorized under the law of the relevant jurisdiction (authorized under section 10.7(e)).
- Appear as a witness for the taxpayer.
- Furnish information at the request of the IRS or any of its officers.
- Receive information concerning a taxpayer from the IRS pursuant to a valid tax information authorization.

31. The answer is C. When a recognized representative has unreasonably delayed or hindered an examination, collection, or investigation, the Internal Revenue Service may request the permission of his immediate supervisor to contact the taxpayer directly for information. Answer "D" is incorrect because a representative does not necessarily have to be an enrolled practitioner for his power of attorney to be valid (for example, a father who is representing a son or an executor representing an estate). See IRS Publication 216, *Conference and Practice Requirements*.

32. The answer is C. Zena is allowed to represent Phillip during the examination of his joint return, as long as Phillip signs a valid power of attorney (Form 2848). In the case of a joint return in which both husband and wife will not be represented by the same recognized representative, the power of attorney must be executed by the spouse who will be represented. Individual representation is allowed. See IRS Publication 216, *Conference and Practice Requirements*.

33. The answer is C. A power of attorney is not required to be submitted by an attorney of record in a case that is docketed in the Tax Court. The Tax Court has its own rules of practice and procedure and its own rules regarding admission to practice before it. Accordingly, the rules of practice in Circular 230 differ from the rules of practice for the U.S. Tax Court.

34. The answer is B. A request for an offer in compromise will not release a tax lien. The IRS will release a lien:
- When the tax debt is fully paid.
- When payment of the debt is guaranteed by a bond.
- When the statute period for collection has ended (In this case, the release is automatic.)

See Publication 1450, *Instructions on How to Request a Certificate of Release of Federal Tax Lien*.

35. The answer is B. Roxanne may be able to qualify for relief as an innocent spouse even when she is responsible for all or part of the tax liability. In the case of an *innocent spouse*, the spouse requesting relief must not have known that income was underreported or that the tax shown on the return was otherwise incorrect. The taxpayer must complete and attach Form 8857, *Request for Innocent Spouse Relief*, to his or her hearing request.

36. The answer is D. A tax preparer cannot make disclosures to solicit additional business from an existing client that is not related to the IRS (for example, disclosures to sell or solicit insurance, stocks, or other financial services). In this case, the preparer would need written consent of the client. IRC section 7216 provides rules and sanctions for inappropriate disclosure of client information.

37. The answer is B. Certified financial planners are not enrolled practitioners for Circular 230 purposes, unless they meet one of the limited practice exceptions (for example, the representation of a close family member, employer, or fiduciary).

38. The answer is D. The IRS cannot seize a taxpayer's property if the taxpayer has:

- A current or pending installment agreement
- A current or pending offer in compromise

The IRS also will not seize a taxpayer's property if it agrees that the taxpayer is unable to pay due to economic hardship (which means that seizing the taxpayer's property would result in his inability to meet basic, reasonable living expenses).
See IRS Publication 594, *The IRS Collection Process.*

39. The answer is A. The Tax Equity and Fiscal Responsibility Act of 1982 (TEFRA) requires that all partnerships not meeting the definition of a "small partnership" be examined at the partnership level rather than at the partner level. Generally, any partnership with 11 or more partners at any one time during the partnership's tax year is considered a TEFRA partnership (Treas. Reg. section 301.6231(a)(1)-1(a)(1).

40. The answer is A. Esther must respond to the summons. A summons legally compels a person, taxpayer, or third party to meet with the IRS and provide information, documents, or testimony. See IRS Publication 594, *The IRS Collection Process.*

41. The answer is D. The TFRP may be assessed against any person who is responsible for collecting or paying withheld income and employment taxes, and willfully fails to pay them. A *responsible person* is any person who has the duty to perform and the power to direct the collecting, accounting, and paying of trust fund taxes. This person may be:
- An officer or an employee of a corporation
- A member or employee of a partnership
- A corporate director or shareholder
- A member of a board of trustees of a nonprofit organization
- Another person with authority and control over funds to direct their disbursement
- Another corporation or third party payer

42. The answer is B. If there is an understatement due to an unreasonable position, the penalty is the greater of $1,000 or 50% of the income derived by the tax return preparer related to the return or claim for refund. IRC § 6694(a)

43. The answer is B. The penalty is $500 for each failure to comply with the EIC due diligence requirements imposed in regulations. IRC § 6695(g)

44. The answer is B. When a question arises about the accuracy of a partnership return, it may be impractical for the IRS to audit each individual partner's return. Under the Tax Equity and Fiscal Responsibility Act of 1982 (TEFRA), the IRS will first audit the partnership as a single entity, with a "tax matters partner" (TMP) designated to serve as the main contact.

45. The answer is C. The OPR can censure, suspend, or disbar a practitioner from practice before the IRS for incompetence or disreputable conduct, such as giving false or misleading information, or participating in any business or accepting assistance from a disbarred practitioner. In 2011, the definition of "disreputable conduct" was expanded to include:

- Willfully failing to e-file returns electronically if they fall under the e-filing mandate, and
- Failing to include a valid PTIN on tax returns.

46. The answer is C. The formal complaint from the OPR is not required to disclose the identity of the employee who drafted the complaint. An official complaint against a practitioner is required to include the nature of the complaint, a demand for an answer to the charges, instructions on how to respond to the complaint, the specific charges against the practitioner, and the sanctions recommended.

47. The answer is A. Cora is allowed to destroy (or shred) the records related to her continuing professional education three years after the date of the EA renewal for which the CPE is credited.

48. The answer is B. The partnership is not a TEFRA Partnership and will not be subject to TEFRA audit rules. Partnerships with ten partners *or fewer* are typically exempt from the TEFRA rules under a special small partnership exception.

49. The answer is D. For Circular 230 purposes, the definition of a tax return includes: an original return, an amended return, and a claim for a refund.

50. The answer is B. If Mattie provides the name, address, and TIN (if the TIN is available) of the lender, the mortgage interest may be entered on Schedule A.

51. The answer is C. A practitioner may recommend or advise a client on a position, so long as the position is not incorrect, inconsistent, or incomplete; is not frivolous; and is adequately disclosed.

52. The answer is C. An enrolled agent who is appealing an official censure may still use the designation of enrolled agent, so long as that person is not disbarred, suspended, or placed on inactive status. A person who has passed the exam but has not completed the application process may not use the designation of enrolled agent to describe his or her status. An enrolled agent who is on inactive status or has not renewed his license may not use the designation.

53. The answer is A. Enrolled agents may not use "certified" when describing their professional designation. The other choices would be allowable representations.

54. The answer is C. Targeted direct mail solicitations are permitted under section 10.30. Section 10.30 specifies that practitioners using direct mail solicitation must retain a copy of the communication, as well as a list of the persons to whom it was distributed, for at least 36 months.

55. The answer is B. Noncriminal tax proceedings brought in federal court are granted confidentially privilege between an enrolled practitioner and his or her client. (IRC §7525)

56. The answer is B. The IRC §7525 confidentiality privilege does not extend to the preparation of returns. Therefore, any discussions surrounding the preparation of a tax return are not privileged.

57. The answer is B. The IRS may assess a penalty of $50 per failure to sign a tax return, up to a maximum of $25,000 per year.

58. The answer is C. Paid preparers are required to sign each return they prepare after it is completed but before presenting it to the taxpayer for signature.

59. The answer is A. An enrolled agent is required to complete a minimum of 16 hours of continuing professional education each year. Two of these hours must be an approved ethics course.

60. The answer is C. The preparer must take reasonable steps to inform the taxpayer within 24 hours of the rejection. In addition, the preparer is required to disclose the reasons for rejection. See Publication 1346, *Electronic Return File Specifications and Record Layouts for Individual Income Tax Returns*.

61. The answer is D. Tax returns with a valid ATIN may be e-filed in most cases. The following individual income tax returns cannot be processed using IRS e-file:
- Tax returns that are for any year other than the current year
- Tax returns with fiscal year tax periods
- Amended tax returns

- Returns containing forms or schedules that cannot be processed by IRS e-file
- Tax returns with Taxpayer Identification Numbers (ITINs) within the range of 900-00-0000 through 999-99-9999

*Exception: Returns with valid Adoption Taxpayer Identification Numbers (ATIN) may be accepted through IRS e-file. See Publication 1345, *Handbook for Authorized IRS e-file Providers of Individual Income Tax Returns.*

62. The answer is C. A practitioner must appeal the decision to the Secretary of the Treasury (or his delegate). Within 30 days after the administrative law judge makes a decision on a complaint filed by the OPR, the practitioner may appeal the decision to the Secretary of the Treasury. The OPR may also appeal an administrative law judge's decision, if a decision was reached in favor of the enrolled agent. In either case, the Secretary of the Treasury, or his delegate, will make a final determination regarding disbarment or other disciplinary complaint against an EA.

63. The answer is B. If a CPA is suspended from practice by a state board of accountancy, he will also be disbarred from practice before the IRS, regardless of whether the suspension was due to a non-tax matter.

64. The answer is B. An owner of a firm that employs preparers will not be subject to the preparer penalty if any of the following applies:
- There was substantial authority for the position taken on the return.
- There was a reasonable basis for the position, and the position was adequately disclosed.
- There was reasonable cause for the underpayment and the preparer acted in good faith.

The determination of whether a taxpayer or a preparer acted with reasonable cause and in "good faith" is made on a case-by-case basis, taking into account all pertinent facts and circumstances. To meet the "reasonable basis" standard a tax return preparer may rely in good faith, without verification, on information furnished by a taxpayer, advisor, another preparer, or other party (See IRC §1.6664-4 *Reasonable cause and good faith exception to section 6662 penalties*).

65. The answer is B. Practitioners who have been disciplined by the Office of Professional Responsibility are not eligible for inactive status. Practitioners must use Form 8554, *Application for Renewal of Enrollment to Practice Before the Internal Revenue Service,* to request inactive status.

66. The answer is A. Agnes is required to submit an e-file application and request a new EFIN. Preparers that acquire an existing IRS e-file business by purchase, transfer, or gift must submit a new IRS e-file application and receive a new Electronic Filing Identification Number (EFIN). See IRS Publication 3112, *IRS e-file Application and Participation*.

67. The answer is D. A taxpayer should keep asset records until the period of limitations expires for the year in which the taxpayer disposes of the property in a taxable disposition.

68. The answer is C. An employer is required to retain all employment tax records for at least four years after the date that the tax becomes due or is paid, whichever is later.

69. The answer is A. A misdemeanor conviction alone is unlikely to cause a tax preparer to face disciplinary action from the OPR. There are four broad categories of preparer misconduct, all of which may result in disciplinary action:
- Misconduct while representing a taxpayer
- Misconduct related to the practitioner's own return
- Giving a false opinion, knowingly, recklessly, or through gross incompetence
- Misconduct not directly involving IRS representation, such as a felony conviction

70. The answer is D. If a taxpayer fails to file a return, and the failure to file is due to fraud, the penalty is 15% for each month or part of a month that the return is late, up to a maximum of 75%.

71. The answer is A. A reportable transaction is a transaction of a type that the IRS has determined as having the potential for tax avoidance or evasion. If a reportable transaction is not disclosed and results in an understatement of tax, an additional penalty in the amount of 30% of the understatement may be assessed. Reportable transactions must be reported on Form 8886, *Reportable Transaction Disclosure Statement*.

72. The answer is C. Since Mollie was owed a refund, she will not be assessed a late penalty on her individual return. If a taxpayer files his or her return more than 60 days after the due date (or extended due date), the minimum penalty is the *smaller* of $135 or 100% of the unpaid tax. Since Mollie did not have any unpaid tax shown on her return, she will not be assessed this penalty. ***Note:** The rules for late filing penalties are different for corporations, partnerships, and other entities.

73. The answer is D. Taxpayers have a right to be represented during the examination process. They also have a right to appeal any and all of the examination if they disagree with the report. However, taxpayers do not have a right to ignore or decline an IRS summons, although they can request representation during the summons process.

74. The answer is A. Tax preparers are required to retain a complete copy of each return they have prepared, (or a list of taxpayer's names and TINs, and the tax years for which returns were prepared). They must retain the copies for a minimum of three years.

75. The answer is B. The reasonable cause and good faith exceptions do not apply to an understatement of income that is a result of an unreasonable position. To meet the "reasonable basis" standard, a tax return preparer may rely in good faith, without verification, on information furnished by a taxpayer, advisor, another preparer, or other party (See IRC §1.6694-2 Penalty for understatement due to an unrealistic position).

76. The answer is A. If a taxpayer files an erroneous claim for refund, the penalty is equal to 20% of the disallowed amount of the claim, *unless* the taxpayer can show a reasonable basis for the claim. This penalty will not be figured on any part of the disallowed amount of the claim that relates to the Earned Income Credit or on which the accuracy-related or fraud penalties are charged.

77. The answer is B. Fraud, as distinguished from negligence, is always intentional. One of the elements of fraud is an intent to evade tax. Some "badges" of fraud that the IRS looks for include:
- False explanations regarding understated or omitted income
- Large discrepancies between actual and reported deductions of income
- Concealment of income sources
- Numerous errors in the taxpayer's favor
- Fictitious records or other deceptions
- Large omissions of personal service income, specific items of income, gambling winnings, or illegal income
- False deductions, exemptions, or credits
- Failure to keep or furnish records

- Incomplete information given to the return preparer regarding a fraudulent scheme
- Large and/or frequent cash dealings that may or may not be common to the taxpayer's business
- Verbal misrepresentations of the facts and circumstances

Generally, the presence of only one indication of fraud is not sufficient to sustain fraud (e.g., unreported income alone does not necessarily support fraud) *Internal Revenue Manual, Part 4, Examining Process.*

78. The answer is B. The fraud penalty on a joint return does not automatically apply to a spouse unless some part of the underpayment is due to the fraud of that spouse. The injured spouse may apply for relief. See Publication 17 for further explanation.

79. The answer is C. In both criminal and civil fraud, the burden of proof rests with the government. The taxpayer's explanations, or lack of explanations, may help distinguish between civil and criminal fraud. A criminal conviction for tax evasion (under section 7201) usually establishes liability for the civil fraud penalty. The civil fraud penalty can be imposed even when the taxpayer is acquitted in a criminal fraud prosecution. *Internal Revenue Manual, Part 4, Examining Process.*

80. The answer is A. Edgar should sign for himself, and the executor of Mae's estate should sign on Mae's behalf. If a spouse dies before signing the return, the executor or administrator must sign the return for the deceased spouse. If no one has been appointed as executor or administrator, the surviving spouse can sign the return and enter "Filing as surviving spouse" in the signature area of the return.

81. The answer is C. Katherine is allowed to sign on behalf of her husband whether or not she has a signed power of attorney. A spouse can sign a joint return for a spouse who cannot sign because he or she is serving in a combat zone, even without a power of attorney. See Publication 3, *Armed Forces' Tax Guide.*

82. The answer is A. A taxpayer can change his or her filing status by filing an amended return using Form 1040X.

83. The answer is B. All the acts of the taxpayer, when seen as a whole, indicate fraud. Fraud, as distinguished from negligence, is always intentional. One of the elements of fraud is an intent to evade tax. The existence of several "badges of fraud" will usually indicate fraud, rather than simply ordinary negligence.

84. The answer is B. If an IRS examiner determines an IRC 6694 penalty applies:

- A detailed report is prepared
- The preparer is provided with a copy

Then the preparer has 30 days to request an appeal before the penalty is assessed.

85. The answer is D. If a primary taxpayer, spouse, (or both) have ITINs, they are in-eligible to receive the Earned Income Credit, even if their dependents have valid SSNs. If a taxpayer and spouse (if filing jointly) have valid SSNs, only dependents with valid SSNs will qualify to receive the EIC.

86. The answer is B. Starting in 2012, Forms W-7, *Application for IRS Individual Tax-payer Identification Number*, must include original documentation such as passports and birth certificates. Notarized copies of documentation will no longer be accept-ed.

87. The answer is D. A censure is a public reprimand. It does not prevent an en-rolled practitioner from filing returns or representing taxpayers before the IRS.

88. The answer is D. All of the above situations reflect a potential conflict of interest for a paid tax preparer. Tax preparers are allowed to represent parties who have a conflict of interest, so long as the preparer has express consent of all directly inter-ested parties after full disclosure has been made. Written consent is required in this case.

89. The answer is A. Sophia may reapply by using IRS Form 8857, *Request for Inno-cent Spouse Relief*, if the collection statute of limitations for the tax years involved has not expired. The IRS will treat the taxpayer's original request for equitable relief as a claim for refund for purposes of the refund statute.

90. The answer is C. If a tax preparer is deemed to have stated a position on a tax return that was due to "willful and reckless" conduct, the preparer penalty is $5,000 or 50% of the income derived, whichever is greater. IRC § 6694 – Understatements of taxpayer's liability by tax preparer:

- IRC §6694(a) – Understatement due to unreasonable positions. The penalty is the *greater* of $1,000 or 50% of the income derived by the tax preparer with respect to the return or claim for refund.
- IRC §6694(b) – Understatement due to willful or reckless conduct. The pen-alty is the *greater* of $5,000 or 50% of the income derived by the tax pre-parer with respect to the return or claim for refund.

91. The answer is A. The penalty is $250 for each unauthorized disclosure of information in connection with the preparation of a return. The maximum penalty shall not exceed $10,000 in a calendar year (IRC § 6713 – Disclosure or use of information by preparers of returns).

92. The answer is C. In 2011, disciplinary authority for the Office of Professional Responsibility was extended to include all paid tax return preparers under Treasury Regulation §301.7701-15(b)(2). The authority to sign complaints and discipline practitioners now lies exclusively with the Office of Professional Responsibility.

93. The answer is A. Circular 230, which is found in Title 31 of the U.S. Code, governs practice before the Internal Revenue Service.

94. The answer is D. An individual who provides only typing, reproduction, or other mechanical assistance in the preparation of a return is not a "preparer" for Circular 230 purposes. A reporting agent who renders tax advice to any client regarding employee classification, or any other tax issue, would be considered a "tax preparer" under Circular 230 (see Treasury Regulation section 301.7701-15(f)(6)). The new Circular 230 §10.2(a) expands the definition of practitioner to include any practitioner who prepares tax returns or provides tax advice for compensation.

95. The answer is D. A preparer may request a PTIN by mail by submitting a paper Form W-12, *IRS Paid Preparer Tax Identification Number (PTIN) Application*. A preparer may also request a PTIN using the online form on the IRS website. A preparer cannot request a PTIN over the phone.

96. The answer is C. Final regulations provide legally binding tax guidance, and carry more weight than temporary or proposed regulations. A U.S. Tax Court memorandum decision is not a type of IRS guidance. The U.S. Tax Court is independent of the IRS. The IRS is not bound to follow any court decision, with the exception of the U.S. Supreme Court, whose decisions are binding on the IRS as well as taxpayers.

97. The answer is B. A preparer is in tax compliance if all returns that are due have been filed and all taxes that are due have been paid (or acceptable payment arrangements have been established).

98. The answer is C. A signing tax return preparer should be the tax preparer who has the primary responsibility for the accuracy of the return. The new PTIN requirements requiring all preparers to obtain a PTIN do not change the existing rules regarding who the signing tax return preparer is.

99. The answer is B. Beatrice is not a preparer under Circular 230 rules, so she is not required to obtain a PTIN. If an employee of a business prepares the business' tax returns as part of their job responsibilities, the employee is not required to sign as a paid preparer. Accordingly, unless the employee prepares other federal tax returns for compensation, he or she is also not required to obtain a PTIN.

100. The answer is B. ERPAs that prepare only Form 5300 or Form 5500 series returns are not required to obtain a PTIN. Also, ERPAs who only provide retirement plan administration are not required to obtain a PTIN.

Exam #2 Representation: Answers

1. The answer is A. Tania is not a tax return preparer and is not required to have a PTIN. All paid tax return preparers are required to obtain a Preparer Tax Identification Number (PTIN). However, employees that simply offer technical or office help are not required to obtain a PTIN.

2. The answer is B. Tax returns prepared by a paid preparer but filed on paper must be submitted with Form 8948, *Preparer Explanation for Not Filing Electronically*. A reason must be provided for each return that is not e-filed.

3. The answer is D. Anyone who prepares taxes for compensation is required to obtain a PTIN, including active attorneys and certified public accountants. However, there is an exception for certain CPAs and attorneys. They do not need to obtain a PTIN unless they prepare for compensation all or substantially all of a federal tax return or claim for refund. A CPA, for example, who only does audit work is not required to obtain a PTIN; nor would a criminal defense attorney, assuming he or she does not prepare tax returns for compensation.

4. The answer is B. The enrollment cycle refers to the three successive enrollment years preceding the effective date of renewal.

5. The answer is E. All of the practitioners listed qualify to represent a taxpayer before the IRS, under certain circumstances. Student volunteers at a VITA site are given a special exemption to represent taxpayers before the IRS. VITA is the IRS's volunteer income tax preparation program, designed specifically to help low income taxpayers. See Circular 230.

6. The answer is B. There are special restrictions on EIC claims by taxpayers that have had previous EIC claims denied. A taxpayer who claimed the EIC due to reckless or intentional disregard of the EIC rules cannot claim the EIC for two tax years. If the error was due to outright fraud, the taxpayer cannot claim the EIC for ten tax years. See Publication 596, *Earned Income Credit*.

7. The answer is C. In 2011 as part of a broader crackdown on identity fraud, the IRS began issuing Identity Protection Personal Identification Numbers (IP PIN) to taxpayers who have been victims of identity theft and who have provided information that verifies their identity. The IP PIN helps prevent the misuse of a taxpayer's Social Security Number or Taxpayer Identification Number on tax returns. The IP PIN is only valid for a single year. A taxpayer will receive a new IP PIN every year for three years after an identity theft incident.

8. The answer is B. Randall needs a PTIN, but he does not need to pass a competency test. All paid preparers need a PTIN. However, certain "supervised preparers" do not need to pass a competency test if they are employed by a law firm, CPA firm, or other tax firm (a firm that is at least 80% owned by attorneys, CPAs, or enrolled agents), provided the returns prepared are signed by an attorney, CPA, or an EA who is employed by the same firm and has a valid PTIN.

9. The answer is A. Form 23 is the application for enrollment. Applicants must undergo a background check prior to enrollment. The IRS says it may take up to 120 days to receive an enrollment card.

10. The answer is A. Form 8857 is used to request innocent spouse relief. Innocent spouse relief provides relief from additional tax owed if a spouse or former spouse failed to report income, reported income improperly, or claimed improper deductions or credits. See Publication 971 for more information on innocent spouse relief.

11. The answer is D. Doug may use the phrase, *"Enrolled to practice before the Internal Revenue Service."* Enrolled agents, in describing their professional designation, may not use the term "certified" or imply any type of employment relationship with the IRS. Examples of acceptable descriptions for enrolled agents are "enrolled to represent taxpayers before the Internal Revenue Service," "enrolled to practice before the Internal Revenue Service," and "admitted to practice before the Internal Revenue Service." For more information, see Circular 230.

12. The answer is D. A PTIN cannot be shared. A PTIN is an individual preparer's number, so each preparer must obtain his or her own PTIN.

13. The answer is A. Practitioners may not use official IRS insignia in their advertising. A practitioner *may* use the IRS e-file logo. A preparer may not combine the e-file logo with the IRS eagle symbol, the word "federal," or with other words or symbols that suggest a special relationship between the IRS and the practitioner. Advertising materials must not carry the FMS (IRS Financial Management Service), IRS, or other Treasury seals. For more information, see Circular 230.

14. The answer is D. Alimony is not considered qualifying income for purposes of the EIC. Qualifying earned income includes:
- Wages, salaries, and tips.
- Union strike benefits.
- Long-term disability benefits received prior to minimum retirement age.
- Net earnings from self-employment.
- *Combat Pay: A taxpayer can *elect* to have nontaxable combat pay included in earned income for the Earned Income Credit.

15. The answer is D. A levy does not apply to the taxpayer's clothing and undelivered mail. Property exempt from levy also includes the following:

- Fuel, provisions (food), furniture, personal effects in the taxpayer's household, arms for personal use, or livestock, up to $8,570 in value for tax year 2012.
- Books and tools necessary for the trade, business, or profession of the taxpayer, up to $4,290 in value for tax year 2012.
- Unemployment benefits and amounts payable under the Job Training Partnership Act.
- Workers' compensation, including amounts payable to dependents.
- Certain annuity or pension payments, but only if payable by the Army, Navy, Air Force, Coast Guard, or under the Railroad Retirement Act or Railroad Unemployment Insurance Act. Traditional or Roth IRAs are not exempt from levy.
- Judgments for the support of minor children (child support).
- Certain public assistance and welfare payments, and amounts payable for Supplemental Security Income for the aged, blind, and disabled under the Social Security Act. Regular Social Security payments are not exempt from levy.
- The taxpayer's principal residence (usually). After 1998, the seizure of a personal residence by the IRS is prohibited for any liability under $5,000. For all liabilities of $5,000 or more, the IRS must obtain approval from a U.S. District Court judge or magistrate prior to seizing a personal residence. (IRC §6334).

An IRS levy refers to the actual seizing of property authorized by a tax lien, so it is a legal seizure of property. A tax lien, on the other hand, is the IRS's *authorization* to act.

16. The answer is A. To claim the EIC, the taxpayer (and spouse, if filing a joint return) must have a valid SSN issued by the Social Security Administration. Any qualifying child listed on Schedule EIC also must have a valid SSN.

17. The answer is D. A practitioner may not charge a contingent fee (percentage of the refund) for preparing an original tax return. Separate fees may not be charged for Direct Deposits, and e-file providers are still required to sign e-filed returns with their electronic signatures (Circular 230).

18. The answer is A. Simply preparing a tax return, furnishing information at the request of the IRS, or appearing as a witness for the taxpayer is not practice before the IRS. These acts can be performed by anyone. Practice before the IRS covers all matters relating to any of the following:

- Communicating with the IRS on behalf of a taxpayer regarding the taxpayer's rights, privileges, or liabilities under laws and regulations administered by the IRS.
- Representing a taxpayer at conferences, hearings, or meetings with the IRS.
- Preparing and filing documents with the IRS for a taxpayer.
- Corresponding and communicating on behalf of a taxpayer.

For more information, see Circular 230.

19. The answer is D. Applicants for renewal of enrollment must file Form 8554, *Application for Renewal of Enrollment to Practice Before the Internal Revenue Service*. To qualify for renewal, applicants must complete the necessary hours of continuing professional education during each three-year enrollment cycle. For more information, see Circular 230.

20. The answer is D. Receipt of taxpayer refund checks is allowed, but the tax practitioner must have a power of attorney in order to do so. A tax practitioner may never cash (or endorse) a taxpayer refund check. A power of attorney is not required in some situations when dealing with the IRS. The following situations do not require a power of attorney:

- Providing information to the IRS
- Authorizing the disclosure of tax return information through Form 8821
- Allowing the IRS to discuss return information with a third party designee
- Allowing a tax matters partner or person (TMP) to perform acts for the partnership
- Allowing the IRS to discuss return information with a fiduciary
- Representing a taxpayer through a non-written consent

These exceptions are discussed in detail in IRS Publication 947, *Practice Before the IRS and Power of Attorney*.

21. The answer is B. A third-party designee may respond to IRS notices about math errors, offsets, and return preparation. The taxpayer completes the Third Party Designee Authorization directly on the tax return, entering the designee's name and phone number and a self-selected five-digit PIN, which the designee will have to confirm when requesting information from the IRS. A third party designee may:

- Exchange information concerning the return with the IRS;
- Call the IRS for information about the processing of the return or the status of refund or payments;

- Request and receive written tax return information relating to the tax return, including copies of notices, correspondence, and account transcripts; and
- Respond to certain IRS notices about math errors, offsets, and return preparation.

The taxpayer is not authorizing the designee to receive any refund check, bind the taxpayer to any IRS contract or agreement (including additional tax liability), or otherwise represent the taxpayer before the IRS.

22. The answer is D. The IRS may accept an offer in compromise based on *three* grounds: (a) doubt as to collectability, (b) effective tax administration, and (c) doubt as to liability.

23. The answer is B. The Internal Revenue Code (or IRC) is the main body of domestic tax law of the United States.

24. The answer is C. Lloyd must notify Kelly of the error and tell her the consequences of not correcting it. But he is not required to amend prior year tax returns to correct the error. A tax practitioner is *required* by Circular 230 to advise the taxpayer when he becomes aware that the client has not complied with the revenue laws of the United States. However, the practitioner is not responsible for fixing the noncompliance issue once he has notified the client of the issue. The tax professional is also not responsible for notifying the IRS of noncompliance.

25. The answer is A. A tax practitioner may not charge a separate fee for Direct Deposit. Charging a flat fee for e-filing is allowed. Contingent fees for e-filing are not permitted. A practitioner may charge fees based on the following:

- Fixed fees for specific routine services
- Hourly fee rates
- Range of fees for particular services
- Fee charged for an initial consultation

26. The answer is B. To be an enrolled agent, a candidate has to be at last 18 years old, not 21. The other statements are all requirements to become an enrolled agent.

27. The answer is C. Erin may qualify for injured spouse relief by filing to receive her share of the refund that was applied toward her husband's debt. Injured spouse relief may also apply when a spouse has past due income tax, child support, or other obligations that are applied toward a tax refund. **Note:** An *injured spouse* is not to be confused with an *innocent spouse,* which is a different legal situation. If certain conditions are met, an innocent spouse may apply for relief from additional tax if a spouse or former spouse failed to report income or claimed improper deductions on a jointly filed tax return.

28. The answer is B. Preparers who anticipate filing 11 or more Forms 1040, 1040A, 1040EZ, and Forms 1041 (fiduciary returns) during the year must use IRS e-file. The requirement also applies to tax preparation firms, which must compute the number of returns prepared by its members in the aggregate. Business tax returns, such as Form 1120 or Form 1065, are not subject to the current e-file mandate (although some very large corporate returns do have an e-file requirement).

29. The answer is C. Any individual who is paid a fee to prepare a return must sign it and fill out the preparer area of the return. This is true even when the client is a family member. An employee working for an employer does not have to sign the return. Rather, the employer is the one who has the ultimate liability for the return's accuracy.

30. The answer is D. Tax returns bearing an ATIN may be e-filed. There are certain tax returns that cannot be e-filed. Returns with paper attachments and other odd requirements must be filed on paper. The following returns cannot be e-filed:

- Prior year tax returns;
- Tax returns with fiscal year tax periods (for business entities);
- Amended tax returns;
- Tax returns with Taxpayer Identification Numbers (TIN) within the range of 900-00-0000 through 999-99-9999. Exception: Adopted Taxpayer Identification Numbers (ATIN) and some Individual Taxpayer Identification Numbers (ITIN) may fall within the range above.

The IRS cannot electronically process tax returns with rare or unusual processing conditions or that exceed the specifications for returns allowable in IRS e-file. These conditions change from year to year. If providers transmit electronic return data with one of these conditions, the IRS rejects the return and the taxpayer will have to file on paper.

31. The answer is D. Internal Revenue Code §7216 is a criminal provision enacted by Congress that prohibits tax return preparers from *knowingly or recklessly* disclosing or using tax return information. The regulations were updated in 2008 to clarify that e-file providers are among the return preparers who are bound by these privacy rules. A convicted preparer may be fined up to $1,000, imprisoned up to one year, or both, for *each violation* of section 7216.

32. The answer is B. When an individual strikes out the jurat on a return, it becomes a fraudulent return. The jurat is an affidavit in which the taxpayer and/or preparer attests to the truth of the information contained in the return and attached return information. Civil penalties for altering a jurat include:

- A $500 penalty imposed under section 6702;
- Additional penalties for failure to file a return, failure to pay tax owed, and fraudulent failure to file a return; and
- A penalty of up to $25,000 under section 6673 if the taxpayer makes frivolous arguments in the United States Tax Court.

33. The answer is D. A taxpayer or business is required to keep records relating to employment taxes for at least four years after the due date of the tax or the date such tax was paid, whichever is later. This includes Form W-4, Form 941, and copies of Form W-2.

34. The answer is A. A censure will not prevent a practitioner from practice before the IRS. Official sanctions include disbarment, suspension, censure, and reprimand. Disbarment is the permanent revocation of a practitioner's privilege to represent taxpayers before the IRS. A censure is a public reprimand. Unlike disbarment or suspension, censure does not affect an individual's eligibility to practice before the IRS. After being subject to OPR sanctions of either suspension or censure, the practitioner may be subject to conditions on his ability to practice.

35. The answer is C. The Office of Professional Responsibility does not process PTIN applications. The Return Preparer Office (RPO) is responsible for reviewing and processing PTIN applications as well as applications for enrollment.

36. The answer is B. In most cases, tax returns are audited for up to three years after filing. However, the IRS may audit for up to six years if there is substantial unreported income (25% or more income is unreported).

37. The answer is D. A power of attorney is valid until revoked. It may be revoked by the taxpayer or withdrawn by the representative, or it may be superseded by the filing of a new power of attorney for the same tax and tax period. For more information, see Circular 230.

38. The answer is A. Taxpayers must sign their returns under penalty of perjury. This means that the taxpayer must make a declaration that the return is true, correct, and complete.

39. The answer is C. Most paid preparers need both a PTIN and an EFIN. Each tax preparer needs to have his own PTIN, which is issued to individuals. An Electronic

Filing Identification Number (EFIN) is a number issued by the IRS to individuals or firms that have been approved as authorized IRS e-file providers. EFINs are issued on a firm basis, and all preparers in a firm may be covered by a single EFIN. Electronic Filing Identification Numbers are issued to individuals or firms.

40. The answer is C. Performance as a notary is not considered disreputable conduct. An enrolled practitioner may also perform duties as a notary public. A practitioner who is a notary public and is engaged in a matter before the IRS (or has a material interest in the matter) cannot engage in any notary activities related to that matter. All of the other acts listed are considered disreputable conduct. In 2011, the OPR expanded the definition of "disreputable conduct" to include:

- Willfully failing to e-file returns electronically if they fall under the e-filing mandate, and
- Failing to include a valid PTIN on tax returns.

41. The answer is B. Tax practitioners may not notarize documents for the clients that they represent before the IRS. If the practitioner is a notary public and is employed as counsel, attorney, or agent in a matter before the IRS or has a material interest in the matter, he must not engage in any notary activities relative to that matter (Circular 230). Tax practitioners are allowed to charge contingent fees in rare cases, but never on an original return. A tax practitioner may represent clients with a conflict of interest so long as it is disclosed in writing to both parties and both parties agree. A tax practitioner may discuss and recommend tax shelters to a client, but the disclosure and ethics rules regarding tax shelters and tax shelter opinions are very strict.

42. The answer is A. Form 8275, *Disclosure Statement*, is filed by individuals, corporations, pass-through entities, and income tax return preparers to disclose a tax position on a tax return.

43. The answer is D. Tax preparers must not endorse or otherwise cash any refund check issued to the taxpayer. A tax preparer cannot withhold a taxpayer's refund check because of a fee dispute. However, a tax preparer is not required to file a client's tax return without first obtaining payment.

44. The answer is B. If an e-file hardship waiver is denied, there is an administrative appeal available. Tax return preparers may request a hardship waiver from the e-file requirement by using Form 8944, *Preparer e-file Hardship Waiver Request*. Form 8944 generally must be submitted to the IRS no later than February 15 of the year for which a waiver is being requested.

45. The answer is D. The taxpayer may not designate refunds for Direct Deposit to credit card accounts. Taxpayers often elect the Direct Deposit option because it is the fastest way of receiving refunds. Providers must accept any Direct Deposit election to any eligible financial institution designated by the taxpayer. The taxpayer may designate refunds to savings, checking, share draft, or consumer asset accounts (for example, IRA or money market accounts). For more information, see Publication 1345, *Handbook for Authorized IRS e-file Providers of Individual Income Tax Returns.*

46. The answer is B. Any tax return preparer who fails to comply with due diligence requirements for the EIC can be liable for a penalty of $500 for each failure.

47. The answer is C. A hard copy (paper copy) is not required. The preparer must provide a complete copy of the return to the taxpayer. Preparers may provide this copy in any media, including electronic, that is acceptable to both the taxpayer and the preparer. The copy need not contain the Social Security Number of the paid preparer. A complete copy of a taxpayer's return includes Form 8453 and other documents that the preparer cannot electronically transmit, when applicable, as well as the electronic portion of the return. See Publication 1345, *Handbook for Authorized IRS e-file Providers of Individual Income Tax Returns.*

48. The answer is C. Private letter rulings are written decisions by the Internal Revenue Service in response to a taxpayer's written request for guidance on a particular tax issue. PLRs become public record once issued; all of the taxpayer's personal information is removed.

49. The answer is B. Any taxpayer who files a tax return that is considered "frivolous" faces a penalty of $5,000, *in addition* to any other penalty provided by law. This penalty may be doubled on a joint return. A taxpayer will be subject to this penalty if he files a tax return based simply on the desire to interfere with the administration of tax law. See Publication 17, *Your Federal Income Tax.*

50. The answer is A. In tax disputes involving $50,000 or less, taxpayers may choose to use the Tax Court small tax case procedure.

51. The answer is C. There are three types of Treasury regulations: legislative, interpretive, and procedural. There is no such thing as a "Congressional regulation" issued by the Treasury Department.

52. The answer is B. If an Authorized IRS e-file Provider uses direct mail, e-mail, fax communications, or other distribution methods to advertise, the Provider must retain a copy, as well as a list or other description of the firms, organizations, or individuals to whom the communication was sent, and provide it to the IRS upon request until the end of the calendar year following the date sent. The preparer must keep a copy of the advertisement and provide it to the IRS upon request. Copies must be retained until the end of the calendar year following the last transmission or use. See Publication 3112, *IRS e-file Application and Participation*.

53. The answer is A. Rejected electronic individual income tax return data can be corrected and retransmitted without new signatures or authorizations if changes do not differ from the amount on the original electronic return by more than $50 to "total income" or "AGI," or more than $14 to "total tax," "federal income tax withheld," "refund," or "amount you owe." The preparer must give taxpayers copies of the new electronic return data. See Publication 1345, *Handbook for Authorized IRS e-file Providers of Individual Income Tax Returns*.

54. The answer is D. The IRS may delay refunds for a number of reasons, including the following:
- Errors in Direct Deposit information (refunds then sent by check);
- Financial institution refusals of Direct Deposits (refunds then sent by check) or delays in crediting the Direct Deposit to the taxpayer's account;
- Estimated tax payments differing from the amount reported on the tax return (for example, fourth quarter payments not yet on file when return data is transmitted);
- Bankruptcy;
- Inappropriate claims for the Earned Income Credit; or
- Recertification to claim the Earned Income Credit.

When a delay occurs, the IRS sends the taxpayer a letter explaining the delay and how to resolve the issue. See Publication 1345, *Handbook for Authorized IRS e-file Providers of Individual Income Tax Returns*.

55. The answer is B. If the IRS rejects the electronic portion of a taxpayer's individual income tax return for processing and the Electronic Return Originator cannot rectify the reason for the rejection, the ERO must take reasonable steps to inform the taxpayer of the rejection within 24 hours. When the ERO advises the taxpayer that it has not filed the return, the ERO must provide the taxpayer with the reject code(s) accompanied by an explanation. If the taxpayer chooses not to have the electronic portion of the return corrected and transmitted to the IRS, or if the IRS cannot accept the return for processing, the taxpayer must file a paper return. See Publication 1345, *Handbook for Authorized IRS e-file Providers of Individual Income Tax Returns*.

56. The answer is A. A late payment on an installment agreement will generate an automatic 30-day notice that the agreement is terminated, which allows the IRS time to make changes to the installment agreement.

57. The answer is A. The ethics requirement for the enrolled agent license renewal is a minimum of two hours of ethics per year, so Francisco has not fulfilled his ethics requirement. Section 10.6(e)(2)(ii) requires a minimum of 16 hours of continuing education credit per year, with at least two hours devoted to ethics. If a preparer takes more than two hours of ethics in a single year, the extra ethics hours can count toward the overall minimum requirement. The ethics requirement is in effect every single year.

58. The answer is A. A Refund Anticipation Loan (RAL) is an agreement between a taxpayer and a lender. An RAL is money borrowed by a taxpayer from a lender based on the taxpayer's anticipated income tax refund. The IRS is not involved in or responsible for RALs or other financial products. For more information, see Publication 1345, *Handbook for Authorized IRS e-file Providers of Individual Income Tax Returns.*

59. The answer is C. Natalie does not have to fulfill the overall 72 hours of CPE required during an enrollment cycle since she was only an enrolled agent for two years. For renewal purposes, the annual CPE requirements only apply for the years in which someone was an enrolled agent. An EA who receives initial enrollment during an enrollment cycle must complete two CPE hours for each month enrolled during the enrollment cycle. Enrollment for any part of a month is considered enrollment for the entire month.

60. The answer is B. The tax preparer may not cash or endorse a taxpayer's refund check. A $500 penalty may be imposed on a return preparer who endorses or negotiates a refund check issued to any taxpayer. This penalty applies even if the taxpayer has given his permission. The prohibition on return preparers negotiating a refund check is limited to a refund check for returns they prepared. See Publication 1345, *Handbook for Authorized IRS e-file Providers of Individual Income Tax Returns.*

61. The answer is A. Tax protester positions are not the same as understatements of liability. If a preparer willfully understates a client's tax liability, he is subject to penalties. Under IRS regulations, understatement of liability means:
- Understating net tax payable
- Overstating the net amount creditable or refundable
- Taking a position with no realistic possibility of success

62. The answer is A. A tax preparer may not charge a fee based on the percentage of the refund for preparing a Refund Anticipation Loan application. If Providers advertise the availability of an RAL or financial product, the Provider and financial institution must clearly refer to the funds they advance as a loan or other financial product, not as a refund. The advertisement on an RAL or other financial product must be easy to identify and in readable print. For more information, see Publication 1345, *Handbook for Authorized IRS e-file Providers of Individual Income Tax Returns.*

63. The answer is A. A family member can represent members of his or her immediate family. Immediate family means a spouse, child, parent, brother, or sister of the individual. Because of their special relationship, family members can represent a taxpayer and practice before the IRS, provided they present satisfactory identification and proof of authority to do so. In this case, the mother would need a signed Form 2848 with the signature of her child.

64. The answer is B. The statutory notice of deficiency, the "90-day letter," gives the taxpayer 90 days to file a petition in the United States Tax Court challenging the proposed deficiency. A taxpayer has 150 days if his address is outside of the country on the day the notice of deficiency is mailed.

65. The answer is C. The confidentiality privilege does not extend to any administrative proceeding with any other federal agency. This privilege applies only to tax advice given to the taxpayer by a federally authorized tax practitioner (EA, CPA, or attorney). The confidentiality protection applies to communications that would be considered privileged if they were between the taxpayer and an attorney and that relate to:
- Noncriminal tax matters before the IRS, or
- Noncriminal tax proceedings brought in federal court by or against the United States.

This confidentiality privilege does not apply to tax shelter opinions or criminal matters.

66. The answer is D. The penalty for filing late is usually 5% of the unpaid taxes for each month or part of a month that a return is late. This penalty will not exceed 25% of a taxpayer's unpaid taxes. The penalty is based on the tax not paid by the due date, without regard to extensions. If a taxpayer files his return more than 60 days after the due date or extended due date, the minimum penalty is the smaller of $135 or 100% of the unpaid tax. If the taxpayer is owed a refund, there will not be a failure-to-file penalty.

67. The answer is B. If a taxpayer does not pay his taxes by the due date, he will be subject to a failure-to-pay penalty of ½ of 1% (0.5%) of unpaid taxes for each month or part of a month after the due date that the taxes are not paid. This penalty can be as much as 25% of a taxpayer's unpaid taxes.

68. The answer is B. Providers may not base their fees on a percentage of the refund amount or compute their fees using any figure from tax returns.

69. The answer is C. Barbara has a right to appeal the judge's decision. If a practitioner fails to respond to an initial complaint, the failure constitutes an admission of guilt and a waiver of the hearing. The administrative law judge may make a decision on the case by default without a hearing or further procedure. During a hearing, the practitioner may appear in person, or be represented by an attorney or another practitioner. The Director of the OPR may be represented by an attorney or other employee of the IRS. For more information, see Circular 230.

70. The answer is A. The practitioner may file an appeal of the judge's decision with the Secretary of the Treasury, and not to the OPR. An administrative law judge presides over the hearing on a complaint for censure, suspension, or disbarment. After a decision for disbarment has been made, the tax practitioner has a right to appeal. For more information, see Circular 230.

71. The answer is D. Covered opinions relate to the advice a practitioner gives a client regarding a tax shelter. IRS regulations provide mandatory requirements for practitioners who provide covered opinions, which are defined as follows:
- Any transaction the IRS has determined is a tax-avoidance transaction.
- Any plan or arrangement that has tax avoidance as a principal purpose.

Under the rules, unless the advice contains a disclaimer, the practitioner providing advice about a covered opinion must comply with all of the following requirements:

- The practitioner must use due diligence in fact finding.
- All pertinent facts must be separately stated and disclosed, and not be deemed unreasonable or immaterial by the practitioner.
- The opinion must relate the facts to applicable law standards without inconsistency.
- All significant federal tax issues must be addressed and disclosed in the written advice.

The practitioner has a duty to also consider the impact of federal tax issues and provide a conclusion about whether the taxpayer's position on each issue is likely to prevail.

72. The answer is D. An IRS power of attorney ends upon death. For more information, see Circular 230.

73. The answer is D. An Electronic Return Originator (ERO) originates the electronic submission of returns it either prepares or collects from taxpayers who want to e-file their returns. An ERO originates the electronic submission by:

- Electronically sending the return to a Transmitter that transmits the return to the IRS;
- Directly transmitting the return to the IRS; or
- Providing a return to an Intermediate Service Provider for processing prior to transmission to the IRS.

See Publication 1345, *Handbook for Authorized IRS e-file Providers of Individual Income Tax Returns.*

74. The answer is D. Generally, confidential taxpayer information can only be disclosed upon a taxpayer's written authorization. A power of attorney is not required in some situations when dealing with the IRS. The following situations do not require a power of attorney:

- Providing information to the IRS
- Disclosure pursuant to a court order
- Authorizing the disclosure of tax return information through Form 8821
- Allowing the IRS to discuss return information with a third party designee
- Allowing a tax matters partner or person (TMP) to perform acts for the partnership
- Allowing the IRS to discuss return information with a fiduciary
- Representing a taxpayer through a non-written (oral) consent

75. The answer is A. Robin may represent both of her clients so long as the conflict of interest is disclosed in writing to both parties and both parties agree. Circular 230 does not ban practitioners from representing clients with conflicts of interest. However, the regulations do require practitioners to obtain written consent to the representation from each affected client. For more information, see Circular 230.

76. The answer is A. Enrolled agents must renew their enrollment status every three years. As part of the application process, the IRS checks the candidate's filing history to verify that he has filed and paid all federal taxes on time.

77. The answer is D. Not receiving a renewal form is not a valid excuse for a waiver of continuing professional education. A waiver of CPE requirements may be requested in extraordinary circumstances. The discretion to grant a waiver lies in the hands of the Return Preparer Office. Qualifying circumstances include:

- Health issues
- Active deployment for military personnel
- Absence from the United States for employment or other reasons
- Other reasons on a case-by-case basis

The request for a waiver must be accompanied by appropriate documentation, such as medical records or military paperwork. If the request is denied, the enrolled agent will be placed on the inactive roster. If the request is accepted, the individual will receive an enrollment card reflecting his renewal.

78. The answer is C. Form 8821 is not sufficient for representation work. Form 8821, *Tax Information Authorization*, is an information request form only that authorizes the disclosure of tax information.

79. The answer is C. The Taxpayer Advocate Service is an independent organization within the IRS whose employees assist taxpayers who are experiencing economic harm, who are seeking help in resolving tax problems that have not been resolved through normal channels, or who believe that an IRS system or procedure is not working as it should.

80. The answer is C. Generally, installment agreements cannot be entered into unless the agreement provides for full payment of the entire tax liability (including interest and penalties) within the earlier of five years or the Collection Statute Expiration Date (Internal Revenue Manual, 4.20.4.2). *NOTE: A request for an installment agreement *cannot be turned down* if the tax owed is not more than $10,000 and all three of the following apply:
- During the past five tax years, a taxpayer (and spouse if filing a joint return) have timely filed all income tax returns and paid any income tax due, and have not entered into an installment agreement for payment of income tax.
- The IRS determines that a taxpayer cannot pay the tax owed in full when it is due, after the IRS is provided information it needs to make that determination.
- A taxpayer agrees to pay the full amount he owes within three years and to comply with the tax laws while the agreement is in effect.

81. The answer is D. The IRS is not required to comply with all FOIA requests. The IRS may withhold an IRS record that falls under one of the FOIA's nine statutory exemptions or by one of three exclusions under the Act. The exemptions protect against the disclosure of information that would harm the following: national security, the privacy of individuals, the proprietary interests of business, the functioning of the government, and other important recognized interests. For more information, see *The IRS Guide to the Freedom of Information Act*.

82. The answer is B. A practitioner may publish and advertise a fee schedule. A practitioner must adhere to the published fee schedule for at least 30 calendar days after it is published. For more information, see Circular 230.

83. The answer is A. The IRS is not bound to follow the decision of every court case. If courts decide against the IRS position on an issue, the IRS will sometimes issue a statement saying that it disagrees or *non-acquiesces* to the court's decision. This means that the IRS may choose to ignore the decision of the court and continue with its regular policies regarding the litigated issue. The IRS is not bound to change its regulations due to a loss in court. The only exception to this rule is the U.S. Supreme Court, whose decisions the IRS is obligated to follow. The IRS publishes its acquiescence and non-acquiescence in the Internal Revenue Bulletin, and then in the Cumulative Bulletin. The IRS does not announce acquiescence or non-acquiescence in every case. Sometimes the IRS's position is withheld.

84. The answer is B. Taxpayers may rely on revenue rulings as official IRS guidance on an issue. A taxpayer may use a revenue ruling as guidance in order to make a decision regarding taxable income, deductions, and how to avoid certain IRS penalties. Revenue rulings may be challenged in court. Revenue rulings are official IRS interpretations and the IRS is bound by them, but the courts are not.

85. The answer is B. The Office of Professional Responsibility has the authority to exercise responsibility and uphold professional standards for all matters related to practitioner conduct, discipline, and practice before the IRS. Answer "C" is incorrect because it is the mission statement for the IRS Small Business Division. Answer "D" is incorrect because it is the IRS's main mission statement.

86. The answer is D. The OPR can issue a notice for judicial proceedings for censure, suspension, or disbarment. Criminal penalties may be imposed on a tax preparer for fraudulent activity, but the IRS refers criminal activity to the Department of Justice for prosecution.

87. The answer is C. The jurisdiction of the Tax Court does not include employment, wagering, and certain excise taxes. The jurisdiction of the Tax Court includes:
- Income tax, estate tax, and gift tax
- Worker classification
- Innocent spouse claims
- Liens and levies
- Awards of administrative costs
- Enforcement of overpayments
- Redetermination of interest
- Modification of estate tax decision

- Litigation costs awards
- Abatement of interest

88. The answer is D. The date of filing is not required. However, it is necessary to state the year or periods involved, such as "2012-2013 tax years." An IRS power of attorney must contain:
- The type of tax and the tax years covered by the power of attorney
- The name and address of the representative
- The name and Social Security Number of the taxpayer
- The signatures of the representative and the taxpayer

The IRS will not accept a power of attorney if it does not contain all the information listed above.

89. The answer is B. A paid preparer is required by law to sign the return and fill in the preparer areas of the form. The preparer must also include his PTIN on the return, but is not required to include his Social Security Number. Although the preparer signs the return, the client is ultimately responsible for the accuracy of every item on it. In addition, the preparer must give the taxpayer a copy of the return.

90. The answer is C. There is no requirement that the practitioner have a permanent business location outside his home. In fact, many e-file providers work exclusively from a home office. An Authorized IRS e-file Provider is a business authorized by the IRS to participate in IRS e-file. The business may be a sole proprietorship, partnership, or corporation. The applicant must:
- Be a United States citizen or a legal U.S. alien lawfully admitted for permanent residence;
- Be at least 21 years old as of the date of application; and
- Meet applicable state and local licensing and/or bonding requirements for the preparation and collection of tax returns.

91. The answer is E. The IRS must give a taxpayer reasonable notice before contacting other persons about his tax issues. This provision does not apply:
- To any pending criminal investigation
- When providing notice would jeopardize collection of any tax liability
- When providing notice may result in reprisal against any person
- When the taxpayer authorized the contact

See Publication 556, *Examination of Returns, Appeal Rights, and Claims for Refund.*

92. The answer is D. Communications about the promotion of a person's participation in a tax shelter are not covered by the confidentiality privilege. A tax shelter is any plan designed for the avoidance of tax. See Circular 230.

93. The answer is A. A taxpayer is allowed to record the examination interview. The request to record the interview should be made in writing. The taxpayer or representative must notify the examiner ten days in advance and bring his own recording equipment. The IRS also can record an interview. See Publication 556, *Examination of Returns, Appeal Rights, and Claims for Refund.*

94. The answer is D. Most cases that are *not docketed* in any court qualify for fast track mediation. Mediation can take place at a conference a taxpayer requests with a supervisor, or later. The process involves an Appeals Officer who has been trained in mediation. Certain matters are excluded from fast track mediation. They include:
- Issues for which there is no legal precedent
- Issues where the courts have rendered opposing or differing decisions in different jurisdictions
- Industry Specialization Program issues
- Collection Appeals Program cases
- Automated Collection System cases
- Constitutional law issues

For more information, see Publication 3605, *Fast Track Mediation-A Process for Prompt Resolution of Tax Issues.*

95. The answer is D. A taxpayer cannot appeal a CAP decision to the court. Once Appeals makes a decision regarding the case, that decision is binding on both the taxpayer and the IRS. A taxpayer cannot obtain judicial review of the decision following a CAP hearing. For more information, see Publication 1660, *Collection Appeal Rights.*

96. The answer is A. Penny may appeal the termination of her installment agreement. If she appeals within a 30-day period after the termination, the IRS will be prohibited from levying until her appeal is completed. For more information, see Publication 1660, *Collection Appeal Rights.*

97. The answer is B. An IRS interview must be suspended when the taxpayer clearly requests the right to consult with a representative. Throughout the examination process, the taxpayer can act on his own behalf or have someone represent him. The taxpayer is not required to be present if the representative is a federally authorized practitioner (enrolled agent, CPA, or attorney). The taxpayer is also not required to be present if the representative is one of the other qualified unenrolled individuals listed in Circular 230, such as a family member or an employee representing an employer. For more information, see Publication 556, *Examination of Returns, Appeal Rights, and Claims for Refund.*

98. The answer is A. A CP-2000 shows proposed changes to a taxpayer's income tax return. A CP-2000 notice is not a bill. It is a request for verification of the income, credits, and deductions reported on the tax return. A CP-2000 is a proposal that offers the taxpayer an opportunity to disagree, partially agree, or agree with the proposed changes. The taxpayer must respond within 30 days of the date of the notice (or 60 days if living outside the United States). If the IRS does not hear from the taxpayer within the 30 or 60 day period, a statutory notice of deficiency will be issued and additional interest will be charged.

99. The answer is C. In most cases, tax returns can be audited for up to three years after filing. However, the IRS may audit for up to six years if there is substantial unreported income.

100. The answer is C. Taxpayers are given ten days from the date of a rejected return to resubmit the return, even if the submission is made after the due date of the return. The "transmission perfection period" is not an extension of time to file; it is additional time to correct errors in the electronic file. When a previously rejected electronic return is accepted by the IRS within the ten-day transmission perfection period, it will be deemed to have been received on the date of the first reject that occurred within that ten-day period.

Also Available from PassKey Publications

The Enrolled Agent Tax Consulting Practice Guide:

Learn How to Develop, Market, and Operate a Profitable Tax and IRS Representation Practice

ISBN-13: 978-0982266045

Available in Kindle and Nook editions and as a paperback

About the Authors

Collette Szymborski is a certified public accountant and the managing partner of Elk Grove CPA Accountancy Corporation. She specializes in the taxation of corporations, individuals, and exempt entities. Elk Grove CPA also does estate planning.

Richard Gramkow is an enrolled agent with more than sixteen years of experience in various areas of taxation. He holds a master's degree in taxation from Rutgers University and is currently a tax manager for a publicly held Fortune 500 company in the New York metropolitan area.

Christy Pinheiro is an enrolled agent, registered tax return preparer, Accredited Business Accountant, and writer. Christy was an accountant for two private CPA firms and for the State of California before going into private practice. She is a member of the California Society of Enrolled Agents and CalCPA.

21870774R00177

Made in the USA
Lexington, KY
02 April 2013